ALL IN ALL

ALL IN ALL

An Actor's Life On and Off the Stage

STACY KEACH

Foreword by Alec Baldwin

LYONS PRESS
Guilford, Connecticut
An imprint of Globe Pequot Press

Lyons Press is an imprint of Globe Pequot Press.

All photos courtesy of the author unless otherwise indicated.

Project editors: Meredith Dias & Lauren Brancato
Layout artists: Sue Murray & Justin Marciano

Library of Congress Cataloging-in-Publication Data

Keach, Stacy.
  All in all : an actor's life on and off the stage / Stacy Keach.
    pages cm
  ISBN 978-0-7627-9145-3 (hardback)
  1. Keach, Stacy. 2. Actors—United States—Biography. I. Title.
  PN2287.K35A3 2013
  791.4302'8092—dc23
  [B]

                                        2013016668

Printed in the United States of America

10 9 8 7 6 5 4 3 2 1

For my wife, Malgosia,

And my children, Shannon and Karolina,

For their love and their laughter

And for always nourishing the light in my soul

And to the memory of my dear, departed parents

CONTENTS

CONTENTS

Foreword

by Alec Baldwin

As a teenage film buff in the early 1970s, I remember an anticipation and excitement when Joseph Wambaugh's first police novel was being made into a movie. And with the great George C. Scott, no less. I rushed to see *The New Centurions* and was immediately struck by the performance of the young actor who played Scott's rookie partner, Stacy Keach.

I didn't know Keach was already a star in the theater world, collecting accolades and awards for shows ranging from *MacBird!* to *Long Day's Journey into Night.* Just weeks before I saw him for the first time critics had called him the finest American *Hamlet* since John Barrymore. I only knew then that Keach was intense, even riveting, and more than capable of holding his own onscreen opposite Scott, both as an actor and a film star.

Now, four decades on, I have a deeper, more nuanced appreciation for what Stacy Keach brings to this art. Yet in many ways my reaction remains as elemental as it was back in 1972—he is both a presence and an actor. I am often loath to make comparisons and contrasts, but Stacy is a miraculous hybrid of the hyper-masculinity of a Brando or Robert Mitchum and the classical training of Richard Burton or Kevin Kline.

The blend of a tough, two-fisted persona with a well-honed Shakespearean technique made Stacy a god in the theater, even if it probably didn't do him any favors in Hollywood, where they often require someone more monochromatic. (I'll leave it to Stacy to detail his endless struggle in Hollywood, with hairpieces among other things.) Many actors glide confidently through their early years only to realize, in middle age, how difficult it is to learn to act in the spotlight. Stacy might have backed off of his technique and left the "heavy acting" to others in order to position himself for a more lucrative movie career, but for great artists like Stacy such compromises are simply not an option. I think we should all be grateful that he didn't jettison both his commitment and the complexity of his performances.

He was on the threshold of becoming a great movie tough guy, in the manner of John Garfield or William Holden, although those names point up the notion that Stacy may have been born in the wrong decade, coming of age when leading men were often either feminized or damaged goods. But Stacy is best known to the masses as Mike Hammer, also a romantic tough guy in the wrong era, roaming the streets of 1980s New York wearing a fedora and trench coat. He played Mike Hammer with a lighter touch than the icon of Spillane's novels and, although it was not as layered a role as the ones he had in movies like *Fat City* or *End of the Road*, he brought to it his ineffable quality—the very same stuff his *Hamlet* was made of. His inner strengths come through regardless of the venue, and that made *Mike Hammer*, a show that otherwise might have been instantly forgettable, the rebirth of an iconic character. Stacy is a working actor, meaning that when he takes a job, he'll pour everything he's got into it.

I'm telling you all this because Stacy won't. Over the course of hundreds of pages, this book contains Stacy's essence, from Hamlet to Hammer, from Richard III to Sergeant Stedenko, from King Lear to Papa Ken Titus. He is a great raconteur. You'll delight in his tales of meeting Burton (though Liz Taylor made the greater impression) and working with Mitchum, of singing with Judy Collins and gambling with John Huston, of false mustaches and near deadly stunts. But Stacy is not a self-seeking man. That guy would have made a different set of choices.

Over the past fifty years, Stacy's passion and persistence have combined with his powerful gifts and technique to make him one of the true wild mustangs of theater history. He is a natural performer who walks out on the stage and is completely in the moment. Immersed in his character, he is nonetheless able to telepathically convey to the audience, "There's no place else I'd rather be than here with you." Through his work, Keach inspires, teaches, and welcomes all at once. How rare!

When I saw Stacy in *Other Desert Cities* on Broadway in 2012, he was not the show's star, yet he was very much the leading man, the sun around which everyone revolved. It's why I look forward to seeing him as Falstaff in *Henry IV* in 2014. Watching him onstage, I said to myself, "That's what I hope I'm still able to do when I'm in my seventies." Stacy Keach remains a role model for me even now. I wonder if he realizes his effect on other actors.

Masculine and sensitive, intelligent and leonine, he is a force. To quote Edward Bulwer-Lytton, "Talent does what it can; genius does what it must."

INTRODUCTION

I GLARED AT THE CAMERA AND SPIT, UNLEASHING A MOUTHFUL WITH AS
much force and rage as I could muster.

It was cathartic, kind of like I was getting even with the gods. Yet I felt
no real anger. This moment was played strictly for laughs, the ultimate spit
take. It was the winter of 2012 and I was out in Queens, filming a scene for
30 Rock. It was a cameo but one I reveled in—after a half-century of acting,
of playing everyone from Hamlet to Hemingway, this was the first time I'd
ever been asked to play a character named Stacy Keach.

The script was a parody of Clint Eastwood's classic Super Bowl commercial "Halftime in America." My role was not to rally the nation's spirit;
Stacy Keach's call to action was to help Jack Donaghy, the ruthless executive
played by Alec Baldwin, unload the world's worst couches. My technique
was to bully American viewers into feeling wimpy if they couldn't handle
tough times and uncomfortable seating.

"When we get hit and are down we don't stay down, we get up and we
hit back with our fists ... or our nunchucks," I growled, before acknowledging that "nunchucking can wear a guy out," and then it's time to "sit on a
couch, an American couch, a Kouchtown couch."

This wasn't just satirizing the Chrysler commercial; it was also pok-
ing fun at me, my tough guy, go-it-alone persona, developed over many
roles but etched in people's minds by my years playing Mike Hammer. It
turns out that—for better and for worse—there's a certain amount of truth
in that image, something I realized about myself in the 1980s after I was
arrested for cocaine possession and landed in England's Reading Jail.

I was already plenty busy performing *Other Desert Cities* on Broadway
eight times a week and narrating CNBC's *American Greed* series, but I'm
always game for more work. When asked what my favorite role is, I invariably answer, "my next one." And the *30 Rock* script was irresistible.

So there I was spending my Monday tromping up and down an alley-way in Queens, braving frigid temperatures and brutal winds without a coat . . . and without complaint. In that first Kouchtown spot, I was a sneering hard-ass. By the second I'd become a frothing martinet.

"When did we get so soft?" I snarled. "You know what this country used to sit on? Logs, girders, poles. Being comfortable, that's not what America is all about."

Before hammering audiences with the slogan—"Sit down or get out of the way"—I capped off my rant by spitting into the camera. It needed to look extemporaneous, but for television the magical moment had to be meticulously planned and perfectly captured. Generating enough saliva for take after take could prove tricky, so the prop man asked if he could get anything to help me. "Do you have any liquid from an egg yolk?" I asked.

He said he could get me as much as I needed, as long as I could stand the taste of it. I could. And I did, hawking up a slimy gob of egg yolk, firing into the lens. Where did I come up with the egg yolk idea? I'm not sure; it's just something I picked up along the way, during nearly fifty years in the business of make-believe.

That night crystallized a thought in my mind, even if the concept of crystallizing egg yolk is rather gross: I have a lifetime of these tales to share, stories that offer insight into what it takes to become an actor, to overcome obstacles (plenty of them self-imposed), and to endure.

I set out to master the classics and then to become a popular artist and discovered that it's a tricky task. As a young actor I was hailed as America's answer to England's great Shakespearean actors, but I felt people didn't see me in my entirety, overlooking my athleticism (I've always loved stunts and fight scenes) and my comedic chops; later on, I earned fame on *Mike Hammer* and *Titus,* and new fans had no idea that I was capable of handling the nuances of *Hamlet* or *King Lear.*

The road has never been smooth, and this book will explore missed opportunities, mistakes made, and the impediments this industry inflicts. It's not a gloomy book, however; I will also celebrate many wonderful roles and memorable friends made along the way. When I was younger my mother would say, "Stacy, you'll know you made it when you're a clue in the

New York Times crossword puzzle." In a career that has brought rewarding roles and notable awards, one of my proudest moments was the first time I showed Mom that the *Times* had "TV's Hammer" as a clue. Hopefully when I'm done filling in all the other pieces of this puzzle, you'll feel like you know me, from start to, well . . . I'm not quite finished yet.

CHAPTER 1

A Different Kind of Fame

TWO CANS OF GILLETTE SHAVING CREAM, SIDE BY SIDE.

Only a fool would make such an obvious mistake. A fool, or perhaps a desperate man whose subconscious was pushing him to get caught. When the curious customs official at London's Heathrow Airport picked up one can and then the other for inspection, I knew instantly it was over. After all, no one packs two cans of shaving cream for a one-day trip.

Busted, like some common perp on *Mike Hammer*. I knew how stupid I had been. Strange as it sounds, however, with the jig up I felt relief, not fear. As I let out my breath, I knew this period in my life was finally over. When the officer asked—after a quick shake of each can—what was in the fake canister, I readily fessed up: cocaine.

I was zipping in from Marseille in the south of France, where I was shooting the TV movie *Mistral's Daughter*, to London for *Mike Hammer* voiceover work, because Columbia Television didn't like the Paris recording studio. It was one day's work, but I was deep enough in the grip of the White Lady that going empty-handed for even a short jaunt seemed unbearably long. So I packed the canister with the false bottom (a present from my wife, Jill), unthinkingly laying it in the suitcase next to my actual shaving cream.

Even had I been paying attention to details, my behavior was absurdly risky. Right as my television career was peaking, here I was smuggling cocaine across borders. (My secretary, Debby, had her own small supply.) Not just this once. Repeatedly. (On trips in the States, I'd sometimes smuggle it in my suitcase and sometimes have packages mailed to me.) Making matters worse, I was flying from one of the drug capitals of the world into a country grappling with drug issues, at an airport where both Tony Perkins and Linda McCartney had recently been busted for drug possession. Still, my addiction would not allow me to see beyond my immediate needs. My motto about cocaine resembled a certain credit card's sales pitch for travelers: Don't leave home without it.

I don't remember the first time I tried cocaine. It likely started out innocently enough, just taking someone up on a friendly offer. In Hollywood in the 1970s it was socially acceptable—you'd attend parties and there'd be bowls of the stuff; at certain restaurants, the maitre d' would come up and say, "Would you like to go to the bathroom and have a snort?"

My initial experiences, about a year apart, were fairly typical—I felt euphoric and alert, seeing the world in a new light, with newfound energy. I had no idea about the drug's potential for damage and destruction. I don't think most people around me did either.

I liked it. That's the thing. I've often said, "Thank God I've never done heroin," because I have an addictive personality. When I was at Yale Drama School in 1964, I was doing a plié in a dance class run by the legendary Pearl Lang, when my right knee suddenly locked. At Grace-New Haven Hospital the doctors found my meniscus totally gone, thanks to my high school years playing football and running track. In those days before arthroscopic surgery, a full operation was required. I awoke in a haze. They gave morphine shots for the pain and I kept asking for more— I quickly found I became very cranky when I didn't receive my shot. In retrospect, it was an early warning sign that I missed.

With cocaine, I was soon intrigued enough to purchase my first gram. Cocaine was something of a status symbol in Hollywood, and for someone whose unusual career path was outside the mainstream, it offered an easy way to fit in, to be instantly popular in a world (not unlike high school) where there is tremendous, overwhelming, often endless pressure to conform. I'd say I could take it or leave it, but if someone offered me a snort at a party, I'd always take it.

I didn't know I was standing atop a spiral staircase and my initial buy was the first step on a long trip down. Ironically, cocaine soon stopped making me feel more sociable, unlike smoking a joint, which felt more akin to having a drink. Cocaine instead took on a medicinal quality, an inhalation of confidence, creativity, and control. I was methodical about my usage, always allocating what I believed was just the right amount to give me that boost I needed to do my job with the proper intensity and focus. Over time, however, the confidence coke provided began disappearing, replaced by a gnawing insecurity. Still, I was convinced I couldn't work without it, even as I had to turn a blind eye to how much money I was spending on this little habit. The drug was seductive, and during my gradual descent, I conjured all kinds of rationalizations and excuses: It tamped down on my appetite and helped keep me in fighting trim, and since I worked out and ate healthfully, I was, on balance, in good shape.

My downfall in 1984 was particularly precipitous because I was emerging from a rough stretch to reach new highs both professionally and personally. In the early 1980s my movie career had hit a rut and settled in there, a little too comfortably. Actually, when I really look back, it had veered off the road in the mid-1970s (around the time I began using cocaine more regularly). Television—which would ultimately prove my savior—was the initial roadblock. I'd been getting meaty roles in compelling movies like *Doc, Fat City,* and *The New Centurions*, but commercial success proved elusive with several life-altering roles—in *The Exorcist* and *One Flew Over the Cuckoo's Nest*—slipping through my grasp. Unable to nab the films, and eager for more exposure and an income that would buy me time to perform where I felt most at home, in the theater—especially with my true love, William Shakespeare—I signed on to star in an ABC cop show called *Caribe.*

I try not to dwell on mistakes and wallow in regret. I'm existential in that regard—things are what they are and you do what you do. And then you move on. That doesn't mean I don't reflect and try to learn from my past. With *Caribe,* I should have weighed my decision more thoughtfully, with a sharp-eyed stare seeing Hollywood as it really was—a place where shallow people made selections based on superficial values, a place where perception ruled the day. Today, television—thanks largely to cable networks seeking sophisticated audiences—has cachet, attracting big name writers, directors, and yes, actors, but in the 1970s, television was definitely the small screen, a home for people who weren't big enough for movies. Let's be honest, I also should have seen that *Caribe*—which was quickly canceled and thus provided no financial security for my theater career—was a lousy show. It became a major dividing line in my career. If I had not moved to television so quickly, I might have had a bigger movie career. Still, the path I took ultimately led me to Mike Hammer, a role with which I will, happily, be forever identified.

My movie career was permanently stuck in neutral by the early 1980s, so I returned to television as the clearest path out of my rut. Television movies and miniseries were flourishing, with good roles, good paychecks, and good casts. I could jump from a Civil War miniseries, *The Blue and the Gray*, with Gregory Peck, Geraldine Page, Colleen Dewhurst, Paul Winfield, Robert Vaughn, Rip Torn, and Sterling Hayden, to a soapy Judith Krantz adaptation, *Princess Daisy*, alongside Robert Urich, Lindsay Wagner, Paul Michael Glaser, and Claudia Cardinale, to the tough-guy detective movie, *Murder Me, Murder You*. That last one was a vehicle for Mickey Spillane's Detective Mike Hammer. It was such a hit that CBS decided to make it into a series. My career was revving up again.

My love life had also shifted gears.

My third marriage was in deep trouble, due mostly to one insurmountable obstacle: My wife, Jill, didn't want children and I most definitely did. That wasn't the only issue but it proved impossible to reconcile.

Troubles at home were wearing me down until I found the answer to my problems on the set. I was in downtown Los Angeles on the set of *Murder Me, Murder You* when I first saw her—when I was going into a phone booth (ah, the good ol' days) and she was coming out. I stopped and said, to no one in particular, "Whoa, who is that?"

Her name was Malgosia Tomassi and she was a European fashion model trying to catch a break in Hollywood; she was playing a nurse in our production. She definitely caught my eye. She was one of the most beautiful women I'd ever seen . . . and I'd seen a lot. A night or two later,

I was heading home from the set in my limo when her old Volkswagen pulled up alongside me at Hollywood Boulevard and Highland Avenue. Malgosia rolled down her window and said, "How long are you going to follow me?" In an instant I made a decision. Maybe it wasn't even a decision. On instinct, I took action. I said to my driver, "Pray for me." I got out, went to her car, and got in. She drove me home and we shared a kiss . . . or three.

Her role on the show ended and I was shooting non-stop, so I didn't see Malgosia for several days until I discovered she was living three blocks from me. And so it began. . . .

I was a star.

I was in love.

I was also a drug addict.

There were times when I'd briefly recognize the dangers, but mostly I was, like so many other addicts, a master of denial. When John Belushi died, it was both sad and scary but John was doing speedballs—cocaine and

One look and it's easy to see why I fell so hard, so quickly for Malgosia.

heroin mixed—so I convinced myself that was something completely different. Bob Woodward, of Woodward and Bernstein fame, called me because he was writing a book about Belushi's downfall and had found out John and I shared the same drug dealer. I don't know how Bob obtained my number. Just that link should have scared me straight, but I easily pushed away those concerns. (Turmoil and tension in my marriage didn't help—drugs were our common ground, while the rift over starting a family grew wider.)

When shooting on the *Mike Hammer* series began, my drug use—and my need to justify it—accelerated. I was in every shot, working twelve- to fourteen-hour days, a relentless cycle. My moderately spaced doses were no longer enough, but I was unwilling, unable to confront the cold hard reality that I was depending on a chemical, that I couldn't function on my own. Logic and reason had vanished behind a puff of fine white powder. I was not Tony Montana near the end of *Scarface*, inhaling mountainous piles of blow. I remained systematic, almost clinical about my use. But each month, each week, I reached for my dosage more frequently. When it started giving me headaches or a nosebleed or two, well, that was nothing to worry about. Another toot would make me feel better.

We debuted in January 1984 and won the ratings war in the time slot, quickly earning a second season. However, having been dubbed a "hot television star" by the *New York Times*, I did not want to slow down, so I raced off to France to star in *Mistral's Daughter*.

Once more unto the stash.

The drug, I argued to myself, enabled me to make it through from beginning to end, bringing the same quality to my acting in the last shot that I had in the first shot. It gave me clarity of purpose and clarity of expression.

Obviously, what was lacking was clarity regarding myself. The reality is that the brutal work schedule was taking a toll, but the cocaine had an even more insidious impact. Exhausted, I would turn to the drug. I'd experience the brief lift but each crash dragged me lower. The crew probably just thought I was wiped out. A few actors on *Mike Hammer* and maybe *Mistral's Daughter* knew I used cocaine, but none knew I was measuring my days, even my hours, by it, relying on it to carry me from morning to night. My work grew erratic, sloppy even (although I wouldn't realize that until much later). I couldn't see it. I couldn't see anything clearly. In that regard, the arrest came just in time, saving me from myself.

Some people have suggested that I wasn't stopped randomly, saying someone tipped off customs officials either to sabotage my career or to give me a much-needed wake-up call. Some saw the handiwork of my producer, Jay Bernstein, believing his messianic tendencies inspired him to get me in trouble just so he could rescue me. The ideas are provocative but the former is unlikely and the latter outrageous. Given the concern over a mounting drug crisis, the London media hysteria (and no one does hysteria quite like London's newspapers), and the celebrity busts of Perkins, McCartney, and others, I think there's a reasonable chance my stop wasn't random, that I was stopped because I was a Hollywood star. No matter what the reason, I was guilty, standing there with more than thirty grams of cocaine in a fake shaving cream canister, plus the smaller quantities on Debby and in her suitcase.

My initial sense of relief dissipated and other feelings rushed in— shame, a protective concern for Debby, and a brief spasm of fear for my career. As the action played out, I felt, oddly, a bit detached, like I was in a scene from a movie. I was taken to a holding cell in the airport before being transferred to a London jail. I made my phone calls—to my attorney, to Malgosia, and to Jay, my producer. I was hauled before a judge—a little old lady, who possessed an actor's timing and delivery. She heard the London officials argue that, given the amount of cocaine, I might be smuggling with intent to deal. She listened to my attorney's explanation that I had flown to London overnight simply to complete some looping for my TV show.

"How much cocaine was in the canister?" the judge inquired.

"33.7 grams, Your Honor."

She paused dramatically and cut her eyes at me. And she asked, in a perfect comedic deadpan, "For one night?"

She set my bail for some enormous amount; I think it was 150,000 pounds. England did not accept a 10 percent payment as is common in America, and according to some arcane rules, it had to be delivered in cash by a certain time or I would not be free to get to Paris and would be responsible for delaying the shoot. Jay started working his phone, but Columbia Television and CBS turned a cold shoulder. He had better luck with Steve Krantz, who was Judith's husband but also executive producer of the miniseries, and thus had the most to lose by my continued detention. From what I was told—and it may have been embellished along the way—the money was wired to London at the last minute and the cash was handed off to a fantastically overweight guy who fought his way through traffic on a motorcycle—with a friend of mine trailing him to make sure nothing untoward happened—to get it handed in on time.

I was free.

I felt vulnerable and fragile, but when I arrived in Paris the cast embraced me and I plunged immediately back into my work. There was no time for introspection. Or perhaps I should say I allowed myself no time for introspection. I wasn't ready yet. I was surprised by how easy it was to work without drugs, how simply I cast off a vice that seemingly had me in a vise. Forced to clean up, I experienced no cravings, no with-drawal. (I fell off the wagon a few times in the following months, but by year's end I was clean for good.) My theory is that while certain people develop physiological addictions to certain substances, others are psychologically addicted, and I fell in the latter category. (If I'd been told to give up my cigarettes, that would have been different—my physical addiction there is definitely strong.)

That understanding came later. I was just looking to move on—my wife, with our marriage essentially over, had already returned to the States to be with her ailing father; now Malgosia joined me in France. The worst seemed behind me. In one way, it was. The arrest humiliated me publicly but also transformed me, yanking me out of my perilous cycle. Everyone was reassuring me that I likely faced the proverbial slapping of the ol' wrist, nothing that would slow down my flourishing television career.

They were wrong. For the next year, the most riveting drama in my life took place off the screen: in the press, the courts, and the prisons of England.

CHAPTER 2

Growing Accustomed to My Face

MY HANDS WERE TIED BEHIND MY BACK, LASHING ME TO A POLE NEAR an abandoned building in the woods; I was too isolated for anyone to hear my frantic calls for help. As the autumn sun started its descent and the temperature steadily slid toward freezing, my anxiety, which had blossomed into fear, threatened to explode into full-fledged panic.

Sounds like a great dramatic scene, doesn't it? Maybe you're even riffling through the reference cards of your memory, trying to retrieve which of my many movies that was from. It wasn't. This was real; this was me as a scared six-year-old, victimized by neighborhood bullies.

As a young boy I was easy prey. I was often the new kid—I was born in Savannah, Georgia, but we moved to Pasadena, California, because my father, Stacy Sr., started working at the Pasadena Playhouse. When I was five, Dad became a talent scout at RKO, relocating us to Flushing, Queens. I spent second grade living with my maternal grandmother in Taft, Texas, then moved with my parents and baby brother James back to California, settling in the San Fernando Valley. And while my given name was Walter, like my dad I went by my middle name, Stacy, which invited easy taunts from even the most unimaginative mini-thugs.

The main target, however, was visual, smack in the middle of my face. I was born with a cleft lip and a partially cleft palate. In the former, the upper lip is split in two and sometimes the gum and bones separate; the latter refers to an opening in the roof of the mouth. (These birth defects form early in a pregnancy from a lack of tissue, but there is not one definitive cause.)

9

Portrait of the actor
as a young kid

In my first four years on this planet, I went under the knife four times. I don't remember much from the surgeries—jumping up and down on the operating table before being put to sleep, the powerful smell of the ether, waking up with stitches in my nose and a craving for ice cream—but even with the doctors' best efforts I was left with the two marks common to cleft lips and palates: a nasal voice and a telltale scar on my lip.

Cleft lips and palates are among the most common birth defects, especially for boys, but when you're a kid, any kind of disfigurement—especially one on your face—makes you feel different, alone. My parents didn't want me to feel handicapped, so they treated me like there was nothing wrong. (We never even discussed the surgeries until I was in college.) I was always encouraged to strive to "be the best" in everything, which helped mold my competitive spirit and my over-achieving nature.

In the big picture this was the right move—I grew up thinking I could do anything, become whatever I wanted to be—but it also left me unprepared for the casual cruelties of other children. That incident where I was tied to a pole took place in Flushing Meadows Park in Queens. It was not out in the wilds, but for a small boy to feel trapped and lost anywhere is terrifying. I remember searching for and eventually finding a piece of broken glass on the ground that I could reach, using it to cut myself free. I don't even remember how I found my way home, but it was dark when I finally arrived, filthy and crying, to find my mother as terrified as I had been.

She immediately took me to the ringleader's house. Billy lived a block away in a ground-floor apartment. When the bully himself answered the door, my mother—a sweet and soft-spoken woman—surprised all three of us when she barked an order, "Get him, Stacy!"

I tackled him and, before he could recover, started banging his head against the ground. When his parents appeared, they were, naturally, shocked. As my mother told and re-told the story through the years, her theatrical training led to memorable embellishments: She'd turn to the

I've always tried to give something back to kids with cleft palates and cleft lips, spending more than three decades as Honorary Chair of the Cleft Palate Foundation.

parents and snarl, "The next time Billy picks on my son, you might have to call an ambulance."

The truth was more mundane but equally satisfying—my mother explained what happened and Billy's mother slapped her son and apologized to my mother. Afterward, Billy and I actually became friendly. Mike Hammer fans might think the lesson I learned was about seeking violent retribution against wrongdoers, but instead I learned how fierce my mother's love truly was.

The bullying didn't stop there. In Texas I came home in tears after being teased because of my appearance, but my grandmother wouldn't downplay my distinctive scar. "You are different, Stacy," she told me. "You are unique." I understood her message but I was never comfortable with that notion, being deemed different simply because of my looks. And self-knowledge didn't stop kids from picking on me—the next year, in California, a group of alleged friends convinced me to climb up on a roof with them; they climbed down and took away the ladder. At that age I was deeply committed to being a normal kid—I worked diligently to correct the nasality in my speech on my own—and later on I would want to be able to create my own persona without being judged by a scar.

For more than thirty years, I have served as honorary chair of the Cleft Palate Foundation and have also served as national spokesman for the World Craniofacial Organization. I've lobbied for fair treatment from insurance companies, which essentially treat cleft repair as plastic surgery; we have fought for coverage for surgery but also for speech therapy and anything else that might follow. Of equal importance for me is the time I devote to writing letters to kids or parents, encouraging them to realize that if you have a cleft you are not handicapped—it is an issue to be faced but one that should not stop anyone from fulfilling their dreams.

Kickball, tetherball, baseball, track, football—you name it, and I played it and usually excelled at it. The easiest way to deflect attention from my scar was to demonstrate physical prowess, so I attacked all sports with an intensity and tenacity that yielded results. Dominating on these playing fields gave me confidence, even a certain bravado. Investing so much in my successes made failure sting more sharply: In eighth grade I earned a spot in the Junior Olympics at the Los Angeles Coliseum. Walking onto the track was thrilling, but intimidating, too. I went from feeling like a star to feeling very, very small.

"On your mark. Get set." Anxious and overeager, I came off the blocks too soon.

"On your mark. Get set." Again, my nerves betrayed me. This second false start disqualified me. I felt humiliated, in front of my parents and this huge crowd. I felt myself shrinking to a lowly worm. (My mom blamed the starter, but that's what moms do.) One redeeming thing about becoming an actor is that I have found a positive use for these memories, summoning them for emotional recall in any scene where my character has failed or been humiliated.

Football brought me even more joy than track but also caused a more tangible and lasting pain. I fell in love with the game watching Friday night high school games in Texas—the Taft Greyhounds—with my step-grandfather Clifford Williams. (I split summers between each maternal grandparent and their new spouses. I loved both sets, though I couldn't mention one in front of the other, which taught me that discretion is often mingled with secrecy, one that in this case was created by broken hearts and shattered dreams.)

I loved playing both sides of the ball, but in high school I found out the hard way that being tough and fast—which made me stand out in pickup games—was not enough, especially because I was on the brittle side.

In tenth grade I played center on offense and linebacker on defense, but my season ended doing a drill called Bull in the Ring. One player stands in the center of a circle; the coach throws the ball to a player on the ring. He must cross the circle without being tackled by the player in the center. I was in the middle and the recipient of the ball was our biggest player, who outweighed me by one hundred pounds, all muscle and bone. He was determined to storm right through me. I was equally set on stopping him. My will was no match for his strength—I was knocked to the ground as if by a real bull, and when I grabbed his leg my body twisted and I bounced up and then landed on my left shoulder, breaking it. The coach pulled my arm and said, "You're all right," and tried to embarrass me into continuing. I loved the sport so much that I returned my next two years, though on offense I moved to end (now called wide receiver). I never had another specific injury, but the pounding my knees endured left me with aches and pains that later cut short my ability to play tennis and other sports and that has plagued me to this day.

Most of the time my athleticism, combined with my determination and drive, enabled me to transform from victim to victor. (By eighth grade I strove for excellence in school as well and in high school I was both class president and something called "Boy of the Year.") I even developed a bit of a swagger, and as I entered my teens I started seeing my scar in a new light, especially when girls found it tough and sexy. As my attitude changed, I rejected further surgeries. The issue would again rear its ugly head (so to speak) when I came to New York. My first agent insisted I needed surgery, saying, "You've got to fix your face if you want to get into movies."

By then I had a strong enough sense of myself to refuse, declaring, "This is who I am."

CHAPTER 3

Tales of the California Keaches

THE DOOR SWUNG OPEN AND WE READIED OURSELVES TO PERFORM another round of Christmas carols, raising money for an organization run by my mother that helped crippled children. I was nine years old, traveling around our neighborhood in the San Fernando Valley with some friends . . . and my three-year-old brother Jimmy.

Naturally I hadn't wanted to take Jimmy—I loved playing with him at home, but like any big brother I hated being responsible for him. My parents had insisted. At this particular house, the massive figure filling the doorway was particularly charmed by my adorable kid brother in his blue jumpsuit. The man, John Wayne, invited us in to his party to serenade his friends, including Zsa Zsa Gabor. When we finished singing and they finished cooing over Jimmy, Wayne gave us each five dollars—the neighbors at every other house had been giving out quarters. As my dad liked to say, after that I asked to have Jimmy tag along every Christmas, and Halloween, too.

My childhood was not completely defined by my cleft lip. It may not have been a normal childhood—Lou Costello was another neighbor (and my father worked as dialogue director for some Abbott & Costello films), my best friend's father was a cinematographer, and we saw people like Frank Sinatra and Spencer Tracy on the set—but it certainly wasn't all about overcoming adversity.

Both parents molded me, but my father especially inspired me with his boundless creativity. He was always performing magic tricks or inventing board games or brainstorming an idea for a new show. At Halloween,

With Mom, Dad, and sweet baby James

he'd spend hours on costumes and makeup for Jimmy and me. One year he transformed me into Emmett Kelly, the sad clown—I loved it so much I asked him do it again the next year.

It was my dad's thrilling life in the Wild West of the imagination that really inspired my career. In 1950, he wrote, directed, and produced *Tales of the Texas Rangers* for NBC Radio. My dad came up with the idea while working for Howard Hughes's RKO; my dad quit RKO, moved to California, and wrote a feature film script about the Rangers. Oddly, the first person to bite on the script was Hughes, who bought it for forty thousand dollars because he remembered his own father having been a Ranger. When Hughes found out his memory

My dad working on *Tales of the Texas Rangers* with Joel McCrea and Homer Garrison

was faulty, he dropped the production, but my dad used the money to buy our house in Sherman Oaks. He expanded the script into a radio series, selling the rights to General Mills. The show was a hit and ran for three years, leading off the Sunday night lineup of Jack Benny, Fred Allen, and Edgar Bergen. It starred the great Joel McCrea, who I'd seen on the screen that year in *Saddle Tramp*.

Listening on the radio made me proud, but nothing matched accompanying my dad to the NBC studio at Sunset and Vine and watching him, McCrea, and guest stars like William Conrad at work. My dad knew what he wanted and gave specific direction. As an actor himself he had a natural touch with the cast and was always very positive in his notes. Joel was cool and nothing rattled him. I was electrified by the way they brought an entire world to life without any visuals, just great storytelling and acting. I also saw how much fun they were having in the studio, producing the sound effects for the horses and essentially playing cowboy. I was hooked. (Amazingly, in 2013, the show was licensed for another go-round on radio.)

My parents were wary of letting me pursue the actor's life. Dad worked hard, bouncing around the country for jobs. My parents were protective because an acting career revolves around rejection, which my dad knew too well. In 1944, he was one of two finalists for the lead in *Keys to the Kingdom*, but the producer chose the other newcomer instead. Gregory Peck earned an Oscar nomination and went on to become, well, Gregory Peck. My dad never had a movie career. He was also initially shortsighted about television, seeing the little black box with the cathode tube first as a mere gimmick and then, accurately, as a threat to his burgeoning radio career. There was often tension at home when money was tight, so my parents wanted more stable careers for their children. Ironically, our confrontation over this would come to a head during my high school and especially my college years when my father was enjoying steady success on TV in an endless parade of series like *The Lone Ranger* and *The Californians*.

—◆—

"You don't even know what truth is." My mother blurted this out one day when she was fed up with the over-the-top whoppers I'd feed to James.

Even today I have to check my tendency to exaggerate when telling stories. My fertile imagination had a positive side—some of my most vivid memories of my summers in Texas are of reenacting the latest movies with my friends, pretending to be John Wayne or Alan Ladd. Playacting came naturally to me, though even as a child I was continually cast in older or authoritative roles, something that would continue in my professional career. In second grade, while I was living in Texas, I made my acting debut in the school pageant, playing Old King Cole. In fifth grade I played Rip Van Winkle. During my twenty-year snooze onstage, I suddenly realized that my beard and rusty gun—to show my aging—were not there. I quietly alerted the kid who was playing my dog and sent him offstage to fetch my stuff. Thinking on my feet, albeit while prone, appealed to me as much as my big speeches or the applause at the end. In sixth grade, I played the Indian chief in a show called *Dawn Boy* (again, the authority figure); I was supposed to shoot an arrow to pierce the clouds and bring rain, but the night of the show my bow broke. Instinctively, I reared back and, in a reverse-Zeus move, hurled my arrow into the clouds. The rains came.

Those were harmless elementary school productions. My parents' mixed messages really began in my teens. They encouraged me to get professional photos taken but wouldn't let me leave school to take acting roles. My dad, having survived the Depression, instilled a more traditional work ethic. My paper route required me to rise before dawn every Thursday, fold papers, and then bike on a dark road alongside semis that galloped along at an alarming pace, making horrific noises, and splashing me as they bumped through puddles. That didn't last long. I had summer jobs as a lifeguard at the municipal pool, shaking shirts at the local laundry, and assembling parts for an airplane parts company. This was not as glamorous as being in the recording studio or on the set with my dad. Not by a long shot.

By the end of high school my attention had really shifted from football to acting. I starred in three plays, culminating with *Our Town*, in which I played the Stage Manager. It was a magical time, with my dad shining all his attention on me—he had played the Stage Manager role and devoted himself to teaching me its nuances. More than half a century

My parents actually loved the idea of these cheesy head shots.

later, I still picture him teaching me how to see things in my inner mind, how to create a big butternut tree or reach down and scoop out ice cream. It was my first, and one of my most important, acting lessons.

I also began venturing into film. First, I collaborated with my friend Joel Tator to write and perform a radio play for speech class called *Dial M for Mergatroid*, a satire of Alfred Hitchcock's *Dial M for Murder*. Then our ambitions grew and we formed a production company, Tator-Keach-Associates (TKA), making short 16mm movies for school assemblies. Joel and I put ourselves in charge as glorious hyphenates: writer-producer-director-actor. We had friends working lighting, sound, and cameras—two brothers shared duties as cameraman, and their dad worked in the business so he gave us "short-ends" from larger reels of film that we spliced together to make bigger camera rolls. Our editor was already working professionally as an editorial assistant.

Our pièce de résistance was *Strange Reflections*, a twenty-minute thriller about an unsuspecting research scientist, Tony (played by yours truly), who "accidentally" gets acid poured onto his face by his girlfriend's younger sister, which leaves him looking like a monster. At the end both Tony and the audience believe that the girl is so ravaged by guilt that she takes her own life; horrified, the sensitive Tony shoots himself. It is revealed that the girl faked her demise to drive Tony to his death, allowing control of the lab to be taken over by the older sister and her true boyfriend. The entire production cost less than seven hundred dollars— most of which went for renting an ambulance for one brief scene. My dad applied my "monster makeup," though you can tell that we filmed on three separate days because my makeup looks different in each scene. I vividly recall having to drive to Laguna to shoot an important scene, sitting in the front passenger seat as "the monster," and drawing very strange, horrified stares from cars and buses driving past.

While this was clearly amateur hour, we had more talent, I believe, than your average crew of kids goofing around with a camera. Joel became a highly successful television news producer in Southern California. Our sound guy, Grover Helsley, had big ears suitable for the job and became a top sound mixer, earning eleven Emmy nominations and three awards. Our man on the lights, Pete Comindini, and editor Dick Dayton founded

As the stage narrator in *Our Town*, trying to put my dad's acting lessons into action

YCM Laboratories, a film restoration company that worked on movies from *Rear Window* to the *Star Wars* trilogy. Brad and Jay Hathaway were our cameramen—Brad worked in government for thirty years but also wrote about theater on the side. We crossed paths again after he reviewed my Washington, DC, production of *King Lear*.

We showed the movie at school and around the community and it received attention from the local newspapers. Roger Corman, still in his early days as a B-movie producer, caught wind of it. He was impressed, I guess, by our moxie—looking back as an adult, I can't imagine anyone would have been impressed by my acting. We graduated and Corman invited Joel and me to rewrite and revamp *Blood and Steel*, a movie his brother Gene had made about a white soldier and a black soldier caught in a swamp as they fought an unseen Japanese enemy. In typical Corman style, Roger wanted a similar movie, simply transferring the action to the North African desert, making the enemy Rommel and

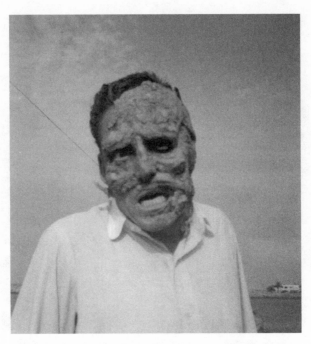

My dad's makeup masterpiece for *Strange Reflections*

the German army. Joel and I were very excited. We called the film *The Road to Berkirk* and envisioned thrilling action sequences featuring large armies, swarming planes, and rumbling tanks. It would be far superior to its schlocky predecessor.

How naïve we were. *Blood and Steel* looked cheap because it was cheap. Roger never could have afforded to make our blockbuster extravaganza, nor would he have wanted to—that wasn't part of his often marvelous aesthetic. (Years later I experienced this firsthand, working with Roger on projects like *Sea Wolf* and *When Eagles Strike* and with his wife Julie on *Legends of the Lost Tomb*.) He wouldn't tell a couple of kids that he was too low budget. So he read the script, looked at us, and said, "Can't make the movie, boys. It does not follow the Aristotelian principles."

The what?!? I couldn't know it at the time, but it was a valuable introduction to the vagaries of Hollywood, a lesson in rejection I would learn again and again and again.

CHAPTER 4

To Be or Not to Be an Actor

WALTER PIDGEON.

What kind of a role model was he for an aspiring actor—indeed, for any teen—in the 1950s? Sure, Pidgeon had carved out a perfectly solid Hollywood career in movies like *How Green Was My Valley* and *Mrs. Miniver*, but like millions of other American boys, I wanted to be Marlon Brando or James Dean. Yet my parents repeatedly held up Walter Pidgeon as an ideal, arguing that he had worked as a lawyer before becoming an actor and always had that as a fallback position.

When I was packing for Berkeley in the fall of 1959, my parents demanded that I devote freshman year to studying—no acting allowed until I earned good grades. I had to study something practical so I chose economics. Ugh. I absolutely hated it. The graphs and statistics just flat out bored me. Suddenly, after years of good grades, I was averaging a C+.

If only I'd had Google back then I could have learned the truth: Walter Pidgeon was never a lawyer. He toiled briefly as a lowly bank runner in Boston, and then chucked this loathsome job to move to New York, where he went into a theater company's office and announced that he could sing, dance, and act. He toughed out lean years in small theaters and small parts in silent film before landing on Broadway in 1925 and then flourishing in the age of talkies. He was actually someone *I* should have been holding up to *my parents* as an example. But even if I had known the story, I might not have been able to change my parents' minds on my own, given that my father wanted to protect me from the rejection and financial struggles he'd gone through.

By second semester my grades were rising, and I was allowed to try acting. The professor who directed shows at Berkeley, William Oliver, would become one of two pivotal people for me that year. The other wasn't actually in Northern California—Laurence Olivier was on the silver screen when he changed my life.

Professor Oliver cast me as a young sailor in *To Learn to Love*. We went to the naval base at Treasure Island to scare up props, which was exciting, though I felt a bigger charge from the attention I received from girls for being in a show. I don't know about the quality of my performance, but I will allow that I looked damn fine in a sailor suit.

Meanwhile, friends invited me to a Laurence Olivier film festival. That day they were showing *Richard III* and, while I came from a theatrical family, I knew little about the classics; my only exposure to Shakespeare had been the movie version of *Julius Caesar*. My high school English teacher, Miss McMillan, had been mortified when she asked who the greatest Shakespearean actor was and I answered, full of teenage certainty, Marlon Brando. I didn't really even know who Laurence Olivier was—without cable television, VCRs, DVDs, and Netflix, movies played in the theaters and then largely vanished. In the late 1950s, Olivier wasn't starring in hit movies, especially ones that American teens were flocking to. I went along just to hang out with my friends. Olivier left me awestruck. I stayed to watch *Richard III* three times. Then I returned for *Henry V* and *Hamlet*. I arrived in college knowing I'd rebel against my parents and become an actor. Now I had a cause: I aspired to be a great classical actor like my newfound idol.

In my sophomore year I stood up to my parents, arguing that I was no Walter Pidgeon, and I was going to abandon their pre-law fantasies and double major in English and drama. My dad moaned, "No, no, no," reacting as if there had been a death in the family, even though he was my original inspiration. My mom consoled herself by pointing out that I could always be a teacher with that kind of education. Professor Oliver turned my parents around. He had given me the choice of starring in John Osborne's recent hit *Look Back in Anger* or the Jacobean tragedy *The Changeling*. Naturally I gravitated to the classic, especially since I've always felt a great affinity for characters with physical deformities, even if they're not sympathetic people; I'm able to call on a deep well of emotion for these parts. As an impressionable newcomer, I mostly channeled Olivier's Richard III, with his malevolence and physical deformities, to play De Flores. Professor Oliver taught me to ignore the archaic language and to dispense with the idea of the grand performance, replacing the bombastic declamation with a naturalistic conversational style. Of equal importance, however, was that he pulled my father aside after the show and said, "Your boy has got talent." After watching my performance and hearing Oliver's assessment, my father accepted that I had both the skills and the stubborn determination to make a serious go at this. Our clash ended and my parents became steadfast supporters.

Acting also meant the end of tedious summer jobs. I had spent the two previous summers delivering furniture for W&J Sloane, and then working at their Beverly Hills store in the rug department, moving carpets around. After sophomore year, when I also played Con Melody in Eugene O'Neill's *A Touch of the Poet*, I was allowed to put my "odd job" days to rest forever. I spent the summer of 1961 at Tufts Arena Theater in Medford, Massachusetts, getting free housing and, I think, forty dollars a week. It was my first time so far from home. My girlfriend there, Susan, had the most amazing blue eyes and also hailed from Brooklyn, so I even journeyed to New York. I loved the travel, the freedom, the chance to explore—years later I would even take roles in less-than-stellar movies to see new worlds.

In my last two years at Berkeley, I not only acted but also directed Edward Albee's *The American Dream* and wrote songs for and directed musical revues. Professor Oliver sharpened my timing, taught me how to play a pause, and how to elicit laughs with even a small gesture. Along with a professor named Mark Shore, he also taught me how vital it was to learn to read and understand the texts before rehearsals.

In the two summers following my time at Tufts, I journeyed north to the Oregon Shakespeare Festival, deepening my knowledge of and appreciation for Shakespeare. (Plus, I got paid fifty dollars a week, a step up from Tufts.) My first year I appeared in *The Comedy of Errors*, *Henry IV*, and *Coriolanus*, plays I had never seen before. We rehearsed one play in the morning, another in the afternoon, and the third in the evening—we were living Shakespeare around the clock, something that led me to a lifelong appreciation for repertory theater, the best training ground for young actors. At that point I was so hungry to act that, once the shows opened, I'd spend my lunchtimes at the local hotel doing a modern play with another actor. I was having the time of my life.

The following year I played Mercutio in *Romeo and Juliet* and Berowne in *Love's Labour's Lost*, but my moment of truth arrived when I assumed the mantle of the title role in *Henry V.* The eminent writer Henry Hewes gave me a stunning notice in the *Saturday Review*, comparing me to Christopher Plummer, already an international star. As I'd find out a few months later, one of the people who read Hewes was America's greatest producer of Shakespeare, Joseph Papp.

At the Oregon Shakespeare Festival in *The Comedy of Errors* PHOTO BY DWAINE E. SMITH, COURTESY OF OREGON SHAKESPEARE FESTIVAL

"Keach, you're a very good actor."

It sounds like a compliment, especially coming from a venerated professor at the prestigious Yale School of Drama. The hint of a sneer belied the truth: The speaker, Constance Welch, meant to belittle me and my performance in *The Devil's Disciple*. Her unstated but obvious implication was that I was not—and in her mind would never be—a great actor.

Yale was definitely one of those best of times, worst of times experiences for me. My parents were, finally, so proud of my acting career that instead of fretting they were boasting. Coming east, however, meant leaving behind my new girlfriend, Kathryn, for a lonelier existence. I lived in a cold and forlorn room, with the bathroom down the hall, above Julie and Charlie's, a New Haven breakfast place, whose odors suffused my apartment. I could live with all that; I even used it as motivation to excel, just like I could fight my way back from a knee injury that made me relinquish another chance to star in *A Touch of the Poet*.

It was my acting class that was ruining my life. It started on the first day when Welch, who seemingly had been teaching since Yale first opened its doors, said everyone would perform a soliloquy. Bristling with confidence after my summer at Oregon, I fairly leaped onto the stage and launched into one of Mercutio's speeches from *Romeo and Juliet*. This lack of humility irritated her—and I should have been more modest—but I think she also raised her hackles because I wasn't intimidated by her reputation and her presence.

This was not, however, a mere clash of personalities. I found fault with Yale's entire teaching philosophy. The school never really knew whether it was teaching people to become actors or to become teachers. Worse, Welch's approach was rigid and stifling. Some exercises were useful—observing a stranger and then creating and performing a biography of that person—but nothing was tailored to an individual's particular strengths and weaknesses. Too many classes simply wasted a serious actor's time—we studied phonetics, writing out the sounds we would speak. It was laborious and totally unnecessary. To this day I get riled up just thinking about it. God, was it awful. I believe in discipline and learning to speak properly, but to create great art you have to break rules or create new rules, but for me, she lacked the imagination to do that. I got more out of a visit from Paul Newman, watching him languidly lounge onstage while talking about the need for

Portraying Henry V earned me my first national press attention. PHOTO BY DWAINE
E. SMITH, COURTESY OF OREGON SHAKESPEARE FESTIVAL

perseverance—he had been rejected for *East of Eden* and didn't become a star until his thirties—than I did from Welch's classes.

So, once again, I rebelled. I stopped attending classes and started one of my own, gathering about a half-dozen interested classmates at lunch for discussions on a wide array of topics, including how laws of science—for every action there is a reaction—intersected with artistic creation. Welch found out and was furious. She flunked me, which I deserved.

But the school awarded me the Oliver Thorndike Acting Award for my performance in *The Devil's Disciple*. It is given to the student who best exemplifies "the spirit of fellowship, cooperation, and devotion to the theater." I like to think I deserved that as much as my failing grade.

There were others at Yale with whom I connected. The professor of directing, Nikos Psacharopoulos, provided sharp-edged but constructive and insightful critiques of my work in scenes by Tennessee Williams, John Osborne, and Anton Chekhov. A few years later, Nikos generously invited me to perform at his Williamstown Theatre Festival.

At Yale, I also met Arvin Brown, who would become artistic director and the driving force behind the Long Wharf Theatre as well as a dear friend. It was Shakespeare's four hundredth birthday that year, and Valley College back in California invited me to create an evening of celebration, paying me the astonishing sum of five hundred dollars. I convinced Arvin to help me put together a one-man presentation of Shakespeare's soliloquies—he still boasts that I gave him his first paying director's job, since I paid him fifty dollars to help me rehearse between classes for two weeks. The show was well received, and my parents, who were there, felt reassured about my embrace of the classical theater, even though my dad's vision of my future was firmly grounded in the movies and television.

Afterward, listening to me moon over Shakespeare time and again, Arvin said, "Why don't you get out of here? If you love the classics and English actors so much, why don't you apply for a Fulbright grant and go to London to study?"

He was right. I wasn't going to be happy spending another two years at Yale. It just wasn't right for me. So I filled out the application and sent it off. I also realized I should pursue other options. One of those put me on a train ride down to New York City.

CHAPTER 5

Shakespeare in the Park with Joe

YOU COULD SAY THAT MY CAREER GOT ITS START IN A SMOKE-FILLED room. But the smoke-filled room is a cliché and not an entirely accurate one—smoke is ephemeral, here for a brief moment, then dissipating into the ether. That room was really filled by the monumental presence of Joseph Papp. It wasn't just the stogie and it wasn't just the charm. It was the personal vision, the impresario's instinct. Papp gave me my first big break and he did it with his own unique flourish.

I had no agent, so in the winter of 1964 I took the initiative, cold-calling Papp with a letter, my resume, glowing reviews from my performances at the Oregon Shakespeare Festival, and recommendations from various directors. I didn't know what to expect; I was just trying to nudge the door open enough to stick my foot in. I had just had those toes—and my hopes—smashed a bit during a failed audition with Robert Lewis, cofounder of The Actors Studio. He hadn't even given me a chance to act. Cold and indifferent, he talked to me for a few minutes and decided against me based on that conversation. Papp stood in stark contrast. Before he even mentioned my audition, he put me at ease with pleasantries about New York and about my trip down from Yale. Once I seemed relaxed, he asked what I planned to perform. I had chosen *Henry V*'s "Upon the King" soliloquy. He offered some encouragement and sat down to watch.

I had only recited a few lines when he suddenly stopped me. Had I bombed that quickly? Before I could grow alarmed, Joe asked, "Are you a member of Equity?"

When I said no, he replied, "Well, you're going to be. You're going to play Marcellus in *Hamlet* this summer."

Wow.

I never asked Joe what he saw in those few lines that made him choose me, though I learned he had already read my *Henry V* review before I sent it. While I don't think he was a particularly great director, he was the ultimate producer and had uncanny instincts, so I guess he recognized some mix of talent and commitment. He certainly believed in me: When the Player King fell ill, Joe gave me a second role in the production, another of the older authority figures I'd play as a young man.

As far as introductions to New York, this was not to be surpassed. I'm not just talking about landing an extra part, the support and advice I received from veterans like Howard Da Silva (whom I'd seen in *Oklahoma* as a boy), or getting to sneak out every night to be awestruck by Julie Harris's mad Ophelia scene. Joe had given me two roles, but he also gave me a valuable lesson about life as an actor, about the importance of a good work ethic, about being ready to seize opportunity, and even about how fun and glamorous it all could be.

In the play, Hamlet is driven by the spirit that visits him. Unfortunately, our Hamlet, Alfred Ryder, was too often visiting the spirits found in a bottle. Joe loved Ryder, and his moment-to-moment acting was mesmerizing, but he often couldn't remember his lines, a daunting problem with this role. There was growing concern among the cast, although during one run-through, when it was raining and we had to go downtown and rehearse indoors, Ryder was totally on his game and gave a magnificent performance.

On opening night, Ryder could barely perform because he was run down and had laryngitis. Joe knew Ryder's understudy, already playing three parts, could not handle the lead role. Richard Burton was simultaneously performing *Hamlet* on Broadway, so Joe "borrowed" Burton's understudy, Robert Burr, who had just subbed for the legendary star to rapturous applause.

I was in the country that day, completely (and wonderfully) out of contact in a pre–cell phone world, so I strolled unaware into the Delacorte to find a stage manager charging at me, shouting, "Where have you been? We've been trying to reach you all day. We called a rehearsal this afternoon and we couldn't reach you!"

I offered to run my lines with Burr, but he was rehearsing a fight scene so we didn't even meet before the performance. When I made my entrance, Burr as Hamlet looked up and said: "Marcellus?"

The line went beyond Shakespeare's intention—he really was, in a way, questioning whether I was he. So when I replied, "Ay, my good Lord," he responded, "I am very glad to see you," with extra enthusiasm.

Burr was magnificent, earning great reviews, including from the leading man he had left behind. On his first night, I was taking off my makeup when the stage manager told me that Burton and Elizabeth Taylor had come to support Burr and now wanted to pay their respects to me. I was in awe and, I'll admit, I was practically drooling as I stood next to Taylor, gazing into her violet eyes.

What a way to start my career. If this was the acting life, I thought, then sign me up . . . even if every night I had to climb up six flights to a crummy walk-up apartment I had sublet from fellow cast member Robin Gammell . . . and even if once I got there I had to do battle with giant cockroaches that looked like alien invaders from some B movie. (I know New Yorkers exaggerate about the size and ferocity of cockroaches the way fishermen do about their catch, but believe me, these could have handled either star in that year's *Mothra vs. Godzilla*.)

Joe had an amazing ability to, as my ex-father-in-law liked to say, turn chicken shit into chicken salad. And he knew what he had found in Burr. So when Ryder tried to return, Joe unceremoniously gave him the boot, refusing to back down even when the feud spilled over into the press. When the opportunity came, Ryder had not been ready. Burr had been. I took note.

I was impressed by and grateful to Joe but I was not intimidated, or even willing to be overly influenced by him. In May, I had been called in for my Fulbright audition. One of the two people overseeing the process was, to my surprise, Joe. He was perplexed, too. "What are you doing here?" he asked, knowing I'd be appearing on his stage the following month. "You don't want to go to England; you want to stay here."

The idea of American actors studying in England was something of an anathema to Joe. He was seeking to create a new style, because he strongly believed that Americans could perform Shakespeare as well as the Brits. I understood his point, but my hero was Olivier, and I believed that to master the great roles I needed classical training. To be in London or not to be in London was, for me, never even a question. To Joe, I said that I wanted to see it through, to seed as many potential paths as possible.

"Okay, fine, you're here, you might as well audition," he said. "But don't do *Henry V.* I've already seen that."

So I had to suddenly switch to Berowne from *Love's Labour's Lost.* A week later a letter arrived, informing me that I had been designated a Fulbright alternate. I was quite disappointed. But during *Hamlet* I learned that someone else had to step aside, and I was in. Joe was happy for me, sort of. He didn't think I should go but he understood, and before I left he gave me another experience by taking me to Philadelphia with the *Hamlet* production; I also got to carry a spear for James Earl Jones in *Othello.*

At the end of the summer, I left Joe and New York behind, excited to embark on the highly impractical dream of becoming a classical actor.

CHAPTER 6

Hello to All That

I WENT TO LONDON FROM NEW YORK BY WAY OF CALIFORNIA. IT SOUNDS like a mistake and it would prove to be one.

I went home to marry my college sweetheart, Kathryn Baker. We had kept our love alive with countless letters during my year on the East Coast, and we thought that everything would be as wonderful and romantic in person as it was on the page. It's easy now to see how foolish and impulsive we were. But young and in love is essentially synonymous with foolish and impulsive, isn't it?

Kathryn and I returned to New York and then boarded the SS *United States*, giddy with excitement about England. We were finally together, but almost immediately, our paths began to diverge. She went to work at Monsanto Chemical and I dove into school and London's theater world. While the marriage would officially last nearly three years, it was over almost as soon as it began.

I barely noticed the problems at home because I had fallen completely in love with the rest of my life. The Fulbright Scholarship landed me at the London Academy of Music and Dramatic Art (LAMDA), which had a brilliant program and stellar professors. The Fulbright provided fifteen pounds per week that had to be used for buying books or theater tickets, which was a learning experience in and of itself. That season featured an unimaginable feast for a young actor: Olivier in both *Othello* and *Master Builder*, Albert Finney in *Black Comedy*, Zeffirelli's innovative *Much Ado About Nothing*, Peter Brook directing *Marat/Sade*, and Peter Hall directing Ian Holm in *The Homecoming*.

I prowled the theaters, happier than I'd ever been, my appetite insatiable. I saw *Othello* so many times I think Olivier thought I was just some

34

freaky-looking usher. One night I managed to get in to watch a rehearsal of *The Dutch Courtesan* at the National Theatre and Olivier came in to check it out. I spent the rest of my night watching him instead of the action onstage.

LAMDA taught everything from the contextual history of Shakespeare's life to how to execute stage falls. I loved practicing falls and fighting with daggers and foils, but the most vital physical lessons were more subtle. The school consciously divided the learning process in two—emotional training and physical training. They taught that the emotional center is in the solar plexus and the physical center is at the base of your spine. We devoted hours to developing these centers: On the physical side, to get our bodies and voices in shape, we studied the Alexander technique, lying on the floor breathing or making a loud "HA HA" sound; for the emotional side we performed mime and worked with masks.

In one stimulating exercise, we each chose a mask, one that would help define our character's behavior. We could make sounds but could not speak. Our teacher yelled out a scenario—"You're on a mountain and must help each other get down" or "You're all stranded in a desert"—and we'd go from there. At certain points we could switch masks and characters, but she'd also lay out new facts like, "The sun is going down and half of you want to go to the left while the other half want to go to the right." She would trigger conflicts, which would invariably end with someone murdering or assaulting someone else . . . all without speaking. It was fascinating, especially when you saw how changing your mask, your outer appearance, changed your decisions and your behavior toward others.

Another favorite class was taught by Roland Fuller, a curator at the British Museum and dramaturg at the Old Vic. We'd sit in a semicircle, and he'd smoke cigarettes and tell the story of Shakespeare's life and times, making it sound as if it had just happened, and he was a member of Queen Elizabeth's court reporting on what he had seen. "When Shakespeare was a boy, he went to Covington Gardens," he'd say, and you'd be totally drawn in. An extraordinary storyteller.

Fuller believed Shakespeare wrote Shakespeare's plays, not anyone else. When I visited Stratford that year, I felt equally certain. I have since come to appreciate the skepticism of some scholars and great

Shakespearean actors like John Gielgud and Derek Jacobi who argue that Edward de Vere, the Earl of Oxford, was the playwright and that Shakespeare was nothing more than an actor-manager who put his name on the plays to protect de Vere's stature. The Stratfordian notion, that a mastery of Plutarch, who Shakespeare studied at school, could provide the needed backdrop for the genius in his plays, is not entirely persuasive. Still, until there is definitive proof that de Vere was The Man, I embrace the image of William Shakespeare as the Bard. "Take him for 'all in all,' I shall not look upon his like again."

Ultimately, the academic debate mattered less than learning to bring these plays to life, a daunting task. Hugh Crutwell would soon leave LAMDA to spend nearly two decades heading the Royal Academy of Dramatic Art, influencing the likes of Kenneth Branagh, Ralph Fiennes, Mark Rylance, and Alan Rickman. For his class I did a live presentation as Brutus in scenes from *Julius Caesar*. After the first one, between Brutus and Portia, he looked me over and said, matter-of-factly, "I don't know what you're doing, son, but whatever it is it's just awful."

I reeled as if struck. I had never been criticized like that as an actor. He then explained that he wasn't feeling Brutus's pain or struggles, that I seemed too removed from the moment. I realized he was right, I had to cross a line, to find a new, more personal, realm of expression. My next go was shaky—I wasn't quite ready to take the risks I really needed to explore the scene's depths—but he encouraged me, saying I was on the right path. I broke through on my third try and this one scene became a turning point in my career.

While in London, I received a fellowship paying for another year of study back in America as well as an offer for a position in the new Stanford University Repertory Company. I wrote to Joe Papp, asking what he thought I should do. He responded tersely, "I believe you can make your own decision. I'll see you when you get back."

He was right. I could decide. London, where acting in the classics is a given, had given me the self-confidence I needed to pursue that course at home. I was ready to throw myself headlong into my acting career.

CHAPTER 7

There and Back Again

THROW YOURSELF HEADLONG INTO ANYTHING AND THERE'S A RISK THAT you'll hit it with a thud and come away slightly dented.

My triumphant return to these shores provided just such a lesson. En route to California, I stopped in New York and auditioned for the Lincoln Center's Repertory Company to debut at its brand new Vivian Beaumont Theater. I already had a regional acting theater that would pay me two hundred dollars per week—to me, that justified all of my work so far. While my father was hoping for a movie star, I just wanted to be a classical stage actor. Still, who could resist the idea of a repertory company in a new theater in New York? I had to at least give it a shot.

I got the job. I just had no idea what I was in for.

Herbert Blau and Jules Irving were both from New York but became known as innovators in San Francisco with The Actor's Workshop, which I had seen several times while at Berkeley. They had taken over Lincoln Center's young repertory company and were determined to conquer their hometown. They were wonderful—Jules more warm, Herb more intellectual—but were quick to blow their own horns. Their self-assured, almost confrontational attitude riled up New York's critics, many of whom didn't cotton to the notion of newcomers showing them how theater should be done. I also think Jules and Herb were blinded by their own ambitions, their need to show that the city's audience hungered for less commercial fare.

The season kicked off with a nineteenth-century play called *Danton's Death*, a difficult play with a massive cast. Call it hubris. Even the theater

A luxurious wig couldn't offset the other problems
faced by the Lincoln Center Repertory Company.

was problematic: Co-designed by the great set and lighting designer
Jo Mielziner, it had awful acoustics and a stage so deep you could have
staged World War III on it. (Subsequent renovations solved these problems.) I was having a good time, anyway. I played a knife sharpener with
no lines, taking a small role while awaiting the plum role of Horner in
the follow-up, *The Country Wife*. In my free time I directed a workshop
of Chekhov's *The Marriage Proposal*, starring Daniel Sullivan (who'd be
the one to make his name as a director), in the small theater downstairs,
which later became the Mitzi Newhouse.

But *Danton's Death* died dismally, roundly panned by many critics.
Time magazine called it "Amateur Night." Even sympathetic writers, like
John Simon, found far more to criticize than to admire. Everyone was
depressed afterward. It cast a pall over the rest of the season. I gave myself
over to *The Country Wife*, studying restoration comedy and shaving my

head for the role. While the *Times* singled me out for praise, the overall reception was fairly hostile. ("Bad Restoration" carped *Time.*) Unfortunately, my most memorable moment came the night I started offstage and someone turned the lights down too soon, and I literally went off the stage. The show had a percussionist, violinist, and harpsichordist in the orchestra pit. I landed on top of the harpsichord with a horrific crash and crunch. The genius who messed up the lights waited until I was struggling to hoist myself back on the stage to turn the spotlight back on. After climbing and crawling, I pulled myself to my feet, gave the audience a wave, and departed. They loved it.

The final two plays, *The Condemned of Altona* and *The Caucasian Chalk Circle*, fared even worse; as much as I admired Blau and Irving, I did wonder about their choice of plays. I was thoroughly dispirited by the season's end and fled New York, eager for a respite from the pressures of the city. I followed the path taken by so many other actors before and after me; I went straight to Nikos Psacharopoulos, the Yale professor running the Williamstown Theatre Festival.

I absolutely loved the schedule there—you spend two weeks intensely rehearsing then just get the play up and work it out onstage. In a small town, you'd run into your audiences in the local bar, which made you feel more connected to them. The living arrangements were also a breath of fresh air after our small Manhattan apartment, although we took that concept a bit too literally. Kathryn and I kept all the windows open at night, allowing cool Berkshire breezes to waft over our bed until the night we were awakened by our shih tzu, Sasso, barking like crazy. A bat was flying around our bedroom trying to find its way out. I went for a broom, but the terrified creature smacked into a wall and hit the floor where Sasso snatched it and shook it to death. After that we kept the windows closed.

That season offered a wild variety of roles: Nikos directed *You Can't Take It With You*, my first chance to act in a modern comedy as a professional. I played the Russian ballet teacher Boris Kolenkhov. I've always loved comedy but was rarely cast in it—people saw me as a "serious" actor and as an authority figure. I played Sitting Bull in *Annie Get Your Gun*, wearing a long wig and faking my way through the singing parts. There were three great dramas: *Marat/Sade*, *An Incident at Vichy* (which I'd later direct), and *A Lion in Winter*, directed by my buddy Arvin Brown, who invited me to act at his new place, the Long Wharf Theatre, that fall. I left Williamstown feeling rejuvenated. At the Long Wharf I did another musical, *Oh What a Lovely War*, and Chekhov's *Three Sisters*. I began a torrid affair with one of my co-stars, Jennifer Darling (who later had recurring roles in *The Six Million Dollar Man* and *The Bionic Woman*), but by then my marriage existed only as a technicality. Soon there wouldn't even be that. More significantly, I reconnected with former Yale classmate Roy Levine, a talented set designer who wanted to become a director. He thought he had the perfect project. In me he found his leading man. All we had to do was convince someone in New York to back the show . . . even if it accused a sitting president of murder.

CHAPTER 8

The Cauldron Bubbles

THE '60S HAD BURST FORTH IN FULL FLOWER AND I—WELL, IT'S NOT like I hadn't noticed, but I'd definitely been watching from the sidelines. Now I would be thrust center stage.

By the time Roy Levine asked me to play the leading role in *MacBird!*, the play—though never before staged—was an underground sensation. The playwright, Barbara Garson, had attended Berkeley, too, but while we'd only been a few years apart, we'd had very different experiences.

While I was there Berkeley's great lefty movement was just beginning; I grew increasingly sympathetic, but I was too tentative in my political beliefs to pursue activism. I was a bit of an odd fit at school. Coming from a staunch Republican household, I had set myself in contrast to my parents' worldview, but not completely. In 1959, when I was old enough to register to vote, I did so as an Independent. At school, I joined the most conservative fraternity, without a Democrat in the bunch, and instantly became their most liberal member. I served as master sergeant in the ROTC, but my hair caused a ruckus—I had to obtain special permission to wear it long for the roles I was playing.

By contrast, Barbara was a true, committed lefty. She was a member of Students for a Democratic Society (SDS) and editor of Berkeley's Free Speech Movement newsletter. One day, while speaking at a peace rally, she accidentally called Lady Bird Johnson "Lady MacBird." It sparked an idea for a skit about an ambitious vice-president's wife pushing her husband to pursue power by means foul or fair. She expanded it into a play, basing her story on *Macbeth*, but also quoting liberally from *Richard III*, *Hamlet*, *Julius Caesar*, and other Shakespeare plays. Using her Free Speech Movement press, she began self-printing *MacBird!* in runs of five thousand, but she could barely keep up with demand. Although the *New Yorker* and other publications wouldn't let her buy ads for something that seemed borderline seditious, people kept finding it. Eventually she landed a publisher, Grove Press, and by the time the play actually opened, more than two hundred thousand copies had been sold.

I signed on to play the Lyndon B. Johnson–like character because Barbara (with plenty of help from Shakespeare) was offering me a fantastic and complex role in a dynamic and entertaining work. I was not from the Brechtian school, where theater is politics—I wanted to make people think but also laugh and cry and feel entertained.

The idea, Roy said, was not to bring Shakespeare "down to a prosaic level" but instead to "raise our leaders to the heroic proportions that their villainy deserves."

To Barbara the notion of Johnson murdering Kennedy (or MacBird and John Ken O'Dunc in the play) served as what Alfred Hitchcock would have called a MacGuffin, an almost meaningless plot device that serves as a catalyst. She didn't believe Johnson had murdered Kennedy—her play was about the corruption of the entire political system, including the Democratic Party and the hyper-ambitious Kennedy clan, and she hoped it would underscore the lies behind Johnson's war in Vietnam.

She was, however, among the first to give full voice to this conspiracy concept at a time when the nation, still wounded by Kennedy's assassination, was filled with whispers about who else besides that patsy Lee Harvey Oswald had been involved. The world was changing rapidly, and trust in government and other authority figures was sinking just as rapidly, but the idea of accusing someone—especially a sitting president—of an assassination was a combustible concept.

When Roy approached me about the show, I instantly recalled everything about where I was on November 22, 1963. I was at Yale, on my way to rehearsal for *The Devil's Disciple* when I entered the apartment elevator and the Muzak on the radio was interrupted with news that the president had been shot. At the rehearsal hall, the cast gathered around a television in a silent stupor. When Walter Cronkite announced that the president had died, we abandoned rehearsal and went home.

A year later I had cast my first presidential election vote for LBJ over Barry Goldwater, whose far right leanings bothered me far more than any misgivings about Johnson. I didn't fully believe the Warren Commission and thought it just as likely that the truth was closer to what Oliver Stone later proposed in *JFK*. I never thought Johnson committed the murder and I never actually discussed it in detail with Barbara or the rest of the cast, since I viewed this as a fictional work of art, a wonderful part, blending the classics I loved with political commentary about the times in which we were living.

It quickly became apparent, however, that many Americans viewed this as an out-and-out accusation. I was constantly driving in from New Haven for backers' auditions at the Theater De Lys, but despite good press in the *New York Times*, *Time*, the *New York Review of Books*, and the *Village Voice*, we failed to secure financial support. Rumors spread that theater owners had been threatened by local officials and that they'd face certain problems if they opened their doors for us. One day, Joe Papp attended a backer's reading and stood up and said that modern American theater was dying, that this brilliant and controversial play was the best hope for its revival, and that it needed to be produced. Not long after, the money came together and Art D'Lugoff stepped up and gave us the home we needed downstairs at his music club, the Village Gate. We made history as his first off-Broadway production. Art tended to book artists he liked, but he also relished the chance to take a stand—he had booked both Paul Robeson and Pete Seeger when they were blacklisted, as well as Lenny Bruce when he was being targeted by the police for obscenity issues. The Village Gate also proved the perfect physical space for us, its intimacy scaling down the play's grandiose notions.

I listened to hours of Johnson on tape and really nailed his accent and his cadences, aided by all my summers spent in Texas. At Lincoln Center I had shaved my head to persuade audiences I was old enough for the role of Horner in *Country Wife;* for *MacBird!* I donned glasses, a false nose, and plenty of padding. I wanted people to realize I was not sixty-five years old, so I played MacBird with great physicality, climaxing with a spectacular fall to the deck for my death. I was still so enamored of the techniques I'd learned in London that I devised a straight forward fall, clutching my chest, saying, "my heart, my heart" and going down hard. (My elbows still hurt from doing it every night but the move routinely brought people out of their seats.)

Given the material's provocative nature, I suggested to Roy that we try a commedia dell'arte approach, putting on white makeup and painting a line around each face, suggesting we were not being literal and giving us a chance to play these parts as larger than life (which Johnson seemed to be even in his everyday existence). Everyone bought into the idea, though it did little to persuade the rest of the country that we weren't actually accusing the president. Over time I also learned to use less makeup and rely more on squinting my eyes like a prune drying to suggest the burdens LBJ faced and hopefully to humanize him a bit.

Rehearsals started, and even though the play was the thing, we kept waiting for outside forces to intrude, for government accusations of sedition, or for the FBI to shut us down. We'd hear that federal agents would be in the audience or that the Secret Service was keeping files on each of us. During previews and the show itself, the White House was bombarded by outraged mail from people (including journalists) who hadn't seen the show, urging Johnson to shut down this treasonous work and prosecute the creators for slander. Other than some oblique criticism, the White House refrained from public or private response, although J. Edgar Hoover did blast Barbara for attempting to "destroy all acceptable standards of personal conduct and sane behavior." (Personally, I think that Johnson would have, on some level, found the play a hoot, and each night I'd imagine him in the front row.)

Even without the Feds, guns drawn, busting down our door, there was plenty of offstage drama. D'Lugoff was harassed by local authorities, and during previews they made him endure a four-hour nitpicking inspection by building and fire inspectors.

Meanwhile, the company that was to print the playbill refused (an executive wrote a letter to President Johnson about it), so Grove Press took on the task. WCBS canceled a feature on the play at the last minute, afraid of being seen as promoting such unpatriotic fare.

Blending LBJ and Macbeth into MacBird made for a memorable role.

Beyond the controversies we were beset by internal strife. Roy Levine had a great vision for the show but as a novice director, he was unable to bring it all together—he was overwhelmed and constantly doing battle with the cast, crew, and producers. The show felt rough and unready, even during previews. Shortly before opening night, the producers fired him and brought in Gerald Freedman to save the day. I had mixed feelings—Roy had worked long and hard to pull this off, but he was like a coach who loses his locker room. We did need help. Gerry proved to be a great choice—he'd directed everything from Shakespeare for Joe Papp to a Broadway revival of *West Side Story* (he'd even been Jerome Robbins's directorial assistant on the original). He was a calming influence and provided all the finishing touches. He and I also clicked. In the future, we'd work together repeatedly, on *Henry IV*, *King Lear*, *Peer Gynt*, and *Hamlet*.

With all the distractions, we had no idea what kind of reception we'd receive opening night. It felt as if we were not only performing a play but also acting out an unsettled nation's feverish nightmare. The reaction far exceeded our expectations. As the audience rose in applause that first night, one man in the front row stood and threw a rose at my feet. It was Joe Papp.

It was an exhilarating moment, especially because the entire process had been so fraught with uncertainty and tension. We'd known we were doing something special, but that night we knew we had a hit. The controversy didn't disappear—the White House still received letters asserting that we should be shut down, people still heckled or walked out during the performances, and there were even bomb threats that temporarily halted the action. The influential theater artist Robert Brustein called it the "most explosive play" of the new theater movement but the press remained divided. Some complaints were valid artistic criticism, but some critics clearly couldn't cope with the show's irreverence toward authority.

I was also getting noticed in ways I couldn't have ever imagined, but the more I became associated with this malevolent vision of the president, the weirder it became. I performed as LBJ on a comedy record, but then I was invited by anti-war protesters to impersonate the president at their rallies, which might have been interesting, but their rationale for having me there was "then we can shoot you." I guess they weren't really peaceniks underneath it all. As an actor, you're always looking for a chance to show your stuff and keep your face before an adoring public, but in a country plagued by too much violence, it was easy to turn down those offers. I was also plenty busy, taping three Shakespeare productions for public television: *Twelfth Night*, *A Winter's Tale*, and, oddly, *Macbeth*, so I'd be Banquo all day then switch to MacBird at night.

I stayed with *MacBird!* from January through August. (The show ran for over a year, until just around the time in early 1968 when Johnson announced he wouldn't run for re-election.) By that time I'd captured the Obie Award and the Drama Desk's Vernon Rice Award for my performance. Awards have never been my main measure of success—I've always preferred personal kudos from someone I admire, a critical endorsement from a critic I respect, or, most of all, the response of the audience for whom I am performing. Still, early in my career, these were a validation of my work. My moment seemed at hand. Maybe I could fulfill my dream of becoming a leading man on Broadway, starring in Shakespeare's plays on the Great White Way. It wouldn't take long for me to be disabused of that notion, to understand that I'd been born several decades too late for that kind of career. This turning point would instead lead me in a different direction, into the modern world, into the movies.

CHAPTER 9

Blount Trauma

"You want to get out of here, Keach?"

The sneering voice belonged to James Wong Howe, the legendary cinematographer, who was intimidating enough for a rookie movie actor, even without his high-top boots and riding crop.

"Yes sir, I do." It was 4:00 a.m. and I was stuck in Selma, Alabama, trying desperately to satisfy Howe while shooting my last scene in my first feature film, *The Heart Is a Lonely Hunter*. It was only a few hours until I had to fly north to my life as a stage actor, where I was about to begin rehearsals for Joseph Heller's play, *We Bombed in New Haven*, at Yale Repertory Theatre.

I was filming a drunken, back-alley excursion that ends up with my alcoholic character Jake Blount slamming his head into a brick wall. Nothing was going right. The original idea was for me to start with my head against the wall and pull back, retreating to where I would have begun the run. Howe would then have the film reversed. Howe was a consummate perfectionist and the shot was not perfect. The crew was tired and tense. Everyone, including director Robert Ellis Miller, was at Howe's mercy, but I was the one racing the clock.

"Why don't you just run into the wall and hit your head," Howe said. "One take and we'll have it."

Of course, I would be dead or in the hospital, but that really didn't matter as long as he got the shot. Welcome to the movies, Mr. Keach.

Still, I might have done it—I didn't know how to handle someone so demanding—but a prop guy produced a rubberized wall for me to bang against. Unfortunately, you could see the "give" in the wall when I hit my head. We had to return to the original plan of reversing the film. Eventually, we nailed the shot, by which point I was exhausted, sore, and better educated about the perils of film: Movies offer the luxury of doing a scene until you get it right, but sometimes you have to repeat yourself only because someone with more power than you didn't like that take. Onstage, once a play begins, the actor is essentially his own boss. So after *Heart* wrapped, I was more wary of the whole movie process and quite relieved to return to the theater.

I was glad to be done for another reason. I never felt comfortable in front of the camera, and my insecurity deepened after Robert invited everyone to a local movie theater to watch dailies. Onstage I had been comfortable projecting larger than life characters like Henry V or MacBird, so the first time I saw myself onscreen, I literally felt sick to my stomach at how far over the top my acting appeared. There was no believability. By the time the lights came up, I had slithered in my seat almost to the floor. In my mind all I heard were jeers, and they were deafening. Robert didn't see it that way. He walked by, simply saying, "Good job, Stace."

I became self-conscious about the "size" of my performance and deliberately underplayed everything, which justifiably irked Robert. My performance turned sterile. I didn't have that internal compass I'd develop later. Eventually, we found the right balance, but as a neophyte film actor, I left dissatisfied.

I didn't want to watch myself in dailies again because it made me too self-conscious. Dailies also made me want to lobby the director for whichever take I thought I performed best in, which no director wants to hear. Staying away created a diplomatic challenge—during *Brewster McCloud*, the cast and crew would drink wine, schmooze, watch the dailies, and discuss the movie, and director Robert Altman took my absence as a personal affront. So gradually I learned to approach directors and tactfully explain why I preferred not to attend dailies.

When the movie was released the next year, my mom loved my performance. That's great, right? Sure, but for years afterward she compared subsequent movies unfavorably. Given how much I valued her opinion, my inability to measure up weighed heavily on me. Meanwhile, my dad said, "When are you going to get the kind of role Clark Gable would have been cast in? Listen to your dad, I know the ropes. You come out to Hollywood, you get an agent, you make yourself available."

Naturally, I rejected his advice, forging my own path, for better and for worse. Some of this was typical father-son rebellion, my need to show I could do this my way. Some of it was genuine devotion to theater, especially the classics—young and without a family, I could afford to be noble and say I'd rather work for pocket change at Yale Rep than be a mercenary in Hollywood. Plus, *MacBird!* was what had opened the door for this movie—the original director attached to *Heart* hired me after seeing the show; when he was fired, Miller saw it and decided to keep me on.

MacBird! also opened my eyes to how exciting new plays could be—even if I wasn't a political person, there was a thrill in knowing your show spoke to, and perhaps for, your generation, that it was trying to open people's eyes to the world around them. *MacBird!* had opened other people's eyes to my ability to do contemporary and comedic work. Playwright George Tabori asked if I was interested in starring in his new play called *Niggerlovers*. The title alone almost made me say no.

George, who was Jewish, was born in Budapest but was living in Berlin when Hitler came to power. He fled to London and, after the war, to America, where he worked as a translator of writers like Bertolt Brecht, as a screenwriter on movies like Alfred Hitchcock's *I Confess*, as a novelist, and as a playwright. His writing frequently examined the relationship between Germans and Jews (he'd eventually move back to Berlin)—one dark satire was called *Mein Kampf*.

His new work was quite different, however. It was two one-act plays, a Brechtian exploration of the way American liberals really felt about race, probing into their darkest paranoia. It was only because of George's daring reputation that I agreed to read the play with such an offensive name. It was flawed, but compelling, and its ideas were certain to force the typical theatergoer to reflect on his or her own beliefs and actions. That was something I couldn't turn down, no matter what it was called.

In one play, *Man and Dog*, George's wife, Viveca Lindfors, played my dog. I was armed and we walked through a black neighborhood; when she disobeyed my orders to attack and protect, I suddenly killed the dog.

The first time we tested the "kill" moment in rehearsal, I leveled the gun just over her head. The director, Gene Frankel, an early member of Actors Studio and a pioneer of off-Broadway, urged me to get the gun in close, to make it real. I moved the gun just behind her head and fired. Viveca let out such a scream I thought I had actually shot her. The stagehands, frustrated by how often the gun jammed with quarter or half loads of blanks, had used a full load. The gun's retort could easily have punctured an eardrum. We stopped rehearsals immediately and when we returned to that scene—several days later—it was with a different gun, one that worked with quarter-load blanks.

One actor was making his off-Broadway debut. He was older than me but had bounced around, working as a dancer at the World's Fair, in a traveling theater troupe, and out in California. He was an eager student of the theater and, just as the cast of *Hamlet* had helped me, I tried to be there for him. One day he invited me for dinner in his tiny East Village apartment, where we sat and talked for hours about movies, actors, and the industry itself. Soon after, I hooked him up with my agent, who helped jump-start his career. The novice's name? Morgan Freeman.

Morgan has graciously repaid me by telling interviewers that he learned a lot from watching me in that play. Once he said he learned that "part of acting is having the security to turn yourself loose and let yourself go in order to reach whatever depths a character has. If your guts aren't hanging out there, you don't offer anything."

I was still learning that myself, and *Niggerlovers* provided a watershed moment in my evolution, a lesson about finding the necessary intensity and the ability to reveal subconscious emotions.

Underneath Gene Frankel's bushy eyebrows was a discerning eye, but beyond his understanding of the play's themes, he knew how to challenge his actors, forcing them to give a richer performance. One day there was something in the script that was bothering me and I said, "I don't feel comfortable with this moment."

Gene froze me with a penetrating glare and sneered, "Who says you have to feel comfortable?"

CHAPTER 10

We Soared, in New Haven

A GENERATION BEFORE I QUIT AT YALE, ROBERT BRUSTEIN WENT through the same cycle of anticipation, frustration, and an early exit. In the mid-1960s, Brustein returned as dean and revolutionized the school, transforming it into the type of institution I would have loved to have attended. I missed out on that experience, but in 1967 Brustein brought me back into the fold in a new role . . . or two, as an actor and a teacher.

Brustein had started a theater in 1966, but that year he relied on outside productions. In the fall of 1967, he launched the Yale Repertory Theatre, featuring a mix of professional actors and Yale students, with some of the actors also serving as assistant professors. During my final weeks in *MacBird!*, he invited me to participate in this premiere season. I was honored and excited.

I taught Shakespeare to first-year students. One student was my brother James, so we decided to live together. This proved to be a debacle. We loved each other's company but we shared an approach to cleaning up: Neither of us believed in it. One day's worth of dirty plates quickly became a week's worth. As the stack grew dangerously high, we'd flip a coin to decide who faced this horrific undertaking, but the loser rarely fulfilled the task and the dishes remained . . . along with the crumbs and scraps that provided many a nutritious meal for our growing population of ants and cockroaches.

I loved teaching as much as I disliked cleaning. My students included James Naughton (who in 1971 would play my younger brother in *Long Day's Journey into Night*) and Henry Winkler, who immediately demonstrated a flair for comedy.

Onstage, I missed the debut, *'Tis Pity She's a Whore*, because I was shooting *Heart*, but I starred in the second show, *We Bombed in New Haven* by *Catch-22* author Joseph Heller, which also featured Ron Liebman, Estelle Parsons, and Ken Howard.

The show drew the attention of not only audiences but also Broadway producers. I was ecstatic about the chance to fulfill my dream, but the producers decided they wanted a bigger name, in this case Jason Robards. Estelle and Ken also were ditched (in Estelle's case for two-time Tony nominee Diana Sands). The play didn't bomb in New York but it was far from a hit, and I admit I felt a touch of pride when the *New York Times* declared that the original production was superior in large part because of my performance. By the time it finished its brief run in December of 1968, Estelle, Ken, and I had all reached Broadway in other productions: Estelle earned a Tony nomination in *The Seven Descents of Myrtle*, Ken made his debut in a Tony-winning musical, *Promises, Promises*, and I became Edmund in *King Lear*.

I had a wonderful season acting in New Haven. In addition to the Heller play, we staged Pirandello's delightfully twisted take on *Henry IV*, *The Three Sisters*, and *Coriolanus*. Performing Chekhov is always inspiring for an actor, and I was glad to return to the role of Baron Tuzenbach in *Three Sisters*, which I had played at the Long Wharf two years earlier. I loved that my character plays the piano for the audience and even wrote an original waltz that we included. I also added to my interpretation in the baron's last scene with his beloved Irina, who has finally agreed to marry him despite feeling nothing stronger than admiration. I wore glasses for the role and left them on the bench where Irina would discover them just before she—and the audiences—heard the offstage gunshots from the duel in which Solyony kills Tuzenbach. I was suggesting that Tuzenbach knew he would die, and perhaps was even committing a form of suicide by participating in the duel. I felt the text warranted it and hoped it would stir uneasy emotions in the audience.

Fascinating but flawed, *Coriolanus* is one of Shakespeare's more ambiguous works, allowing directors to use it for right-wing and left-wing agendas. (We played it relatively straightforward.) My brother and Henry Winkler were in the cast, but most notable was Coriolanus's enemy Aufidius, played by Harris Yulin. Harris reminded me of a young

Harris Yulin and I have been friends for more than four decades.

Richard Burton. Like me, Harris was a lover of Shakespeare and an invet-
erate jock, endlessly athletic and competitive. On our own we rehearsed
our swordplay for long hours, dueling and sweating, sweating and dueling. It helped define our warrior characters but it was also great fun and a
bonding experience. It resulted in a lifelong friendship in which we have
shared the stage or screen many times and, if I may be so bold, in the best
stage fight in any production of *Coriolanus* that I have seen.

I was probably too young for the role of Coriolanus. That summer I'd
play even older, as Falstaff in Shakespeare's *Henry IV.* A *New York Times*
article looked at *MacBird!, Coriolanus,* and Falstaff and asked, "what . . . will
be left for him to do when he is 50?"

I didn't have time to worry about what I'd be doing decades down the
road; I had my hands full right then. A movie director saw my picture in
that *New York Times* article and decided to give me my first starring role.
My roles in Shakespeare in the Park and the movie were going to overlap.
It would be a busy summer.

CHAPTER 11

On the Road

IN THE SUMMER OF 1968, FALSTAFF, ONE OF SHAKESPEARE'S GREATEST creations, was born anew each day in the passenger seat of a wood-paneled station wagon hurtling down the Taconic Parkway. That was literally where I began getting into character.

Gerald Freedman and Joe Papp had offered me the part in *Henry IV, Parts One and Two* the previous fall. I'd started preparing at Yale by teaching the play to my students, affording me a chance to study alongside them. Then I watched Orson Welles's masterful performance as Falstaff in *Chimes at Midnight*, released in the United States in 1967. While other great Shakespeareans like Ralph Richardson had played Falstaff as the braggart warrior, Welles personalized the role, given where he was at that point in his career; he didn't have any second skin. I saw how Falstaff actually reacts to his own impulsive behavior, reflecting on something that he has just blurted out. My success as Falstaff relied heavily on what I learned from watching Orson.

Of course, I was much younger than Orson, coming to the role at a very different point in my life. I also worked on the part from the outside in, building my character from how I felt inside the padding and makeup required. The body suit was shockingly heavy, but it helped me feel how Falstaff was weighed down by time and regrets. Getting into makeup was time consuming. That's where the station wagon came into play. That summer I was simultaneously up in the Berkshires starring in my first movie, Aram Avakian's *End of the Road*.

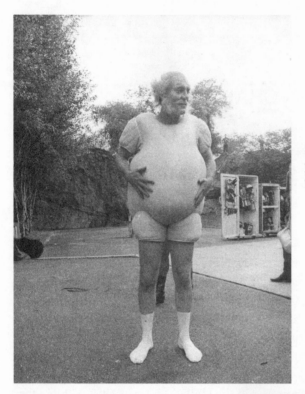

Playing Falstaff as a young man required a wee bit of padding.

Putting my Falstaff makeup on in the car en route from a day of filming

The timing was terrible but being young and invincible has its advantages, so I shifted into overdrive. During the day, I'd act in the movie, shooting in an abandoned button factory in Great Barrington, Massachusetts. Late in the afternoon I'd climb into the back of a station wagon and collapse on a mattress for an hour-long nap. Then my driver would awaken me and I'd move to the front seat. Using the glove compartment as a dressing table, I'd don my makeup for Falstaff while cruising along the Taconic, my nose jiggling whenever we hit a bump. By the time we reached the end of this road, I'd have transformed from someone in a hip 1960s indie film to a creature of the Elizabethan theater. We'd drive right into the park. I'd step into my costume and then it was time to go out and spar, verbally, with Sam Waterston, who played Prince Hal. (One of my co-stars in the movie was Harris Yulin; near the end of the summer, he was rehearsing for an off-Broadway play so he'd often share my ride.)

What I remember most clearly about performing Falstaff was the heat. Acting outdoors in the summer is always a challenge, but add in a fat suit, a wig, and leather costumes and, well, I guess I could have had a best-seller about a surefire diet plan. Sweating a small ocean each night, I lost a lot of weight that summer, though my primary fear was that the glue on my false nose would dissolve and the front of my face would tumble to the floor. It never happened. Striding offstage afterward, drenched and exhausted, I felt like I'd just come off the field after a hard-fought football game. The most indelible memory came the night we performed both parts together. We began Part One late, so by the time we finished Part Two nearly eight hours later, just after Hal has become king and banished Falstaff, streaks of daylight began flickering along the outlines of the theater. It was an exhilarating moment, one I shall always cherish. Most nights I'd simply climb back onto my mattress in the station wagon and sleep the whole way to Great Barrington, then steal a few more hours before shooting began all over again.

End of the Road would have been a wild ride even without the crazy commute.

Aram Avakian was an experienced editor (everything from Edward R. Murrow's *See It Now* program to *The Miracle Worker*), but he had never directed a feature before, having been dumped from *Lad, A Dog* when he wouldn't make the sentimental family film Jack Warner wanted.

Aram wanted to work totally outside the studio system. In a sense, he was paving the way for the great film auteurs of the 1970s. His friend, the writer Terry Southern, knew someone named Max Raab, who had made a fortune in the garment trade but wanted to get into show business. He told Southern, who had already co-written *Dr. Strangelove* and the as-yet-unreleased *Easy Rider*, to find a movie to do and he'd come up with three hundred thousand dollars. Southern had read John Barth's college campus novel, *End of the Road*, and he and Aram decided to adapt it.

Barth's novel had been set in the 1950s, but after Martin Luther King and Bobby Kennedy were killed in the spring of 1968, Aram moved the story to the present, to show an America that was coming apart, largely undone by violence. This decision resonated, since the unraveling seemed to continue even while we were filming. Terry left in August to attend the Democratic Convention in Chicago with the French writer Jean Genet. When he returned, our evening conversations shifted from Shakespeare to Terry's hair-raising tales of the protests and police aggression.

The budget was pretty small so Aram cast unknowns—James Earl Jones, Harris, myself, and Aram's wife, Dorothy Tristan. To save money on a cinematographer, Aram and Southern watched reels of directors of commercials who were hoping to break into features. One cameraman, who had also made documentaries, stood out. Gordon Willis got his first chance on our little movie and from there he went on to have a profound impact on American cinema with his brilliant use of lighting for Francis Ford Coppola, Alan J. Pakula, and Woody Allen.

Gordon also had a profound impact on me. I was suddenly leaping from minor player to star, yet I still felt uptight in front of the camera, worrying about it probing my inner soul. When I told Gordon how I felt, he casually responded, "Let me introduce you to Mitchell."

I looked around and saw no one. Gordon had personalized his Mitchell reflex camera. It was something he'd done for himself but he saw it could help me. He said, "Mitchell, this is Stacy Keach. You'll be shooting him for the next few weeks."

Whenever I was on the set, I'd say, "Hi Mitch, how's it going?" and it helped relax me, even if I seemed a little crazy to everyone else. I was also unaccustomed to the hurry up and wait process that makes film so different from theater and still got frazzled by it. I had to undo my theatrical habits of working externally, starting with the voice and movement first. In movies, I was learning, the camera does external work for you. "Get inside," Aram repeated like a mantra.

End of the Road gave me a chance to work again with James Earl Jones, who played the flamboyant Doctor D. Jimmy's persuasiveness as an actor is awe-inspiring, which could make life difficult for me. In our first scene together, I stand on a train station platform in a catatonic stupor; I was not to react in any way to Jimmy, even as he cursed and cackled and danced around me. When he growled his first line, "Your mother's breast is like cold stone," I nearly lost it. His antics then grew wilder and more fantastic and he amped it up with each take. My only recourse was to conjure up images that transported me away from his outrageously funny behavior: anything from sitting around the dining room table with my grandmother to trying to figure out how to change the tire on my car.

We experienced some tension during the shoot because Aram had his own way of coaxing performances out of his cast. For some reason, he was really hard on Harris, who was new to movies. I asked him to ease up, but he just shrugged me off. Harris didn't really seem fazed. One day we had to walk down a long hall together. Right before we started Harris said, "I'm going to do something crazy." I told him I'd go along with whatever he did. As the camera rolled he just started skipping. I later learned Aram was really ticked off, thinking Harris was trying to get back at him, but in the end he realized that Harris had created a revealing moment for his character and left it in.

Soon after, I had a scene with Harris that was supposed to be rife with tension since my character is having an affair with his character's wife. In real life we were becoming even closer as friends, spending our spare time making Super 8 movies together. To elicit the emotions needed, Aram proceeded to ignore me and all my suggestions, making me feel uptight and isolated—I took it out on Harris, which is what Aram wanted all along. Generally, though, Aram simply let us act—it wasn't his area of expertise—and our conversations revolved more around how our movie connected to the world around us.

The one tricky situation arose because his wife, Dorothy, was making her film debut as Harris's wife and my lover. Before one particularly intimate scene, she couldn't bear to have Aram staring at her so I had to say, in front of the amused crew, "Miss Tristan and I are going to make love and we'd like you to leave."

Communication was an issue in a larger sense. The cast never really understood the director's vision for the overall picture. Terry had written a great screenplay but what he had written, and even what we ultimately shot, was not really what wound up on the screen (though Terry, despite being left out of the post-production process, reportedly loved the movie). Aram had his own agenda and never really communicated it to us and, of course, he was most comfortable in the editing room, where he was a master at shaping a story to his own purposes.

I'd had real problems during the shoot because I felt my character, Jacob Horner, was some new kind of heavy, a protagonist who symbolized what was wrong with our country and was without any redemptive qualities. Horner was ugly because, like people in the new America, he refused to extend himself to anybody. Showing the dishonesty of his facades was tricky on film. When I saw the final version, I noticed Aram had cut the bits of levity I had thought crucial and had fought for, yet he had also made Horner empathetic while remaining representative of our culture. He found the performance I thought I gave and it was one of the best of my career before or since.

That taught me a lesson in patience and in believing in your director, even if sometimes the cuts a director and editor make leave you wishing you'd never signed on to their movie. I also began appreciating that film acting is about the moment-to-moment reality, that you can't really build a character along an arc like you can in the theater. Onstage, the director guides you until the show starts and then you are in control of your character. If I do something in a film, say, a gesture or a tic in Scene 2 to pay off in Scene 6, but the director uses a different take from Scene 2 or cuts it altogether, then I look like an idiot in Scene 6.

While Aram's editing underscored the truths in my performance, it didn't always serve the movie well. Some radical and surrealistic touches

Playing opposite a dynamic performer like James Earl Jones in *End of the Road* was both a thrill and a challenge.

were brilliant, but some were so stylized or ahead of their time that the audience felt lost, not enlightened. The catatonic scene I mentioned earlier—when I stood silently on a train platform while childhood photos and images from the recent political upheaval flew by—was brilliant, silently revealing that the only way I could handle all this tumult was to sink into a catatonic state. Yet it was overwhelming for some audiences, startlingly different from what they were used to. Far more shocking was the scene in which a man simulates sex with a chicken—everyone was acting out in the 1960s and Aram wanted to show what would happen if we followed this to an extreme. He may have taken it too far. There was also the infamous, graphic botched abortion scene. The movie was slapped with an X rating, most likely because of the chicken and abortion scenes, though Aram thought his anti–Vietnam War stance also hurt. The fight over the rating—along with Aram's endless re-editing—delayed the movie's release until 1970.

Life magazine gave it a huge spread in November of 1969 (we were bumped from the cover at the last minute when Paul McCartney appeared to refute the Paul Is Dead rumors), which seemed to create a backlash among the critics. Several praised it, but plenty, including Pauline Kael of the *New Yorker*, loathed it. Ultimately, the critics mattered less than the women fainting in or fleeing the theaters. I remember a screening in New York just before the movie was released, and you could hear people retching.

Aram didn't care that he had made his film unwatchable for many people; he felt the botched abortion summed up where America was heading. The film's power hinges on that scene to a large extent—it is the sad and painful resolution to an indifferent world in which people are preoccupied with the trivial and the mundane.

I was proud of my first starring role even though a movie that could have reflected and spoken for our generation, like *Easy Rider* did, instead had a short run in largely empty theaters. (I was quite pleased in 2012 when director Steven Soderbergh used his clout with Warner Bros. to get the film released on DVD for the first time, alongside a half-hour documentary he made about the movie.)

In the fall of 1968, I didn't know that yet. I did know my great opportunities were pulling me in two directions, between movies and theater. Falstaff led to a phone call that would underline that challenge.

CHAPTER 12

Caught in a Catch-22

MIKE NICHOLS HAD DIRECTED TWO MOVIES: *WHO'S AFRAID OF VIRGINIA Woolf* and *The Graduate*. When his casting director told me Nichols wanted me for his next project, Joseph Heller's classic anti-war satire, *Catch-22*, I floated out of the room. Nichols had seen me as Falstaff and was impressed by my ability both to play someone older and to play an authoritarian. He wanted me to play either General Dreedle or Colonel Cathcart in the movie. His uncertainty would prove disastrous for me.

With this offer in my back pocket, I returned to my beloved Shakespeare at Lincoln Center's Vivian Beaumont Theater, as Edmund in *King Lear*. Lee J. Cobb was making his first attempt at Shakespeare in the first Broadway version of the play since Orson Welles starred in it back in 1956. Cobb was no Welles, but this still became the longest Broadway run ever for the show. Meanwhile, I waited for Nichols to decide whether I was going to play Dreedle or Cathcart. Finally, two weeks before we were to fly to Mexico, my agent called and said Nichols had decided I wasn't right for either part. I was crushed. Then something changed his mind again—I think he had a private look at *End of the Road*. The next day I was back in the picture, playing Colonel Cathcart. I should have known better than to get excited all over again.

In a sense I was a victim of my own creation. I loved the idea of not being typecast, of playing wildly divergent characters, and from elementary school on I'd always excelled at playing older roles, at wielding an authoritative voice, such as in *The Country Wife*, *MacBird!*, and as Falstaff in *Henry IV*. I quickly learned that what worked in the theater might not

63

in movies, in a world of close-ups. Or maybe the problem was simply a director who was unsure of what he wanted.

On the plane I kept looking at this cast—Tony Perkins, Bob Newhart, Art Garfunkel, Dick Benjamin, Jon Voight, Chuck Grodin, and, of course, Alan Arkin, who had been so wonderful in *The Heart Is a Lonely Hunter*—thinking that this was going to be a highlight of my young life. But even as I sat talking to Jon Voight, I started sensing something was wrong—Nichols was friendly to everyone else but noticeably standoffish with me. Looking back I think he decided to take me to Mexico as a tryout. If it didn't click immediately, he'd ditch me.

On location life grew worse. We walked through the sets with Nichols telling each actor in great detail what he'd be doing in his set. When we reached Cathcart's office, I was positively giddy with anticipation. My balloon was quickly punctured as Nichols tersely said, "We'll work that out later. Let's move on."

At a table read Nichols laughed at every line that everyone said, or so it seemed. Laughter is contagious, especially when it's emanating from the boss man, so everyone began guffawing along. Then I read my first line. Total silence. If there were crickets in Guyamas that was all you'd have heard. Sweat rained off my forehead. Was I imagining all this? Was I paranoid? Alan Arkin reassured me, saying "I'm sure everything is fine."

The next morning I was ordered to report for a special rehearsal with Tony Perkins. Soon after, Nichols and producer John Calley fired me. Nichols said, "We don't think you have an ear for the part." Really, he was justifying the fact that he had made a casting mistake to begin with, which John told me separately, acknowledging, "You're too young." It was true. Orson Welles ultimately played Dreedle and Martin Balsam replaced me as Cathcart. Both had already celebrated their fiftieth birthdays. Compounding my misery, there were no flights out that day, so I was stuck at the site of my epic failure. I was absolutely disconsolate. My ego was shattered. I thought I was going to slit my wrists. I was a young actor and this was a huge movie, and I'd been thrown overboard after just three days. I know it sounds silly to lose a job and start muttering about suicide, especially with my stage successes, but I thought my movie career was taking off (which I knew my father badly wanted), and this blindsided me. Jon

Voight consoled me and encouraged me all night and even checked up on me after I'd returned home. I've always been indebted to him for that.

The firing took its toll in another way. Back in New York I received a call from Bob Altman, who was not yet established as a director. He had mostly done industrial films; of his two previous features, he had been fired from one, and the other, *That Cold Day in the Park*, had just bombed. He once wanted to make a movie version of *MacBird!*, but because he had seen a Los Angeles production starring Phil Bruns, he'd been talking about casting Bruns, which frustrated me. That movie never got made. So I was a bit wary about my relationship with Altman.

Bob called and said, "I've got this anti-war war movie, a comedy, and I've got a lead role for you. I don't really have a script. We'll improvise."

Having just returned from an anti-war war comedy with a part that wasn't clearly defined, I was hesitant to say the least. Still, getting right back on the movie horse would have been tempting if not for another phone call a half-hour later. My agent had a play by Arthur Kopit called *Indians*. It had been staged by the Royal Shakespeare Company in London and was coming to the Arena Theatre in Washington, hopefully en route to Broadway. And they wanted me to play the lead, Buffalo Bill.

"Oh boy, that sounds good," I said. This was a script that I could read—and I loved it. Plus I'd be working with Gene Frankel again, back onstage. So I said no to Bob Altman.

It can be read as a happy ending. *Catch-22* was a critical and commercial failure and Martin Balsam became the first actor in an American movie to be seen sitting on a toilet. That could have been me. Instead, I played Buffalo Bill in Washington and then on Broadway, earning a Drama Desk Award and a Tony nomination. That was a great triumph for me.

There was a catch, of course. The Altman part I rejected went to Donald Sutherland. The character was Hawkeye Pierce. The movie was *M*A*S*H*.

CHAPTER 13

How Can You Catch the Sparrow?

IT COULDN'T BE LOVE AT FIRST SIGHT BECAUSE IT HAD ALREADY BEEN love at first listen. Like so many other men, I'd had a crush on Judy Collins for years, since I first heard her sing back when I was at Yale. Judy was one of those performers you felt like (or fantasized that) you knew just from her music and her public persona. When I finally met the real Judy Collins, I have to admit I acted a bit starstruck and swoony, unable to get past the fact that this woman I'd admired from afar was now working with me on the stage. It was a humbling experience.

We met on the set of *Peer Gynt*. The play itself was entirely my doing. At lunch one day in early 1969, Joe Papp and his associate producer Bernie Gersten (the future head of Lincoln Center Theater) asked what show I'd like to do in the park that summer. "*Peer Gynt*," I blurted out immediately.

The play, written in verse by Henrik Ibsen, is quite difficult to pull off, but I loved the challenge of evolving from a young man to an old one over the course of an evening. Combinations of roles always fascinated me and I wanted to say I had played Falstaff and Peer Gynt, something the English greats—Olivier, Gielgud, Richardson—had not done. I felt I was contributing to the lexicon of classical acting by mixing and matching roles in a new way. Also, the title character's fanciful nature, love of storytelling, and penchant for exaggeration fit my personality. To prepare, I studied Ibsen and experimented with different make-ups to cover Peer's journey as he ages over the course of the play. Director Gerry Freedman wanted to cast Judy Collins as Solveig, Peer's love interest, who sings several songs. Gerry reassured me that he'd be able to compensate for any acting shortcomings Judy might have, explaining that the singing was the key to the role and Judy's voice was peerless. Having worked with Gerry on *MacBird!*, *Henry IV*, and *King Lear*, I trusted his judgment and was soon glad I did. (Judy was hesitant as an actress at first, but she quickly grew into the part.)

Our rehearsal process was so intense that I quickly moved past my initial awkwardness around Judy; acting in love can create instant intimacy. I was struck by how knowledgeable and interested she was about theater and culture in general. The more I knew her as a real person, the stronger I felt about her. One night she invited me to dinner and before the meal was over we were in a relationship, one that would last four years, through the most critical years in my career.

I was newly single, having just broken up with Maeve McGuire, whom I had met filming Shakespeare for public television two years earlier. (She'd had a small role in *End of the Road* but was becoming known for the soap opera *The Edge of Night*.) Judy, meanwhile, was ending things with Stephen Stills, although he did not go quietly into the night. One evening Judy and I returned home from dinner to find him on the steps. He said he needed to talk so I sat in the taxi and stewed in my own jealousy. I was relieved when Judy turned him away. Stephen's next effort to win her back from me was far more substantial. In August, his new band, Crosby, Stills & Nash, performed at Woodstock, singing "Suite: Judy Blue Eyes," which Stephen had started writing for Judy as their relationship was disintegrating. Perhaps he hoped it would woo her back. By the fall it was a Top 40 single and utterly inescapable—Judy and I would get into a taxi and there it was . . . again. That I found really intimidating—even though he couldn't pull her away from me, he definitely exacted some revenge by writing a masterpiece of a song that we wanted desperately to avoid. (Years later, however, Stephen and I got to know one another and now we greet each other with a hug.) Woodstock, meanwhile, was a trip. I got to meet Janis Joplin and share a cup of tea with Jimi Hendrix. Even the traffic jam on the way up was a sight to behold. The rolling acres of humanity forced you to experience everything slowly and deeply. However, we did not stick around to hear Crosby, Stills & Nash perform— Judy decided she didn't want to be there so we drove to Williamstown, where Nikos was directing our *Peer Gynt* co-star Olympia Dukakis in *The Cherry Orchard*.

Judy and I lived together in her West 79th Street apartment until we found a new place together farther uptown, where we lived with Smokey, a black-and-white malamute puppy I'd given Judy for our first Christmas together. Her son Clark also lived with us before he went off to boarding school. I was somewhere in between a friend and a surrogate father for Clark, a wonderful boy whose company I enjoyed. Judy was concerned about his emotional state after an ugly divorce from her first husband— she has since written that none of the schools or therapists helped him, but that she later realized that he was already battling with the genetic pre-disposition for alcoholism handed down through her family. I was always in favor of treating him like a normal kid, sending him to either public or private schools with other normal kids. One of the most traumatic moments for both of us came when we learned he'd nearly been killed in a sledding accident at boarding school. I was co-starring in a public television movie about the Wright Brothers with my brother James and shut down production so I could be with Judy and Clark in the hospital.

Often, however, Judy and I were on the road together. We had met when she ventured into my world, but almost immediately I began journeying with her into both the world of political activism and that of music. In early 1970, I accompanied her to the infamous trial of the Chicago Seven—who included Abbie Hoffman, Jerry Rubin, and Tom Hayden—in which the men were charged with inciting riots outside the 1968 Democratic Convention in Chicago. The eighth man in the original group, Bobby Seale, was first bound and gagged in the courtroom by Judge Julius Hoffman, then sent to jail.

The entire scene was madness. Rubin and Hoffman showed up one day wearing judicial robes; Phil Ochs, when called to testify, said he'd bought a pig to nominate as a presidential candidate. When it was Judy's turn on the stand, she teamed up with the Chicago Seven's lawyer, William Kuntzler, to subvert the proceedings. Kuntzler asked her about a song she had sung at the Yippee Press Conference, and Judy began singing "Where Have All the Flowers Gone," much to the dismay of Judge Hoffman. When she was forbidden to continue, she instead recited the entire song.

At lunch with Kuntzler, Hoffman, and Rennie Davis, I was impressed by how happy they were—they were not victims at all; they were energized, knowing that they were making an important statement for America and Americans. I had already been outraged by the Vietnam War, but under Judy's influence I became more politically outspoken. One night while starring in *Indians* on Broadway, I invited the audience to join the cast in an anti-war march after the show, joining forces with the casts of other shows. In 1972, I directed an anti-war rally in Washington, overseeing the appearances of Kuntzler, Jane Fonda, Donald Sutherland, and others. (The protest was the same week that J. Edgar Hoover was lying in state in the Capitol.)

Needless to say, my parents, true conservatives from head to toe, were not ecstatic about my new relationship. They eventually settled into an uneasy peace with Judy, but there was always tension. In 1972, Judy gave a concert in Santa Monica and said to the crowd that something horrible had happened that day, that our government had bombed Haiphong Harbor. From out of the silence suddenly emerged a lone person clapping and cheering for President Nixon's bombing campaign. My dear mother, ladies and gentlemen. Around that same time, I performed for two nights with Vanessa Redgrave in Berlioz's operetta *Beatrice and Benedick* in Los Angeles. At the curtain call, Vanessa stepped forward and asked the audience to join her outside the theater for a candlelight vigil protesting the Vietnam War. She flipped off her shoes and strode through the audience with me at her side, knowing my parents were in the audience shifting uncomfortably in their seats.

One of my most cherished memories of my travels with Judy had nothing to do with the activism itself. In San Francisco we joined Warren Beatty, Joan Baez, and Joni Mitchell at a rally to support George McGovern's presidential campaign. Afterward a small group of us went out to eat together and when we finished Judy, Joan, and Joni regaled us with one song after another. It was extraordinary, mesmerizing, and magical.

Joan and Joni were definitely more sociable than another legendary talent I met through Judy: Bob Dylan, who shared a manager, Harold Leventhal, with the three women. Harold had Dylan, Judy, and myself over for dinner. Dylan sat in virtual silence throughout the entire meal.

Suddenly, after it was over, he erupted with stories about sitting in the back of his Rolls-Royce writing songs.

Judy and I immersed ourselves in each other's lives. I'd travel with her on the road to her concerts (she dreaded touring) and even go into the recording studio with her. In fact, I was privileged to sing on one of her greatest records, one of the greatest records of all time. But first I had to suffer.

Judy was interested in encounter group therapy and persuaded me to explore it. She thought it would help me deal with some of the bitterness I was still feeling after the whole *Catch-22* experience. The groups were so brutal and so aggressive in trying to push you to examine your past that I just felt uncomfortable; the fact that group leaders often looked to seduce the female clientele lent a sleazy air to the sessions. (We also checked out Esalen Therapy, but once everyone started getting naked and climbing into the hot tub I decided that wasn't for me either.) Encounter groups were going to leave me *needing* therapy so I stopped going. One night Judy was at a session where things turned ugly and people turned on each other; her producer suggested that Judy calm things down by singing. Into her head popped "Amazing Grace" and when she sang the room was transformed; soon everyone was hugging and kissing. This needed to be recorded.

We went to St. Paul's Chapel at Columbia University. First, they had tried with backing instruments, but Judy wanted to replicate her encounter performance so she sang a cappella, alone at first and later joined by a chorus of professional singers mixed with friends and family—her brother Denver John, Harris Yulin, and me. With our voices echoing off the chapel's walls, it was a transcendent evening, one that the recording beautifully captured.

I even co-wrote a song with Judy, though it never achieved the same stature. I made a movie called *The Traveling Executioner*, which filmed in part at Kilby Prison in Alabama. The state had recently cleared out all the inmates before tearing down the prison, yet they'd done it so quickly that the inmates' journals, writings, artwork, and other stuff was left scattered around the cells. I decided to collect it and make a short film about life in the prison called *The Repeater*. We asked Bob Dylan if we could use his

Falling for Judy during *Peer Gynt*

song "Time Passes Slowly" but, without explanation, he said no. So Judy and I wrote "Easy Times," which she also performed live and included on her album *Living*.

Judy also joined me when I had to travel—to Alabama for *Traveling Executioner*, to Spain (with Clark) for *Doc*, and to Stockton, California, for *Fat City*. In fact, I had the feeling that Judy might have had something to do with my being cast in *Doc*—director Frank Perry was a huge fan of hers and also hired Sandra Cole, who designed the clothes for Judy's concerts, as costume designer, and Denver John in the role as the Kid, whom Doc mentors.

Judy and I never really publicly discussed the demise of our relationship. Our lifestyle certainly contributed strain, pulling us in different directions. Judy later wrote that she was struggling with her drinking and bulimia, which began in the summer of 1971, but which I was unaware of at the time. My blindness to her struggles is revealing in and of itself, about her ability to hide these things, my inability to see her pain, and how far apart we were growing. We had already taken separate apartments to give ourselves time to sort things out—I was living near the Museum of Natural History—when our true crisis arose. Judy discovered she was pregnant. I wanted to have the baby. Judy did not, given her inner turmoil, Clark's issues, and how our relationship was already ricocheting up and down.

From her perspective, her decision was the end of the discussion. She had an abortion. From my perspective, it was the end of us. We never recovered from the fight over that decision. Things soured and soon enough our relationship was over.

Eventually, Judy and I recovered our equilibrium and became friends, partly because of our siblings. We had set up my brother James with her sister Holly, and they married and had a son Kalen, so we became uncle and aunt to the same child. Judy is also a wonderfully supportive and warm person—I wish I could have such good relationships with all of my exes. Much later, when Clark died, I reached out to her and our bond has been even stronger since then. Now Kalen has children and so we are great-uncle and great-aunt together. She and her husband, Louis Nelson, a classy and charming man, came to see me perform in *Other Desert Cities*.

At the time, however, I was traumatized, first by the unraveling of our relationship, and then the abortion and the break-up. Distraught and even disoriented, I fled to California, returning home. While I'm glad I settled back down there, the move—driven by emotion—was a miscalculation. My film career was stalling and leaving New York took me away from the theater for years, which for me was akin to wandering the desert, lost and thirsty. Those years, in the mid-1970s, were my least productive years and, not surprisingly, the time when I began turning to cocaine for relief. It would take falling in love with Malgosia, nearly a decade later, to save me.

CHAPTER 14

Once Upon a Time in the West

IN *TALES OF THE TEXAS RANGERS*, MY FATHER CREATED JACE PEARSON, AN iconic figure of the American West, the lawman who solves problems and carries out justice. That was 1950. Plenty had changed in two decades, and when I took on the American West—first as Buffalo Bill in the play *Indians*, then as Doc Holliday in the movie *Doc*—I was, like my father, creating characters who were products of their time.

Indians playwright Arthur Kopit told the story, both comic and tragic, of Buffalo Bill and his Wild West show. He stuck close to the facts, but he was also writing allegorically about American arrogance in the Vietnam War. I thought Kopit used Buffalo Bill to explore our country's identity crisis—Buffalo Bill was a great and flamboyant showman who was torn between two worlds. Americans have lofty ambitions: We want to be seen as both the good guy, the hero, *and* as the big man, the power broker. In that sense Buffalo Bill—star of his own Wild West show, a friend and supporter of the Indians, yet someone who made his name when he helped destroy their world by his ruthless slaughter of the Plains bison—was like MacBird, a bombastic vulgarian with an ego bigger than his conscience.

The play ends with a wonderfully theatrical moment when Buffalo Bill strips off a mask to reveal his true self, only to find another mask underneath, and another beneath that. I've always loved that sort of schizophrenic dichotomy in characters, including Hamlet. Finding all the colors in between two diametrically opposed states, I was splitting in two myself at that moment, undergoing an identity crisis after *Catch-22* about whether I was only a stage actor or a film actor, too.

I'd always enjoyed researching my roles, but playing a historic figure really allowed me to indulge my studious side. I devoured books on Buffalo Bill and even traveled to Cody, Wyoming, to see the town he helped build. The show had already played in London before I signed on for a run at the Arena Theatre in Washington, DC, but Arthur was dramatically rewriting it, and we worked together on shaping Buffalo Bill. We did have one major argument. At the end I wanted to show that Buffalo Bill was riddled with guilt about his role in the death of so many Indians. I wanted blood on his face, blood on his hands. It was powerful, especially in those war-torn times, but Arthur thought it too crude so I dropped the idea.

We performed the Washington production at The Arena, a theater in the round and a perfect space—it felt like a rodeo ring, ideal for Buffalo Bill's show. When we moved to Broadway it was a more spectacular production, but the proscenium sapped a little of the show's manic energy. The reviews were positive but focused more on the politics than on the artistic side of the show; for a downtown audience that might have been good, as shows like *MacBird!* certainly packed the house, but a Broadway crowd doesn't want a polemic about how America screwed the Indians, so they largely stayed away. We were disappointed to last only four months.

The play was definitely political, but it was also highly entertaining, even while commenting on the artifice of entertainment. I made my grand entrance on a "horse," made out of light plaster, with a flowing tail and a hole between the front and rear that I stepped into. Legs dangled in stirrups on either side. The reins operated the neck of the horse. It was a brilliant theatrical device and created the illusion of a horse and rider. On opening night I was so nervous that I yanked too hard and snapped the horse's "neck," leaving me holding its head in my hands. The audience loved it and some people who came a second time asked why I'd dropped that bit.

In a trial scene later in the play, Buffalo Bill sits on a box with his back to the audience to watch the action. One night someone forgot to nail the box to the stage. It was a raked stage, meaning it sloped down toward the audience. So when I sat the box started sliding and I soon went flying, backward, off the stage and into the crowd. I could have been badly hurt, but thankfully people still really dressed for Broadway then, and I landed on a magnificently plush fur coat in the lap of a woman in the front row. Again, everyone thought this was part of the performance, and they all cheered as the people sitting around her helped propel me back onto the stage.

Most nights everything went smoothly and while the run wasn't as long as I'd hoped, I did win a Drama Desk Award and earn a Tony nomination. I didn't win, and I think I took it for granted, presuming it was just the first, even though I haven't swayed the Tony voters since. I think it should have meant more to me, and I may not have been grateful or proud enough at the time. Still, I'm not a tremendous fan of our obsession with awards—art isn't sports; it isn't meant to be a competition, and I think this creation of winners and losers oftentimes distorts the way we appreciate (or don't) the artistic effort and integrity of a play or movie.

I gave an interview during that time in which I talked about how I was apprehensive about moving from an ensemble actor off-Broadway to becoming a Broadway star, how I found the pressures to be a distraction, how I was suddenly facing the choice of accommodating or fighting demands from producers, neither of which helped me immerse myself in my role. Some of that was modesty, and some was tentativeness about taking on greater responsibility for a production's success, but I was definitely ambivalent about stardom. I wanted to play great roles, no doubt, but I was not someone who hungered for the trappings of fame. This ambivalence may have undermined my "career" and prevented me from getting some movie star roles that could have changed my life, but it also led me to some of my favorite plays, movies, and TV shows.

I followed my Broadway debut with an offbeat movie that was a period piece about executions, then played a small part in which I was confined to a wheelchair and unrecognizable beneath makeup that made me look wizened and ancient. And those were my mainstream choices.

In *Traveling Executioner* I had a fabulous role; I played Jonas Candide, a carnival showman turned executioner, who traveled from prison to prison across the South in 1918, with his own portable electric chair. It sounds almost absurd, but it was a realistic and layered role. As I mentioned, after filming in the prison in Alabama, I was inspired to write and direct the short film *The Repeater* about the lives of the prisoners. Obviously I had no idea that I would one day find myself in the same grim situation.

While filming I met a man famously associated with another prison. I was having dinner one night with the director, Jack Smight, and his wife, when she noticed who was at the next table and went over to Johnny Cash and June Carter to say hello. Soon enough they invited us all over for a drink. We spent the evening talking music and movies. Johnny was incredibly charming. Years later he was in California where he saw a sign that said "Stacy Keach Productions." He stopped in and met the original Stacy Keach. I was in prison then, and my dad was obviously grief-stricken about my situation, so Johnny spent an hour listening as he poured his heart out. Then he sent me a copy of his new autobiography, *Man in Black*, in which he wrote about his own battle with addiction. He inscribed it, "Peace in Your World."

The Keach clan: Mom and Dad, James, Jane Seymour and their kids, Malgosia, Shannon, Karolina, and me

A decade later, Johnny was invited to guest star on the first season of *Dr. Quinn, Medicine Woman*. Who should be directing the episode but another Keach, my brother James. Johnny returned for three more episodes. When James married "Dr. Quinn," Jane Seymour, and they had their first child, they named him John after his godfather. (Kristopher, their second son, was named after his godfather, Christopher Reeve, with whom I worked before he became *Superman*.) Johnny and June became so close with James and Jane that eventually they asked James to bring Johnny's life to the silver screen, which is how James became executive producer of *Walk the Line*. It's kind of astonishing to trace the seeds of this relationship back to an accidental meeting in an Alabama hotel.

"If Mr. Saunders did die on Tuesday I can't do anything about it; he still owes me for a week's rent. That money's going to have to come from someplace," I said as the ancient Abraham Wright, calmly talking to a woman who ran one of the many rest homes for this voracious and vicious billionaire. A second later I was berating her, "That's money right there in your hand. I want my money! Give me that money!"

I had regretted passing up *M*A*S*H* for the career opportunity, but working in just a small role for Bob Altman on *Brewster McCloud* showed me how much fun I had really missed out on. He created our characters and our scenes, but left it to the actors to improvise all the dialogue. Whether I was bullying my new driver, Brewster, or anyone else I encountered, I loved the freedom of breaking loose with all that verbiage. I enjoyed experimenting with my lines to find the right rhythm and tone—and with a character like mine there was no such thing as over the top. (Brewster was played by Bud Cort, whom I'd worked with on *Traveling Executioner* and who had just fallen into an odd but lasting friendship with Groucho Marx, which provided him with no end of entertaining stories between takes.)

My mouth was free, but my face was not. I disappeared beneath a mask that aged me by nine decades to play Abraham Wright, the 120-year-old brother of Wilbur and Orville. We filmed in Houston, which was excruciatingly hot in the summer under any circumstances, but especially under that mask. Between takes I'd have to duck into the car and crank up the air conditioning just so I wouldn't melt.

From the outside, it probably seemed as if I was dedicating myself to driving my agent nuts. At the moment that I was finally gaining some recognition, I was not only disappearing behind makeup in quirky films but also plowing ahead with projects that seemed downright certifiable. The experimental electronic music composer Eric Saltzman created a piece called *Nude Paper Sermon*, in which I delivered a monologue over his dissonant music while completely disrobing in front of the audience. I performed this at Hunter College and needless to say I didn't invite friends and family, but it did feel good to push myself beyond my comfort zone.

I devoted more time to writing a screenplay I hoped to direct based on *Outer Dark*, the second novel by a young writer named Cormac McCarthy. I loved McCarthy's characters and his sense of suspense, but it was foolhardy to think someone would finance a gothic horror story set in Appalachia that starts with incest then moves on to murder and cannibalism. Even after I rewrote Cormac's ending to make it more tolerable, it was so relentlessly dark that no one wanted to produce it.

My next acting project—playing Wilbur Wright in *The Wright Brothers* for public television—was also far from a traditional stepping stone. I was no longer rebelling against my father and his hopes for my Hollywood stardom; I simply wanted projects that interested or challenged me and wouldn't say no just because one didn't advance my career. I did lay down one condition for *The Wright Brothers*—I'd only do it if my younger brother could play my character's younger brother. James was cast as Orville and we had such a great time together that we decided to seek out another similar project. Jokingly we said, "We've played the Wright Brothers, how about the wrong brothers" and set about making a movie about Frank and Jesse James. It would take us nearly a decade to bring *The Long Riders* to life.

As with *Indians*, I reveled in the research that went into playing a real person. This project was special because we were able to shoot in the Wright Brothers' actual home and bicycle shop in Ohio, and in the bunkhouse and on the airfield in Kitty Hawk, North Carolina, though the plane I flew those first few historic feet had a Honda engine and was built in San Diego.

Even when I took what might be considered a genuine stab at movie stardom, playing a fabled Wild West hero, it was far from straightforward. *Doc* was a modernist revision of Hollywood mythology, a western with just one shootout, which lasted perhaps thirty seconds.

Doc Holliday, a dentist with a first-class reputation as a gunfighter, is obviously a delicious combination for an actor to play. (There are some biographers who believe Holliday, like me, had a partly cleft palate and lip, but others disagree. It's a fascinating coincidence but I honestly didn't use it in playing the part.) My good friend, Harris Yulin, played Wyatt Earp and we also researched the legend of Earp and Holliday in Hollywood, reading about and watching movies like *Gunfight at the OK Corral*, with Burt Lancaster and Kirk Douglas.

Pete Hamill wrote a wonderfully poetic screenplay for *Doc*, which moved away both from traditional westerns and from the thrillingly violent spaghetti westerns of the 1960s. Unfortunately, I don't think the director Frank Perry truly got it. He was great with images but not so strong on behavior; Harris and I deliberately underplayed our characters, trying to move away from mythmaking toward a realism that would provide grounding for Hamill's impressionistic writing. Perry never understood or appreciated the understated tone of the performances, so the movie feels out of sync with the events it depicts. He also cut scenes that revealed more of Holliday's character, including a drunken scene where Doc stumbles through a graveyard, finding his own tombstone, digging a hole for himself with his hands, before lying down and going to sleep. Gone as well was a framing device at the beginning and end of the movie in which a white-faced Doc (he was dying of consumption) plays solitaire on top of a huge butte before dancing with an imaginary vision of his true love Katie Elder (Faye Dunaway). These were beautifully written and shot, strangely mysterious, stylish and daring. The film flopped at the box office, a monumental disappointment, especially because unlike *End of the Road* or *Traveling Executioner*, I thought this one had more commercial potential.

During the filming Judy came to visit, bringing her son Clark. Judy has written that things were awkward for her, seeing me having to act

Doc may not have fulfilled all its ambitions but acting with Faye Dunaway was a pleasure unto itself. PHOTO CREDIT: BRIAN HAMILL

like I was in love with Faye Dunaway, but despite Faye's magnetic allure, I wasn't tempted. She was having a torrid affair with Harris, which made for plenty of tension the day her other lover, Marcello Mastroianni, came to visit the set. We were filming a big scene and I think everyone knew what was going on.

We had one other visitor during filming. My agent called to say someone was coming to see me about a movie role. That someone, however, was not just anyone. It was John Huston.

CHAPTER 15

The Treasure of John Huston

I WAS EAGER AND NERVOUS, LIKE A HIGH SCHOOL KID ON PROM NIGHT. Instead of the big dance, however, I was getting ready for my biggest movie to date. I was in Stockton, California, preparing to shoot *Fat City*, and my director was coming over to discuss the script. I hadn't felt this way before meeting with the men in charge of *End of the Road*, *Traveling Executioner*, or *Doc*—nothing against them but they weren't larger than life. John Huston was.

Huston had directed his first film in 1941, the year I was born. And he'd started with *The Maltese Falcon*. Not only that, he'd begun the year with an Oscar nomination for the screenplay of *Dr. Ehrlich's Magic Bullet*. By the time we met, he had a dozen to his credit for writing and directing (including wins in both categories for *The Treasure of the Sierra Madre*) and even one for Best Supporting Actor.

It wasn't really the awards, of course. He'd played a huge role in the ascent of his good friend and drinking buddy Humphrey Bogart from film heavy to American icon. (He wrote Bogie's first leading role, *High Sierra*, then directed *The Maltese Falcon*, *Key Largo*, *Treasure of Sierra Madre*, and *The African Queen*.) He was immensely talented and had a grand vision for his art forms, both writing and directing, but he was also a unique character, a wholly unstoppable force of nature. He'd been an amateur boxer, had studied everything from painting to ballet, had ridden with the Mexican cavalry, and had worked as a journalist. I'd heard all about him and I was wondering if he'd live up to his billing. He did. And then some.

John arrived at the house that had been rented for me with script in hand, but he dropped it as soon as he spotted the pool table. He quickly challenged me to a game. We decided on 8 Ball, "stripes and solids." John broke and smashed the cluster with such force that three balls found pockets. He nonchalantly ran the table. I never got a shot. "Just lucky, I guess," John said, smiling. "How about another? You break this time."

I fared marginally better but still lost handily. He could have done it all night except that he was distracted by the sight of my backgammon set. He sat down, lit up a Monte Cristo #1—in my mind's eye, John always has either a backgammon set or a box of cigars tucked under his arm— offered me one, which I accepted, and began shaking the dice cup like a bartender mixing an exotic drink. As we played, John graciously pointed out where I was making wrong moves. When I'd won a few games, he convinced me that I was ready to play for money.

"Dollar a point," he suggested. There was no way to back down, even as I worried I was about to get taken. Had he let me win those games? Would John Huston hustle his leading man simply to up the dramatic tension in a backgammon game? I'd say yes.

Still, I loved the adrenaline rush of games, especially when something was at stake. As a boy visiting my grandparents in Texas, I remember watching the grownups playing dominoes down at the local grain warehouse—whenever the train arrived on the tracks just outside they'd stop the game to load and unload sacks of grain, but then they'd turn right back to their game. I'd played poker in junior high, mostly for nickels and dimes (there's nothing more exciting than gambling on the sly). In high school I joined my friends in marathon gin rummy tournaments. In college I switched to hearts, at which I became fairly proficient; I also learned backgammon, albeit not well—to become adept you must know how to maximize your opportunities and minimize your risk, meaning you must study the game. At that time I only played backgammon casually, devoting more energy to shooting pool in the local Berkeley pool hall (which welcomed you with a sign declaring DON'T WORRY, IF YOU FLUNK OUT OF SCHOOL, YOU STILL HAVE A TRADE!). While at Lincoln Center, Daniel Sullivan and I, along with a few other members, would collect our meager checks each payday and immediately repair to my place for poker games that often stretched on until four o'clock the next morning. We weren't earning much but we couldn't resist. Even today, I love putting a little wager on a football game.

So I took John on. He beat me—no surprise there—but only by a few dollars, nothing spectacular. In the midst of it all he even managed to slip in some observations about the film we were about to make. Finally, at some ungodly hour, he said "See you tomorrow, Stace," and was out the door.

Games, but especially backgammon, became the focal point of my friendship with John. His mind was always active and he was also wildly competitive; the gambling wasn't about the money for him—it was the chance to win, or to lose, he found intoxicating. He loved the sense of taking chances and weighing risks. Once I was in London filming *Luther* and he was directing Paul Newman in *The Mackintosh Man*, and we met up for an evening at a casino. He sat down at the blackjack table and within ten minutes amassed a mountain of chips. I drifted to another table and played a few hands; by the time I returned the mountain was less than a molehill. John had dropped a bundle, but as he strode to the exit, he smiled at me and, with utter indifference, said, "Win some, lose some."

I think competition helped him dispose of nervous energy and focus on the task at hand when he needed to—today, he'd have been an Angry Birds or Bejeweled addict, for sure. I'm the same way—I'd played chess with Harris Yulin during *Doc* and later would do it with Peter Gallagher during *Milena*. I can't read between takes, because I don't like to disappear into another world. As I've gotten older, I've started playing solitaire and online backgammon, something I'll even do when I'm backstage between scenes during a play. (Chess requires too much concentration to play in the theater.)

On the set John and I would play backgammon between shots. Originally we played only at lunch, but soon we started slipping in games between setups, after we had rehearsed but while we waited for the crew to arrange the set. My co-star Jeff Bridges once commented that he felt jealous of our gaming bond, though he might not have felt like he was missing out if he knew that by the middle of the shoot I owed John five hundred dollars.

John Huston taking my money, yet again, in a game of backgammon

Our games made producer Ray Stark crazy—there was tremendous tension between Ray and John. One day Ray stormed over and demanded the board. John responded with his usual cool, "Why, Ray, everything's going fine."

"No, everything's not fine, John . . . we're falling behind schedule. You're not concentrating."

"I can assure you, Ray, I am concentrating, and my concentration is aided by a relaxing game between setups."

Ray reached for the board, disturbing our game, and John rose to his feet, grabbing the other end of the board. What followed was like "gimme-tussle" between two children. John finally acquiesced, and Ray, as if he were a parent, said John could only have it back if he stayed on schedule. The next day John rumbled, "We're on time today, Ray—give me the board."

Ray may have seemed like a taskmaster, but he was also a gregarious fellow who worked at building camaraderie by organizing communal dinners. Jeff Bridges would make salads, Susan Tyrell handled hors d'oeuvres, and I was supposed to make dessert. Ray taught me how to make lemon soufflé. The first time was a soggy mess, though it tasted fine, and I actually became pretty good at it. After dinner, Ray would show old movies, especially John's films, including *Reflections in a Golden Eye*, which they'd worked on together.

If John and I couldn't play on the set, he'd simply come to my house for more pool and backgammon. John could last until three in the morning and then get up on three hours of sleep with no problem, even though he was thirty-five years my senior. When we traveled to Los Angeles for scenes at Columbia Studios, my luck finally turned, and by the end of the shoot, I owed John a mere eighty dollars. At that point I considered it a victory.

John also loved telling stories, especially on the set. I'll never forget the day Audie Murphy died. Murphy had been a decorated soldier in World War II and then a celebrated actor, starring in John's *Red Badge of Courage*. When John learned that Murphy had died, he just shut down production on *Fat City*, sat down with his cigar, and said, "Well, we've lost Audie."

Then he started telling tales. The most surreal one was about how Audie was late to work one day because he was freaking out after the gun he kept under his pillow went missing. John took particular delight in delivering the story's punchline: "It turns out he forgot he had left it in the bathroom when he'd gotten up in the night."

Life with John wasn't all fun and games—the movie itself was extremely depressing. When John first discussed *Fat City* with me, I wasn't sold on the material. With my career unsettled, starring in a bleak film did not seem like a pragmatic decision. Also, instinctively, I was hoping for a more heroic role, not Billy Tully, a broken-down drunk of an ex-boxer spiraling down the drain. It was an intriguing choice for John at that moment in his career, given that his fortunes had been steadily declining since his last great movie, *Night of the Iguana*, in 1964. Like a reluctant politician who agrees to serve his president, I said yes simply because it was John who had asked me.

It was a wise decision. John trusted actors and allowed them to work through their own choices. This encouraged me to follow my instincts in figuring out how to reveal my emotions. In a crucial scene, say, the one in which Susan Tyrell and I argue heatedly in our apartment, John would say "a little more" or "a little less" between takes, but he'd let Susan and me hash much of it out ourselves, although usually he was easing us toward what he wanted all along.

John loved shooting rehearsals, when we were more relaxed and sometimes stumbled our way into an electrifying moment, one that would be difficult to replicate when we were acting "for real." Yet John also didn't hesitate to spring a surprise—even a painful one—to get results. I had to box against a professional light heavyweight, Sixto Rodriguez. I thought I was ready. I was an avid fight fan, having rooted for Carmen Basilio, Rocky Graziano, Sugar Ray Robinson, and of course, Muhammad Ali. I'd recently starred in *Long Day's Journey into Night* with Robert Ryan, who boxed in college and starred as a down-and-out fighter in the classic *The Set-Up*, and he gave me pointers about bobbing and weaving. "It's all in the shoulders," he'd say. "Don't be static. The camera doesn't like it." And

I'd trained for this movie with former light heavyweight champion Jose Torres, who worked me on the speed and heavy bags and had me do long runs, bending down every few minutes to pick up imaginary stones.

Sixto and I worked with John on choreographing the big fight scene so it would look as realistic as possible. We filmed it, but after John watched the dailies, he wasn't happy so we tried again. Then, he asked for one more take. Just before we started, he sidled over and said, with a sly smile, "All right boys, let's forget the choreography; just go out and box."

Sixto flashed a grin and said, "Just hit me as hard as you want."

Easy for him to say. I swung away but it did no good; he had arms of steel that blocked anything I threw. Suddenly, and with great finality, Sixto's right hand surged out of nowhere and just clocked me. John got the shot he wanted.

In the film, my character, Billy Tully, helps Jeff Bridges's Ernie Munger get his start. I didn't have many scenes with Jeff, and we had distinct and separate experiences making that movie. Our crucial scene at the movie's end was a quiet one, with neither character able to articulate his thoughts. We were also side by side at the coffee counter, which was too bad in a way because Jeff has extremely expressive eyes, which made acting opposite him in our other scenes feel virtually effortless. Off screen, we hit it off, and on the day we shot our walnut-picking scene, we discussed him playing Culla in my movie of Cormac McCarthy's *Outer Dark*, another reason to rue the fact that it never came to fruition.

Fat City was an incredible experience and, I believe, a great movie, one of my finest achievements. It could have attained the stature of a film classic, but Columbia Pictures felt John's original cut showed a world that seemed hopeless, so executives made him trim close to twenty minutes from the movie. One scene from John's original cut—we gathered to watch it at Ray Stark's home—was a flashback. In Billy's last moment of glory at the end of the movie, he sits dazed in his corner, thinking back to when he was a champ, introduced to a cheering crowd. The audience realizes Billy once was someone special, not just a washed-out pug, which makes his downfall more tragic. Then, after the fight, Billy returns home only to be told he has to get out of his apartment. He is almost knifed in an alley and winds up sleeping amidst cardboard boxes, hitting

Paul Newman and I at the *Fat City* party COURTESY OF COLUMBIA PICTURES

absolute bottom in a way that provides a catharsis and makes the final scene with Jeff's Ernie Munger all the more touching. The scenes were cut to minimize Billy's fall and make it less depressing, but it left viewers feeling incomplete instead. I always hoped those scenes would be found and restored on a DVD.

The actor was jittery—as we left the trailer to begin shooting, he told me how nervous he was, uncertain whether audiences would accept him in this role. I was stumped; I didn't have a clue about how to ease his mind. Had it been a novice looking for advice, I would have found helpful words—I was acting in my eighth movie and was growing more confident before the camera. This was no newbie, however; it was Paul Newman. We were on the set of *The Life and Times of Judge Roy Bean*, the subversively farcical western John had chosen immediately after *Fat City*. (Not only did John give me this role, he also showed his support by coming to see me in *Hamlet* in Central Park—tickets were so hot I couldn't even get one for this legendary director, so he sat on the staircase the entire evening.)

Paul was playing against type, as a grizzled ol' character, and he really didn't know if he could pull it off. This was the first time we'd met, but when he'd spoken to my class at Yale and in his onscreen persona, he'd projected the cool confidence that made him famous, so I was surprised to see this concern. I don't know that I was helpful, but Paul and I did become friendly. When Paul was in London shooting John's *The Mackintosh Man*, he brought Joanne Woodward to visit me on the set of *Luther*. He regaled me with ideas for a script about race car drivers—that was one of Paul's passions and I grew to love it too; the movie never happened, but Paul and I remained friendly.

In *Judge Roy Bean*, however, Paul and I played mortal enemies. Since he was Paul Newman, I was the one revealed as mortal, with bullets shot clear through me. Still, John had given me a doozy of a role, Bad Bob, the hammiest part I'd had since *Brewster McCloud*.

Bad Bob is an albino outlaw with long white hair; I gave him a maniacal laugh and twitchy fingers. I had my eyes fitted for red contact lenses but as dawn broke over the Tucson Mountains, the wind kicked up so much desert sand that my eyes became badly irritated—which meant that they looked red even after I ditched the contacts. Edith Head designed an all-black costume that made me feel madly confident, and John got me a frisky horse to rile me up further. He also encouraged me to chew the scenery as much as I wanted. In my mind, I pictured Bad Bob as a rabid dog, one whose nervous system operated independently of his brain—hence the laughter and the twitching.

Bad Bob rides into town seeking Judge Roy Bean, declaring, "You go tell that snake scum judge I intend to burn his eyes out and feed him to the buzzards." He shoots a horse and orders him cooked—"smother him in onions"—then drinks from a boiling coffee pot. In his second death threat to the judge, he promises to use an "ivory-handled knife to cut your head off and sell it to a friend in the carnival. It is my intention, Beano, to rid the ground of your shadow and to take my pleasure of this town."

In other words, I got to have more than my share of fun before Paul Newman killed me off.

The Mareth Line may not be the greatest picture but it gave me a chance to act with Henry Fonda and John Huston (plus Samantha Eggar).

John loved to let his actors find their way, yet he was always filled with opinions. Except when he wasn't. About five years after *Roy Bean,* I was cast in a movie so bad the studio kept changing the name to try and re-market it. It has been called: *The Greatest Battle, The Biggest Battle, Battle Force,* and *The Mareth Line.*

It is a flat-out awful movie but it had a terrific cast and some great moments. I was playing a quasi-good Nazi soldier, Henry Fonda played an American general, and John Huston played an Irishman. Orson Welles served as narrator. Unfortunately, director Umberto Lenzi was Italian and didn't speak English. This, as you might imagine, led to some communication issues.

I was fretting about my German accent—I didn't want to do too much—but obviously couldn't get a clear answer out of the director. So I asked John, since he'd directed me twice before. John, however, was there as an actor and struggling to figure out his own part. So he shrugged me off, saying, "I'm only an actor here. I didn't ask you about my accent. Talk to the director." When I pointed out the difficulty with that suggestion, John responded wryly, "Then learn Italian . . . or find a translator."

On both *Judge Roy Bean* and again on this movie—a portion of which was shot in an estate in Bel Air—we continued our greatest battle, the one on the backgammon board. Every time, however, I came out on the losing end.

Years later, I was returning home from a vacation in Puerto Vallarta, Mexico, and I ran into John at the airport. We greeted each other warmly and caught up on our lives. Then we discovered we were on the same flight back to California. Naturally, John happened to be carrying his backgammon set, just in case, I guess. Once on the plane, we settled in to play. For some reason, this was the one time we decided not to play for money . . . and this was the one time I won almost every game.

CHAPTER 16

Outrageous Fortune Met by
Slings and Arrows

I PUT MY BOOK TO THE SIDE. IT WAS TIME TO STEP OUT OF THE PAGES and into the moment. I was ready. I felt as though I had been living my entire life for this. This book was my journal, in which I'd scribble down my thoughts and preoccupations in the half-hour before it was time to go onstage. I'd collect my thoughts and then rid myself of them so that I would be fully open, able to react spontaneously and without any pre-meditation to what the other characters put forth. The goal was to make every performance feel like the first time I had lived these experiences. I always strive for that on stage, but I had never done this writing exercise before, nor have I ever done it since. There was only one character in my career for which I felt compelled to go to such lengths: Hamlet.

This was June of 1972, the summer dreams are made on.

First, I stepped out onto the stage at the Delacorte Theater in Central Park as Hamlet. Clive Barnes called me "one of the great Hamlets of our time" and "the finest American classical actor since John Barrymore."

In July, *Fat City* was released. Roger Ebert called me "electrifying."

August brought *The New Centurions*, which was, in terms of box office, my most successful movie to date.

Before 1972 was over, I'd earn the most votes for Best Actor from the prestigious and influential New York Film Critics Circle and be offered a pivotal role in what would become the groundbreaking and box-office film sensation of 1973. All this, and I was just thirty-one years old.

As Pistol remarked to Falstaff in *The Merry Wives of Windsor,* "The world's mine oyster."

Unfortunately, before 1972 was over, I'd also learn that not every oyster contains a pearl. Sometimes all you find is a slimy, slippery glob of mollusk. Learning to appreciate whatever you find inside the shell of life is definitely an acquired taste.

\~

For me, *Hamlet* was, oddly enough, the offspring of Eugene O'Neill. In 1971, my old friend Arvin Brown invited me to star off-Broadway as Jamie Tyrone in *Long Day's Journey into Night* with James Naughton, whom I had taught at Yale, as my brother, and Geraldine Fitzgerald and Robert Ryan as my parents. Robert was a great mentor, not about acting, but about the perils of the movie business; he said I'd be lucky to have a half-dozen movies come to fruition in the way I hoped, and I should learn to be content with the ones that worked. Of course, as a young buck, I thought my career would be different, but Robert's advice proved prescient.

Arvin's light and amiable touch quickly brought us together as a family, even though O'Neill had created a thoroughly dysfunctional one. My greatest challenge was that my character Jamie goes out to get drunk and is offstage for an hour-and-a-half, which is a lot of time to sit and fidget backstage. I'd heard that Jason Robards, when he originated the role, stayed in character by leaving the theater for a drink; one night, I tried living up to the legend but it was discomfiting—with alcohol in my system, my concentration was thrown off, and I felt disconnected from the rest of the cast. After that night I simply sat backstage and listened to the play over the intercom.

Arvin, Geraldine, James, and I were each honored by the Variety Critics Poll and our cast recording was nominated for a Grammy. After such a stirring success in New York, Arvin asked me if I'd like to return to his Long Wharf Theatre (where I'd performed four years earlier) and take my shot at *Hamlet.*

Well, any (male) stage actor, but especially one besotted by Shakespeare, dreams of two roles: Hamlet when you're young and King Lear when you're old. Don't get me wrong, I've been fortunate to play some

James Naughton and I got quite comfortable with each other back-stage during *Long Day's Journey Into Night.*

great characters in the movies, on TV, and onstage, including some of Shakespeare's other classic creations like Falstaff, Richard III, and Macbeth, but these two roles are special. They are Shakespeare at his peak, offering endless depth and nuance combined with dynamic action and great soul-shaking speeches. The catch is that you have to land your shot at these roles at the right age—perform Hamlet too soon and you might seem callow, wait too long for your Lear and you might lack the stamina the role requires. I leaped at Arvin's offer and headed off to make *Fat City* and *New Centurions* in the months in between.

In *New Centurions*, I played a rookie cop who is partnered with a world-weary veteran and who gradually absorbs how much the job costs police officers. The movie was based on a book by an active cop, Joseph Wambaugh. To make it as realistic as possible, I went to the police academy with my fellow rookies (including Erik Estrada and Scott Wilson) and was put through the paces—push-ups, sit-ups, rope climbing—all for the camera but all done for real. George C. Scott, who played my partner Kilvinski, didn't have to endure the training, but we all accompanied real LAPD officers into the most dangerous neighborhoods on real calls. I saw more dead bodies than I ever imagined I would, and I was haunted by one grotesque experience in which a corpse's head was trapped in a wire headboard and the officer we were with had to delicately set it free. Nights like that helped me understand why my character began drinking and why his marriage (to a character played by Jane Alexander) fell apart. On the bright side, Carey Loftin, who was the greatest stunt driver and coordinator in Hollywood, taught me a few tricks—how to fishtail, how to take the corners—so I could do all my driving, something I've always loved doing. And watching George act taught me about finding the truth in a scene; he would just lose himself in the moment and not try to put any spin on it. (He hated losing that focus and would become annoyed when the crew failed to keep the public—who often yelled out to "Patton"—at bay.)

The studio, however, could only stand so much veracity. In Wambaugh's story, my character Roy finally puts his life back together in large part because of a new love . . . with a black woman. Columbia Pictures thought that would be too much for mainstream America and asked if the woman could at least be made Puerto Rican, since her skin would then be lighter. Fortunately, Wambaugh stood his ground and Rosalind Cash wound up with the part of Lorrie. The love of a good woman proves irrelevant in the end, as Roy gets killed on the job.

Even being in the fake police took its toll. In one nighttime scene, I was thrown into MacArthur Park Lake but the duck droppings were so treacherous that I slipped and wrenched my knee. My leg swelled up and I was immobilized by pain. The show, the director reminded me, must go on, and I still had to chase someone through a tunnel. So I called my doctor, and they threw me in a car and sent me to his office where he was wielding a needle the size of a stiletto. It was filled with cortisone. He jabbed that sucker right into my leg. The pain was still excruciating but I made it through the night, which seemed to be all anyone cared about. Over time, the knee degenerated and I had to have surgery and eventually have it replaced, though before the replacement I called up all that pain to help me get into character for the crippled Richard III.

Balancing out the pain, *New Centurions* also introduced me to a new source of pleasure—during the shoot I stayed at a house on the beach in Malibu. Sure, I grew up in southern California, but living by the beach

Mom and Dad showing their support for me as *The New Centurions* opens

spoiled me—waking up to the soothing sound of the surf, being able to leave your front door and seconds later be plunging into the waves. It was both restful and invigorating. So a few years later, I found a six-acre parcel of land with a small house on Winding Way, a dirt road off the Pacific Coast Highway that had just a few homes on it. We were remote enough that there was no city water from Malibu and we had to install our own water tank and keep it filled—though, after bad storms, trucks couldn't make it up the dirt road, which lent a pioneer feel to the place. (Eventually, the city made it a public road and paved it. By the time I left Malibu around 2004, the whole city was more crowded and touristy.) I also loved the fact that my friend Edward Albert Jr. had a ranch just down the road, so instead of going to a neighbor for a cup of sugar, I could walk over when I felt the urge and borrow a horse.

At the start of *Hamlet,* a ghost appears and his presence looms large over the moody prince. The ghost's name is also Hamlet. In the play that makes sense because the apparition is the murdered king. It is also fitting in real life because those who have already played Hamlet will haunt any actor tackling the role.

You have an obligation to tradition, but you are also at the mercy of every audience member who has seen another Hamlet. Given my love of research, I probably doubled my burden, reading deeply about the legendary performances by William Charles Macready, Edwin Booth, Edmund Kean, John Barrymore, Maurice Evans, John Gielgud, and, of course, Laurence Olivier. (I had also acted alongside Robert Burr in 1964 and seen Richard Burton that same summer.)

To some extent, Hamlet plays you, but I did make some specific choices. I aimed to keep my performance simple, elegant, and clear. I was fortunate to tackle this role first in a small space, because the intimacy caused me to get inside my character and not declaim the lines, to make it as if the audience was eavesdropping on Hamlet's thoughts.

I also wanted to break with the notion of Hamlet as an indecisive neurotic. Some people believe Hamlet is a teen, others that he is thirty (my age at the time)—and the text supports both—but either way I saw Hamlet as a man of action, but one who is undone by his impulsive nature. He makes too many decisions, plunging in one direction and then another; as he continually plays at acting insane, he slowly blurs the line for himself.

The other key for me was to find the humor in the role, something I've always believed to be essential, especially in the most dramatic roles. You open the door to tears with laughter, humanizing a character, not with jokes but by revealing to the audience something in a situation they would recognize in their own lives.

Arvin's deft directorial touches enhanced the show. He used the small space to create an intimate, almost suffocating atmosphere for my character. When Hamlet is advising the Player King, Arvin had the Player King break out with the speeches he'll use in his show. In the *New York Times* Clive Barnes lavished praise on Arvin, myself, and the entire cast. We had another visitor from New York as well—the man who had first put me in *Hamlet* back in 1964: Joe Papp.

Joe, who loved *Hamlet* and was nearly obsessed by it, was impressed with my performance. He felt it was worthy of a New York production, and, it goes without saying, of his prodigious talents. The catch is that he wanted me to leave Arvin and nearly everyone else behind.

"I will get you an all-star cast," he promised. "I will surround you with the best of the best."

I had been distraught when New York producers had done this to Estelle Parsons, Ken Howard, and me with *We Bombed in New Haven*. I was ready to say no to Joe, to say we were a troupe and it was an all-or-nothing kind of deal. He would have shown me the door if I had tried that—you didn't give Joe Papp ultimatums. Arvin was the one who talked me out of it, telling me I'd be a fool to toss away this opportunity and that everyone involved would understand. He also pointed out that from Joe's perspective it was the right decision.

I said yes. And Joe lived up to his word. He assembled a cast for the ages. When he read off the names to me I was overwhelmed.

Claudius: James Earl Jones
James was formidable and powerful. He is quite intimidating, a crucial attribute because a weak Claudius can undermine the show.

Gertrude: Colleen Dewhurst
Colleen was regal, and powerful enough to be a good match for James. She had the bearing of a queen.

Polonius: Barnard Hughes
He was funny but also charming, which is vital for Polonius, because he otherwise becomes an unsympathetic windbag, and the audience is glad when he gets killed.

Laertes: Sam Waterston
Sam brought great finesse and grace to our duel with rapier and dagger at the play's end. I was as proud of that scene as anything else I've done.

Osric: Raul Julia
Raul was a genius comedian with impeccable timing. He was also incredibly dedicated—he was simultaneously performing in Two Gentlemen of Verona *downtown and would race up to the park by car each night to get changed and onstage just in the nick of time.*

Gravedigger: Charles Durning
Charles had a great affinity for the common man, which brought a much-needed humanity to the role.

This was also a group that made me feel like I was coming home. It was my fourth time working with director Gerry Freedman and my fourth time at the Delacorte. I'd worked with Jimmy Jones there back in 1964 and again in *End of the Road* in 1968; I'd acted in *Indians* with Raul, Sam, and Charles and with the latter two in *Henry IV;* two other friends from *Indians,* Tom Aldredge and James Sloyan, had smaller parts in *Hamlet.* From the New Haven production, Joe did import Kitty Winn, who played Ophelia with depth and delicacy, and Linda Hunt as the Player Queen. Barnard Hughes and I hadn't worked together, but he'd played Marcellus to Richard Burton's Hamlet back in 1964 at the same time I was playing Marcellus in the park.

We did nearly the full play, with a running time of almost four hours, an exhausting and exhilarating experience. Since I knew most of my lines, I read even more widely to ready myself, studying everything from a Russian version of the show to Freudian interpretations of the characters. Some people accused me of being a "technical" actor, but all this background would be synthesized into a unique, and hopefully, bravura performance. I wanted each performance to be an exploration, a journey to find something new. The research helped, but the truth was that acting opposite these people enabled me to find new depths to my own character—the new cast made it fresh, and Kitty and I even re-staged our entire scene.

The one actor I didn't know at all was Colleen Dewhurst. I'm sure she would be intimidating in any circumstances, but there was a twist. Colleen had just divorced George C. Scott, after a tumultuous (and public)

For *Hamlet,* Joe Papp surrounded me with an all-star cast including Colleen Dewhurst as Gertrude and James Earl Jones as Claudius.

break-up at around the time I was becoming friends with George during *New Centurions.*

Strained relations between Hamlet and his mother Gertrude play well onstage, and most nights the real-life tension heated at a low simmer. But on one memorable occasion, about halfway through the run, our conflict suddenly escalated. Colleen must have been in a foul mood because she'd been stewing all day. Finally, during our confrontation in the closet scene, she slapped me hard. Shockingly hard. This was no stage slap—it was not part of our show or something we had ever rehearsed or discussed. No, she just hauled off and hit me. My face stung and I was shaken up. While the behavior was entirely justified in the context of the scene, I was enraged—she had crossed a line and I would march right over it after her. So I grabbed her by the hair and shoulders and flung her onto the bed. She bounced off the bed and onto the floor. I moved in on her when I heard the sound of Polonius's voice, forcing me back into the flow of the action. I rammed my sword through the curtain with such force that the set piece crashed down. It was unnerving for me both to have another actor lose herself like that and to be pushed beyond my own sense of self-control. Yet it played as absolutely electrifying theater, a savage Oedipal confrontation.

Backstage afterward I went to confront Colleen but before I could utter a word, she said, "Stacy, my apologies for that moment but you were so brilliant in that scene the only thing I could think to do was slap you, knowing you would take the moment and use it."

Colleen never said that. It's actually what I wish had happened, followed by a teary reconciliation and a closer relationship. In actuality, we never spoke of the moment at all, remaining—much to my chagrin— distant and uncomfortable around each other for the rest of her time there. (She left before the run was over.) And our inability to communicate left us unable to figure out a way to re-create that stage magic.

Still, despite those minor issues with Colleen, and the fact that police radio calls in the park occasionally broke in over our wireless microphone system, this was the greatest experience any actor could hope for. I had set out to scale the mountain that was *Hamlet* and I had done so.

The one disappointment was that Joe didn't take the production to Broadway, which was clearly what he had in mind when he assembled that cast. He was only willing to make that investment if he had all his big guns, and James Earl Jones had another commitment. "Joe," I protested, "The show is called *Hamlet*, not *Claudius*." Joe would not budge.

I had once told the *New York Times* that I had promised myself to only take parts "which challenged and stretched me" and that I'd rejected more commercial Broadway shows because my goal was to play the great parts and "to become the best classical actor in America."

Now the *Times* had offered me that crown. The obvious question once you reach a summit is, "Where do you go from there?" If you plan ahead, perhaps you are in a range of mountains with more peaks to scale. If, like me, you are singular in your focus, then you look around from this pinnacle and see nothing, nowhere to go but down, a steep and rocky path.

With an unfortunate touch of condescension, I had added in that interview, "Do not get me wrong—I love films—but I want to develop my range, not my image."

This came in part from my year studying in London, where the students at LAMDA thought we were actors, believing the Royal Academy focused on creating stars, a dirty word. I was finally realizing this was a false premise, but I was too late. Being America's finest classical actor would not earn me a living—in Hollywood it wouldn't even open any doors, as my agent so brusquely reminded me after *Hamlet*. "Get out of your ivory tower and get to Los Angeles," she said. Yet opportunities there were slipping away, too.

There were two stunning blows, one right after the other.

The first arrived with the New York Film Critics Award. This was a prestigious and hugely influential award, one that back then swayed many Academy voters and typically led to an Oscar nomination. The previous six winners had captured a Best Actor nomination and four—Paul Scofield, Rod Steiger, George C. Scott, and Gene Hackman—had taken home the statue. (My two friends, Jon Voight and Alan Arkin, were the others.)

I won. And then I didn't.

I had the most votes but I didn't have a majority—Marlon Brando was a close second for his role as Don Vito Corleone in *The Godfather*. Suddenly, a plurality was not enough; the critics decided a majority was required to win. I've since been told that one reviewer, who had panned my performance, used the closeness of that first vote to push through this sudden rule change. Brando and I apparently battled it out across several more ballots before, somehow, a compromise candidate was found: Laurence Olivier in *Sleuth*. Soon after, Olivier garnered an Oscar nomination. I did not.

As I've mentioned, I'm not a huge fan of these awards competitions— and I say that as someone who won an Obie and a Drama Desk Award that year for *Hamlet*—but I believe this nomination would have helped my movie career.

I would not have needed that boost but for another incident that fall. I read for the part of the young priest in *The Exorcist,* performing with Ellen Burstyn and Linda Blair for writer William Peter Blatty and director William Friedkin. I knocked it out of the park. I just knew it. And I was right—that afternoon my agent called with the job offer . . . but she got a bit greedy, as agents are wont to do. The money was too low, she complained, so she had not agreed to the deal. She'd make a counteroffer on Monday. Over the weekend, Friedkin saw the Broadway smash *That Championship Season* and met the playwright, Jason Miller, who, Friedkin decided, had that certain something. He offered Jason the role. On Monday my agent found out she was too much, too late. I missed out on a role in one of Hollywood's biggest blockbusters and Jason wound up with an Oscar nomination.

Around this time, John Huston was generous enough to say of me, "Stacy is not just a star, he is a constellation. The audience will come to see whatever characters he portrays." John was a smart man but he was dead wrong on that one. *Doc* had been a flop. Audiences did not come to see me as Tully in *Fat City. New Centurions* made money but it had George C. Scott atop the marquee and even that didn't break the top twenty for box office receipts in 1972. *Judge Roy Bean* did, finishing sixteenth, but that's because audiences would come to see Paul Newman as whatever character he portrayed.

My career as a movie star shuddered to a stop, just as it was getting started.

I'd grow increasingly frustrated by this shift, especially since it meant working incessantly in smaller movies to earn a living, which left little opportunity for theater in the years to come. By taking the road less traveled, I was still able to hone my craft until I was again able to earn the roles I wanted, in television and then back onstage, having endured the "slings and arrows of outrageous fortune."

CHAPTER 17

One Fell Out of the Cuckoo's Nest

IT'S A GOOD THING I WAS NOT THE KIND OF GUY TO SIT AROUND AND wallow in self-pity, because I easily could have drowned in it: My relationship with Judy Collins soured then ended, my movie career dried up as quickly as a puddle in the summer sun in Texas, my one shot at resurrection was abruptly yanked away, and I made poor decisions in my personal and professional life. Even another go-round with *Hamlet* left a bitter taste in my mouth. On the other hand, it's a bad thing that I was not the kind of guy who was open to introspection about my frustrations and insecurities, because it was in the mid-1970s, as all these things started going wrong, that I began to use cocaine.

Life is strange, and looking back on your own from a great distance can warp your perceptions even further. The projects I landed in 1973 and 1974 made me feel diminished—plays for radio and television or movies that were either low-budget with woefully underwritten scripts or so very British as to ensure they wouldn't find an American audience. I was constantly being excoriated by my agents and managers who told me I was violating Hollywood's unwritten rules. They would have preferred that I sit on the sideline and hold out for A movies. Of course, they weren't doing such a hot job of landing me a role in those movies, but they didn't want to hear that.

Here's the truth of the matter: I am an actor. I have always been obsessed with acting. It's what I do and who I am. So I must act.

Big stars get to be choosy; the rest of us get out there and hustle. Look at IMDb: In over fifty years, Paul Newman amassed eighty-two acting credits in his filmography, Dustin Hoffman has seventy-three, and Al Pacino just fifty. By contrast, a great character actor like Charles Durning, the foil for Pacino's star turn in *Dog Day Afternoon*, was in 208 films; Murray Hamilton, who played Mr. Robinson in *The Graduate*, said yes to 153 gigs; and yours truly, who had that cameo in Paul's *Roy Bean*, well, I'm at 187 and counting—and that, of course, doesn't include the dozens of plays or all the nonfiction voiceover work.

If a script interests me, or a character intrigues me, or the cast features someone I've always wanted to work with, or the location is somewhere exotic, then sign me up. I'm not going to stay at home and wait for a call that may or may not come. Sure, some of these projects were frustrating to work on, or fell apart in the editing room, or otherwise just flopped at the box office. In most cases I enjoyed the role I was playing, and I learned something about myself in the process. All these years later, I'm able to look back at a treasure trove of memories I might otherwise have forfeited for the distant hope of a shot at movie stardom.

When the world feels like a cold and lonely place, well, that's when you're ready for Samuel Beckett.

After losing out on the chance to take *Hamlet* to Broadway and on the Father Karras role in *The Exorcist*, I had few options, but I did have an open mind to go with my open calendar. So one of the first things I did was Beckett's radio play, *Embers*, for WBAI in New York. The play is about loss, the struggle to communicate, and the need to go on regardless—prototypical Beckett in other words, but also quite suitable for where I was and where I was heading.

I was heading to Los Angeles, where my first project was only nominally more high profile than a Beckett radio play, but equally enjoyable and challenging: I played Napoleon Bonaparte filtered through the eyes of George Bernard Shaw in *Man of Destiny*. The play, which co-starred Samantha Eggar, was produced for public television by Norman Lloyd, who started as an actor in the Mercury Theatre founded by Orson Welles and John Houseman, then appeared in several Alfred Hitchcock movies, became good friends with the director, and became producer and director on *Alfred Hitchcock Presents*. (As an actor he found a new audience on *St. Elsewhere* in the 1980s.) I had a great time playing Napoleon amidst larger than normal furniture to make me look small, but I took the role in part so Norman would allow me to try my hand at directing on another project.

I chose Arthur Miller's *Incident at Vichy* and put together a great cast of actors I knew well—Harris Yulin, Richard Jordan, René Auberjonois, Barry Primus, and Bill Hansen, who had acted in the show with me at Williamstown. Knowing the material and the cast made me feel comfortable and gave me the freedom to focus on eliciting the performances I needed. It went so well that a few years later Norman invited me back to direct Pirandello's *Six Characters in Search of an Author*, which I decided should take place on the set of a television production. The concept worked, but this production was much more challenging. Norman had hired his old buddy John Houseman to star opposite Andy Griffith. (I cast my brother James in the role of the Son.) John had a wonderful demeanor, but by this point was better suited to being a presence like in his Smith Barney ad—"they make money the old-fashioned way, they eaarrrn it"—than to actual acting. His perpetual failure to memorize his lines drove Andy crazy; Andy was known for his aw-shucks *Mayberry RFD* persona, but he was a first-class actor who was always prepared and had little tolerance for those who weren't.

Still, I loved the work and would have done more if I had the chance. I'd directed Pirandello in exchange for the chance to direct a futuristic *Julius Caesar*, but the company folded before that could happen. As an actor who was struggling financially and jumping from job to job, I never had time to pursue more low-paying directing jobs, much as I might have enjoyed them. Later on I did direct a *Mike Hammer* episode and was always involved with the direction of each show.

I also acted for American Film Theater, in *Luther*, a filmed version of the John Osborne play that had been a huge hit with Albert Finney. Unfortunately, this production was rife with problems. Originally we were to film in Wittenberg, and I had visions of myself nailing the 95 Theses to the church door there. Budget cuts eliminated that side trip from England. Then producer Ely Landau overruled director Guy Greene

Luther was a man of the cloth but I always remained a man of the people. PHOTO CREDIT: NANCY L. DUBIN

and me—we wanted to make a movie, where Luther's soliloquies would be an interior voice heard by the audience but Landau wanted a filmed play and insisted I speak the soliloquies aloud. Additionally, Greene, a former cameraman of some repute, had hired the great Freddy Young as cameraman but then couldn't resist offering his own opinion on every shot, creating on-set tension.

I felt quite at home with an all-British cast that included Patrick Magee, Robert Stephens, and Judi Dench. I loved being back in London. One night, I attended a performance of *Long Day's Journey into Night* and went backstage to meet my god, Laurence Olivier. He was quite gracious to me, which obviously felt wonderful—one Shakespearean actor talking to another—but then his dresser came in and Olivier said to him, "Ah, let me introduce you to Stanley Kreach."

He could have kneed me in the gut and gotten the same reaction. I wasn't about to correct his lordship. I felt somewhat redeemed several years later when we both appeared in the television miniseries *Jesus of Nazareth*—we had no scenes together but when I saw him on the set he knew me, by face and by name.

I had one more golden goose flutter out of my grasp in those years. I was keeping myself busy doing low-budget fare like a fun but forgettable heist comedy called *The Dion Brothers* with Frederic Forrest and Margot

Kidder, a disjointed thriller called *Watched* with Harris Yulin, and a television movie called *All the Kind Strangers*, which co-starred Robby Benson, John Savage, and Samantha Eggar.

Look at that list and you can imagine how high I allowed my hopes to soar in 1973 when Kirk Douglas called. Years earlier, Kirk had starred onstage in *One Flew Over the Cuckoo's Nest*, which I happened to see during dress rehearsal from the balcony of the theater in New Haven when I was at Yale. Kirk had bought the film rights, which he eventually turned over to his son Michael. Kirk liked my work and said, "I want you to play this part, McMurphy."

Kirk wanted me to meet with Michael, so Judy Collins, who I was still with, and I went out with Michael and his longtime girlfriend, Brenda Vaccaro. Then I met with their director at the time, Hal Ashby. Hal loved the idea of me playing McMurphy. Author Ken Kesey was still writing the script and the movie at the time was, like his book, being told from the point of view of Chief Bromden, but the McMurphy role was still something to salivate over.

Then the studio decided Kesey's script read like a protest film and wasn't commercially palatable. He was shoved to the side. Soon Ashby was gone too, replaced by Milos Forman. Milos invited me to breakfast in Santa Monica, where he was quite gracious in explaining why I was no longer ideal for the part.

Devastated, I asked who I was getting pushed aside for. The answer was Jack Nicholson, "if he can get out of this movie he's doing," Milos said. "If not we'll come back to you."

That very night I was drinking at Dan Tana's on Santa Monica Boulevard and there was Jack. I sat down with him and asked, "Are you going to do this movie?"

He said, "Well, I don't know, Stace, I just don't know."

My frustration boiled over and I turned resentful and pushy, "Don't be a jerk, Jack, you better take this part. If you don't, I sure will." With a flourish, I stormed out of the place. I haven't seen Jack since. My apologies, Jack. I was the one being a jerk.

CHAPTER 18

Career Careening, *Caribe* Capsizes

BY NOW IT APPEARED THAT THE ROLE I SEEMED BEST SUITED FOR WAS The Invisible Man, since no matter how good the role was at this point, nobody noticed. In 1974, Gordon Davidson invited me to bring *Hamlet* to the Mark Taper Forum in Los Angeles. I said yes immediately—this assuaged my fear that leaving New York meant the end of my stage career and gave me the chance to show everyone out in Hollywood what I could really do. There were two problems. First, while I felt fully comfortable in Hamlet's skin, this production didn't measure up to the one in Central Park. Second, no one in Hollywood cared much about live theater and especially the classics. I felt ignored and adrift. I had appeared in nearly two dozen plays between 1965 and 1972; but after this I would not appear onstage for four years.

Soon afterward, I returned to England to co-star in the film *Conduct Unbecoming*. It was a good chance to get away and to land somewhere I felt both at home and appreciated. As with *Luther* I was again surrounded by impeccably trained actors: Richard Attenborough, Trevor Howard, Michael York, James Faulkner, and Christopher Plummer. I managed to make my English accent smooth enough to be mistaken for a local. There's no real secret to mastering it. It's observation and practice, then repeat. I'd watched many of Olivier's movies, but I'd also done a great deal of listening during my year as a student in London a decade earlier. Back then we performed all over the United Kingdom, paying close attention to the differences between the Welsh and the Scottish, between someone from London and someone from the north of England. We even took a map and broke it up into regions and then tried speaking the same basic sentences with the proper dialect for each area. It was a valuable training lesson.

I enjoyed talking Shakespeare with Chris Plummer in the make-up room and between scenes, and was impressed with how deeply everyone committed to their characters. Even when their blood alcohol levels soared, they still performed impeccably. Richard and Trevor would drink wine steadily through lunch at the Shepperton Studios commissary; Trevor in particular loved his lunchtime libations, yet no matter how lubricated he seemed, he'd shift from slurring his speech to being a proper English military man the moment we were back on the set. I'm proud of that film; it was quite successful on its own terms, unlike, say, *Dion Brothers* or *Watched*, but, even so, nobody in America saw it.

While I was in England, I also got married. I know it sounds like an afterthought, but this marriage was probably doomed from the start. Marilyn Aiken worked for my agent in California, and she was extremely attractive; when I moved to Malibu after breaking up with Judy, I really needed to buffer my pain, and this was a rebound relationship. Not long after Marilyn and I started dating, we were married in a civil ceremony in London. Then I was off again racing from one role to the next, preoccupied with resuscitating my career. Not surprisingly, we drifted apart fairly quickly.

It was not the only ill-conceived relationship I entered on that trip. One day my business manager called with an offer for a starring role in a cop show called *Caribe*. The series, meant to rival *Hawaii Five-O*, was being produced by Quinn Martin, a legend in the field, whose company cranked out hit after hit—*The Fugitive*, *The FBI*, *Cannon*, *Barnaby Jones*, *Streets of San Francisco*—setting a record with at least one series in prime-time every year from 1959 to 1980.

I was torn about doing a TV series, but my manager insisted that I'd make a lot of money, which I'd need since I was newly married, had just plunked down a fortune for a place in Malibu, and hoped to sock away enough cash to allow me to return to the stage. Finally, he said, "Let me have Burt call you."

The phone rang, and Burt Reynolds was on the other end. Here's a guy who knew all about getting exposure—remember when he created a stir in 1972 by posing for *Playgirl?* I've always admired Burt, and we had

With Carl Franklin before
we knew *Caribe* would
capsize so quickly

a nice chat, before he turned to business. "Stacy," he said bluntly, "you're a great actor but nobody knows who you are. Do the series."

I did. It was a disaster. So, it's all your fault, Burt.

❦

The Caribe Force was, well, who knew what the hell it was. It was some kind of police force. The producers changed the show's name seven times—at one point it was *Caribbean Beat* (which sounded as if I'd be playing steel drums each week)—and couldn't explain the concept clearly. Those should have been warning signs that I'd made a huge mistake.

On October 4 of that year, ABC executive Michael Eisner called Quinn Martin and asked if he had a winter replacement series. Martin had nothing more than a name but promised a series. Three days later he produced a broad outline and some general plot ideas. Trusting Martin's reputation and desperate for a hit, Eisner ordered up *Caribe* almost immediately. Martin called in writer-producer Tony Spinner; his hastily assembled staff of writers cranked out thirteen stories in one day. They wanted Robert Wagner for the lead but ended up hiring me, forcing them to rewrite the scripts to tailor it more to my personality.

They wanted to begin shooting on November 18, but I was in England getting married so we didn't start until December 9, just over two months before the first episode aired. In between I almost bailed out because I wanted more humor and some hint of originality added to the scripts—it turns out the staff had merely pulled the storylines out of old files from other shows. In the press I'd later call the show "premeditated mediocrity."

I played Lieutenant Ben Logan. Carl Franklin played Sergeant Mark Walters. We seemed to be the entire force—there was no sense that we were connected to the CIA or the FBI or anything, we were just two random guys running around the Caribbean busting people. Franklin, who had done Shakespeare in the Park and would go on to direct movies like *One False Move* and *Devil in a Blue Dress*, gave an interview as the show was debuting acknowledging that while he played an islander, his character's "native origin was not too clearly defined."

Since I'd only seen the scripts that were written for Wagner, I showed up thinking I was playing a slick, smoothly dressed playboy who gets all the girls, only to find that Spinner had rewritten Logan as a hip, tough guy to better fit me. On the bright side I got to pick out cool leather jackets and silk shirts.

Communication and planning were in short supply. Quinn had a police headquarters built in Florida, even though Tony Spinner had written nine episodes that did not feature a police headquarters. Quinn also wanted Logan to live on a boat that he'd use to travel to crime scenes, overruling Tony, who protested that no law officer would be so impractical. Quinn wanted to shoot all over the place, without considering the expenses and logistical difficulties involved in going from country to country. The government in the Bahamas wanted script approval. Haiti wanted a tax per foot of film shot. Quinn arranged for a barge that would travel with the crew and cameras, which largely went to waste as we shot only in the US Virgin Islands and in Puerto Rico before settling mostly in Florida. It still wound up being the most expensive show of the season. Oh and by the way, neither Quinn nor Tony was on location most of the time, the unit manager left, and an associate producer got stuck in charge. Not surprisingly, we were always behind schedule.

The symbol of how screwy the whole situation became was my mustache. One day, Tony flew in a subordinate carrying a portable phone in a briefcase, looking like something out of *Get Smart*. It was for me. On the other end of the hotline was Quinn. The early ratings were not inspiring and Quinn had research showing how to fix the show. "Stacy, we're not attracting enough female viewers," he said. "We want you to wear a mustache."

This, in his mind, would solve everything. The notion that the scar on my lip made me not ready for primetime stung, but I was a team player so I readily agreed. There was no time to grow a mustache so I had to wear a false one. We were shooting in the Everglades, where the humidity was 1,000 percent, and almost immediately one end of the 'stache began drooping. It started sliding off my face, stopping the action so we could fasten it back on. This made it challenging to stay in character and to shoot an entire scene. Finally, I called Tony and Quinn and told them that while I understood the manly appeal of facial hair—this was the 1970s after all—I could not stick with the mustache since the mustache could not stick with me.

The show was canceled and I overheard the following from someone from QM Productions: "Quinn says, 'It's all because Stacy wouldn't wear the mustache.'"

Quinn Martin never produced another successful series, but I was the one who really paid for this fiasco. I had compromised my youthful ideals and blatantly pursued fame and money—I had really stepped in it. The *San Francisco Chronicle*, which had written that the next time "ABC should ask for a script," was kind enough to say my career "will survive this sort of trash." They were overly optimistic.

I found myself ostracized by executives, directors, and actors, including my friends . . . or people I had mistakenly thought were my friends. They thought I had sold out, and on the outside they were right, yet I was doing it in part to allow me the luxury of pursuing stage roles that paid a pittance. Instead, I had traded that for a financial security that instantly vaporized, leaving me scrambling for work and without the time for theater.

My frustrations in these years led me to step up my drug use, which obviously was a disaster, yet there is an irony here. If I had become a bigger movie star then, perhaps I would not have found my way back to the theater to do ambitious plays like *Richard III*, *King Lear*, *Frost/Nixon*, and *Other Desert Cities*. That is something I would have deeply and truly regretted. And the (bumpy) path my career took ultimately led me to Mike Hammer. It just took me a little while to get there.

CHAPTER 19

The European inside Me

WOULD YOU HAVE ANY INTEREST IN APPEARING IN AN ACTION MOVIE with James Bond?

When your agent puts the question to you that way, the answer is easy, especially if your career is stagnating.

It was not some high-budget, Hollywood blockbuster but I'd been a big fan of that Bond, Roger Moore, since *The Saint*. The script for *Street People* was fairly well written (even if it felt like a *Godfather* rip-off in parts) and my scenes as Roger's sidekick were filled with charm and flair.

An Italian-made movie, it was part of a significant lifeline from Europe that helped me through the nadir of my Hollywood career. It was good to be an American abroad in the 1970s. The international film market was vital and there were great opportunities for American talent —in Hollywood I was a mere commodity; everywhere else I was an actor— and starting in 1975, I worked on seven European productions in four years.

Street People filmed in Italy and northern California. Making the movie, with Italian director Maurizio Lucidi and a mixed crew and cast, proved fun but chaotic and what emerged from the editing room was an incoherent mess. The ending is a perfect example: In the final scene, Roger and I are on a country road in Italy. He pushes my car off a cliff, stranding us. Why? I have no idea. I'd bet no one making the movie knew either—it was enough that it was in the budget and it looked good on camera.

This haphazard approach did produce one memorable scene: I get into a bad guy's car under the pretense of buying it and drive around with him throughout San Francisco, smashing the car to bits. It makes no sense but it's highly entertaining. It was also a spur of the moment thing—we had no permits and the streets weren't closed off. Before I got in, Lucidi told me to talk—"just count, 'uno, due'"—so my mouth would be moving and we could loop dialogue later on. Using all the tricks stuntman Cary Loftin taught me on *New Centurions*, I screeched around corners, cut off unsuspecting civilians, and banged into cars and walls.

Roger's character had hired me as his driver after seeing me in a Formula One race. We went to a track outside Rome where the car's owner—understandably apprehensive about a novice behind the wheel—requested that I just drive his beautiful machine a few feet. They showed me the controls, the gears, and the brakes, and I told the second assistant that I just needed to "get the feel" of the car. Then I shot off down the speedway. The feeling of power was addictive, and I didn't notice—at least at first—the owner running after me, yelling and screaming in Italian. I brought my new toy to a perfect stop in front of the camera crew, who gave me a round of applause. Now I understood why Paul Newman and Gene Hackman fell in love with race cars.

I loved working with Roger, who is a better actor than he ever gave himself credit for—he was always self-deprecating and felt he got lucky in his career because of his looks. It was a shame because he could have stretched himself beyond roles in which he felt comfortable. I will admit that on some level though, he was James Bond. When things went awry on the movie—and there were plenty of lost-in-translation technical snafus—Roger never lost his cool. He was suave and savvy, and he could hold a room with his wit and his storytelling, whether we were with the crew in San Francisco or in a hotel in Rome where he introduced me to Liza Minnelli, who was in town for a concert. Roger also gambled like Bond, with a debonair air and an innate ability to seduce Lady Luck, so that while my backgammon battles with him were mellower than they had been with John Huston, I lost with the same distressing frequency.

I chose my next flop, I mean film, because of the source material. I've always loved hard-boiled crime fiction and have jumped at the chance to play characters written by its great practitioners. Fortunately, I'm too stubborn to fall into the "once bitten, twice shy" pattern, because for me it took until the third time—after Jim Thompson's *The Killer Inside Me* and, later, James M. Cain's *Butterfly*—to find the one that worked, with Mickey Spillane's Mike Hammer.

The Killer Inside Me was just too dark. No matter how majestic the Montana scenery is, and how fascinating Lou Ford might seem as a character, it's hard to draw an audience to a movie with a relentless focus on a sadistic sociopath. The producers really tried—they proposed renaming the film *The Nicest Guy in Town* (not sure who they thought that would fool), and they insisted on adding a childhood filled with abuse to make Ford a more sympathetic violent murderer. I was actually called on to help fix some of the problems in post-production. The original director, Robert Weinbach, wasn't really a director—he'd gotten the rights and written the script and found himself in charge then fallen so far behind schedule that the producers fired him. They asked if I wanted to take the helm but I recommended Burt Kennedy, who had directed me in *All the Kind Strangers*. Later, the producers asked me to rework his cut to create this childhood abuse leitmotif throughout the movie. It was a great experience working on an old Moviola machine, with two equally aged editors sorting through the short and long strips of film, trying to paste together the story we wanted. I think we improved the film, but it was still too unappealing and thus another commercial disaster.

— ~ —

There are times for pride and times for practicality. If you're being considered for the lead role and instead they offer you something much further down the ladder, extenuating circumstances definitely can make your pride slide down the gullet easier.

Lew Grade invited me to his office in London for breakfast. He was incredibly excited about producing a humanizing miniseries about Jesus Christ—"he was a carpenter, he worked with his hands," he kept repeating—and he thought I might be right for the part of the Savior. The director, Franco Zeffirelli, had other ideas—he cast me as Barabbas. I felt privileged just to be part of the greatest cast to tell this story:

Laurence Olivier, James Mason, Ralph Richardson, Christopher Plummer, Cyril Cusack, Ian Holm, Michael York, Peter Ustinov, Anthony Quinn, Rod Steiger, Anne Bancroft, Donald Pleasence, Olivia Hussey, Ian McShane, and James Earl Jones.

Still, I was a little wary about my part. Barabbas was the Jewish revolutionary whom the Jewish mob before Pontius Pilate chose for freedom instead of Jesus, and the story was historically told in a way designed to incite anti-Semitism. Zeffirelli put my concerns at ease when we met the day before I was to begin shooting. His office was filled with photographs of every visual depiction of Jesus from every great painting in the world; literally hundreds of books and photos lay on tables, chairs, desks. I felt I was standing at the center of the Renaissance, surrounded by spiritual inspiration. Franco poured himself into understanding the context as much as he did into creating a visual feast for his audiences. He explained that his focus was on revealing my character's humanity; Franco's passion was infectious, particularly when he described the political righteousness he felt Barabbas embodied. He wanted to tell the story of a man whose political views, however justified, landed him in prison, and whose fate, in relation to Christ's, was equally fraught with tension.

Franco also made a brilliant decision in casting Robert Powell as Christ. Powell's amazingly expressive blue eyes revealed his character as more man than God, vulnerable and accessible. I loved spending time in Franco's trailer with Powell, watching the two spar verbally. At first I thought there were serious problems but this was how they communicated, how they inspired one another. It was an eye-opener, teaching me that by passionately challenging an idea or a point of view, by questioning the whole premise of an interpretation, you can attain clarity, a clarity that is more deeply felt, because it was hard won.

We shot in Tunisia and every order had to be translated from Italian into Arabic, English, and often several other languages to accommodate the blended cast and crew. Every day we'd have to stop shooting scenes about Jesus because of the Muslim call to prayer, an irony we all relished.

Meeting Anthony Quinn (who later became a close friend) and some of the other legends was a thrill, though there was one disappointment. Rod Steiger played Pontius Pilate, another onscreen enemy, and I was eager to work with him. Since moving to Malibu, I'd become friendly with Rod and Martin Sheen; we'd meet at the Malibu Coffeeshop for breakfast, sitting and discussing job offers we'd received or those we'd lost. (Marty and I also attended the same church.) Rod was generous and opinionated. There was a certain bitterness about the industry, a sense that he'd been overshadowed by Marlon Brando in *On the Waterfront*, even though he'd been nominated

As Barabbas in Zeffirelli's epic *Jesus of Nazareth*

for Best Supporting Actor (and even though getting overshadowed by Brando was routine for every actor). But he'd spent a lifetime avoiding being pigeonholed—he even turned down a studio contract and a starring role in *Marty* to maintain creative freedom—and so he was a great inspiration for me. However, by the time I was to film my scene with Pontius Pilate, Rod had had to leave for his next project, so they used a stand-in to shoot over his shoulder and our dialogue was spliced together. Still, it was a great project, truly living up to the word "epic," and the fact that it is still shown somewhere in the world, especially around the Easter holidays, is deeply satisfying, although to return to the practical side, some residuals would have been nice.

CHAPTER 20

You Never Forget the Taste
of Human Flesh

My career was cratering. No A-list Hollywood directors were looking at me as the next star; it was just a jumble of small parts and lackluster scripts. That is how my life looked from the outside in those years, and it's what I sometimes thought in the still of the night. Yet even after stardom had slipped away, I led a pretty charmed life, though that's always easier to fully appreciate in retrospect. In a three-year span, starting in 1976, I appeared in nine movies, three TV movies or miniseries, two episodic series, and one short film, which gave me the chance to roam the world: Tunisia, Italy, England, Spain, Sri Lanka, Canada. The finished products ranged from good to bad to truly ugly, but while my disappointments were real, they were not the entirety of the reality. And my hard work paid off in totally unexpected places: A stoner film put me in my first big commercial hit, and all that globe-trotting gave me the financial cushion to return home, by which I mean, to the stage.

～～

London too felt like home, especially after Italy and Tunisia. Michael Apted, a wonderful and intelligent director, had seen me in *Conduct Unbecoming* and cast me as another Brit in *The Squeeze*, a moody and gritty film in which I played an alcoholic, burned out ex–Scotland Yard detective. It didn't translate in America but it was well regarded and successful in England. Then I was off to Almeria, Spain, to film the desert scenes in *The*

Greatest Battle (*The Mareth Line*), which, as I've already discussed, didn't even translate well on the set. Still, I learned an invaluable lesson from Henry Fonda, though that came while we were filming at an estate in Bel Air. It was a dinner scene, with Henry playing an American general, John Huston playing an Irish industrialist, Samantha Eggar playing an Austrian actress-beauty, and yours truly as a "good" Nazi. Our conversation centered on why Hitler refused to shake hands with Jesse Owens at the 1936 Olympics and the imminence of war. All of Henry's coverage was shot first thing in the morning. Most actors—especially an older star of his magnitude—would then take off for the day and let their stand-ins read their lines off-camera for the rest of us. Not Henry. He stayed until seven o'clock at night running lines. It taught me about work ethic and the difference it can make. It's something I try to pass on to younger actors. Even when I've taken movie and television jobs simply to pay my bills or to allow me to return to the theater, I still endeavor to give my work my all, both for my own sake and for everybody working around me.

I'd work hard but if the script or the shoot went awry, I learned you couldn't always fight it. On the submarine disaster flick *Gray Lady Down*, Charlton Heston and I spent our time between takes talking Shakespeare, and I swapped Williamstown Theatre tales with Christopher Reeve, who was making his movie debut with a bit part. Then I'd go on the set and deliver overwrought clichés like, "Whatever it takes, we'll get him out of there" as best as I could.

That screenplay was pure poetry compared to *Mountain of the Cannibal God*, which gave me one of the funniest lines of my career—even though it was meant to be a tense and dramatic moment. I don't think any actor could have pulled off the line, "You never forget the taste of human flesh."

Still, this one was definitely not about the script, which told the sordid saga of a woman (Ursula Andress) who ventures into the jungles to search for her missing husband and the treasure he may have discovered in a forbidden land, a mountain jungle populated by deadly animals and hostile cannibals. I had taken the part for the chance to explore Sri Lanka, easily the most exotic and spectacular place I've ever filmed a movie.

The appeal for the producers was probably the sensationalism of the topic—one main character is disemboweled and eaten in the final

Exploring Sri Lanka and spending my days with Ursula Andress made *Mountain of the Cannibal God* worthwhile . . . almost.

moments, just before the delectable Ursula has her naked body slowly covered in paint by young native girls.

Those scenes were filmed in Malaysia, after my character died and I'd returned to America. My death scene was the perfect indicator of how clueless the producers really were. I was supposed to slip and tumble to my death off a waterfall while Ursula's character's brother (played by Antonio Marsina) stood by refusing to help. (Don't ask why, you're better off not bothering with the shaky machinations of the plot.) When they produced a yellow rubber mannequin to stand in for me, I protested that they should at least get something flesh-colored to bounce along the rocks. "The sun is dropping, we don't have time," our director, Sergio Martino responded. "Give me your shirt." So I had to strip to the waist to provide a passable cover for the dummy.

Ursula came closer to actual danger while we were on location. We were filming a scene where a cobra is supposed to appear in the weeds and Claudio Cassinelli has to grab the snake from behind the head and kill it. (His character kind of appears out of nowhere midway through the movie but at least that gave me one strong actor to play off.) It was carefully staged with snake handlers showing him what to do. The snake's jaws had been sewed shut. Even so, Claudio remained terrified and tentative. It took perhaps twenty takes before he could even grab the snake. He finally got it. The next day we were filming a scene in the river where our raft crashes against the rocks, and we have to swim to the riverbank. In the middle of the shot, a deadly cobra started climbing on Ursula's back. Only this time it was for real, and Claudio instinctively grabbed the snake like he had finally learned to do the day before. He saved Ursula's life.

When I finally saw the movie, I actually felt a bit sick. Martino, apparently to appease the gore-hungry distributors in foreign markets, had stuck in actual footage of scenes of a tarantula being killed, a monitor lizard being gutted, and a monkey being eaten by a python. The latter was especially controversial because there was speculation that the monkey was essentially presented to the snake for the purposes of the shoot. The movie was banned in the United Kingdom until 2001, and I can't say that the British missed out on anything.

If I had known about these plans ahead of time, I would have turned down the script. Having endured this film and the mixed bag that preceded it, however, I at least finally had the luxury of returning to the theater, playing a character whose every line is a classic.

CHAPTER 21

From the Shadows

MY NOSE, MY NOSE, MY KINGDOM FOR A NOSE. IT IS THE MIDDLE OF THE night, yet the world is lit in vibrant color. I am frantically racing around San Francisco, going from phone booth to phone booth, calling one person after another, desperately seeking help. I cannot find my nose and I need to be onstage in a matter of minutes.

Finally, I find my oversized proboscis in a trash can. The stench is overpowering, yet I must affix it to my real one. I am thrust into the theater and then out onstage. It is smoky and the glare from the lights is blinding, all these dark figures are standing around and ... I have no idea what to say. I no longer even know what play I'm in.

I wake up from this actor's nightmare just as the laughter and catcalls begin. I've had this dream numerous times across the decades, but it started when I was wearing the most prominent nose in theater history, the one swooping off the face of Cyrano de Bergerac.

I did not have this nightmare when I returned to the stage in the fall of 1978, for the first time in four years, starring as Cyrano, opposite Stefanie Powers in Long Beach. In fact, it was a relief, almost cathartic to be back. I had been so busy with films, I had forgotten how much a stage actor feeds off the audience's energy, how much it nourishes you.

The nose is, of course, central to the role. I'd worn false ones before—as MacBird, as Falstaff—but this one had to be just right. I'd seen schnozzes that dipped down, but Cyrano is a romantic, filled with hope and longing, so I wanted mine to go up at the end. Yet I also wanted it to be a little off, to be crooked, something that was a real deformity but that also looked lived in and realistic.

As for the famous balcony scene, I received an intriguing tip from the man most associated with the role, Jose Ferrer. "Make sure you have light in the balcony scene!" he told me. Although Cyrano is hidden in the shadows so Roxanne can't see him, Jose insisted that it was crucial that he be lit so the audience could see his emotional reactions. Unrealistic? Sure. Self-serving? A bit. But it served the play well.

Stefanie and I were a smash, connecting so well onstage that her beau, William Holden, was initially jealous. I was so excited to meet him, I didn't even realize that until after we'd become friendly. We got great reviews, even back in New York, which fueled a drumbeat for a Broadway transfer. This felt like a dream, the chance to play one of theater's greatest roles on center stage.

Alas, there was a newspaper strike in New York, which meant no possible press, which meant no investors and no show. Instead, we took the production to my alma mater at Berkeley, and it was right before that debut when I first had the nose nightmare.

The fear of embarrassing myself onstage may have been strong in my subconscious, but my experience with *Cyrano* was so invigorating that I was determined never to let myself stray so far from the stage again, a vow I kept except for the years around my arrest and time in jail.

᠆᠊᠊᠆

I have to admit I had been a bit of a theater snob—one reason it took me so long to return to the stage, besides the need to earn a living, was that I had been waiting for a great role in a classic play, like *Cyrano*. Having rediscovered the vitality of acting live before an audience every night, I was determined to be more open-minded. Not long after *Cyrano*, I was offered the chance to return to Broadway as a replacement in a slick commercial thriller, *Deathtrap*. There was still a stigma attached to taking over a role in a successful production, but I was past caring about what anyone else thought—I was going to be in a Broadway hit and that was enough for me. I watched John Wood's performance before I took over, but my favorite lesson came from venerable producer Alfred De Liagre, who loved the role of frustrated writer Sidney Bruhl so much that he got up onstage and acted out the part for me. He was great. I actually stole a lot of his behavior.

The next year I had a chance for more serious fare when Bill Bryden staged a Eugene O'Neill festival at the National Theater in London. Bill invited me to star in *Hughie*, O'Neill's short two-hander, which is largely the monologues of Erie Smith, a down-on-his-luck hustler.

This was a triumphant return for me—I had starred in the play as my final student project at LAMDA. This time around, the nicks and bruises inflicted by Hollywood—not to mention the lessons I'd learned losing money to John Huston and Roger Moore—enabled me to dig deeper into Erie's battered psyche. Bill and I re-imagined Erie's entrance—actors often saunter into the hotel lobby where the action takes place. I burst through the doors, nearly frantic, as if I was being followed, creating a powerful tension from the opening moments. I felt especially gratified when Sir Ralph Richardson came backstage and said, "Young man, that opening was absolutely stunning."

Fortunately, Sir Ralph was not there the night I committed one of my more memorable gaffes onstage: Every actor drops lines, but on this occasion I suddenly jumped ahead four entire pages. The eyes of the actor playing the night clerk bulged, alerting me to what I had done. I shifted gears, reversing back to where I should have been but then spent the next several minutes simultaneously acting and desperately trying to sort out what I'd do when I got back to the future.

The small moment was far less nerve-wracking than the next theatrical challenge I set for myself: singing in a musical for the first time in more than fifteen years, this time while walking on a tightrope.

In 1981 I went out on the road as the lead in *Barnum*. Many actors don't like the road, but movie life trained me to take home with me, so I was comfortable with the travel. It was the demands of the part that weighed heavily on me.

I knew I wasn't going to be a belt-it-out vocalist—I was more the Rex Harrison or Richard Burton talk-singer—but I had to at least sound passable, especially on the ballad "The Colors of My Life," so I took singing lessons and also found a way to make the song quiet and reflective in a way that suited both the moment and my abilities. Cy Coleman, who'd written the music, also took me up to his apartment one day to help me master "There's a Sucker Born Every Minute."

Meanwhile, I'd been so impressed by the way Jim Dale pulled off the show's physical stunts that I went to circus school in Los Angeles to master the tightrope. Then I came to New York to get additional help from Big Apple Circus founder Paul Binder, who was simultaneously teaching Tony Orlando as he prepped to replace Dale on Broadway.

Still, I struggled. One day I fell off from six feet up and landed directly on my chin, which became quite swollen. My embarrassment was acute because soon after I had to perform as Barnum at the annual Easter Egg Hunt at the White House. I looked more like a clown than the circus mastermind.

Each day during rehearsal, I mounted the tightrope, started singing, and fell off before reaching the other end of my walk. Through previews I was growing increasingly frustrated and nervous, until the first time I successfully pulled off the feat ... which happened to be on opening night.

There was a burst of applause, but it wasn't from the audience—it was from my fellow cast members, who knew how much work that journey had required. I quickly learned, however, that if I made it across the first time, the audience thought there was some trick to it—when I fell off just before the finish, picked myself up, wobbled a little on the second time and then made it, that's when the audience really responded. On those occasions where I fell off twice in a row, I didn't take a chance on a third strike. Instead, I played it light, earning laughs by reaching my arm up and letting my fingers do the walking the rest of the way. It was the kind of wonderful theatrical moment that makes acting onstage worthwhile.

CHAPTER 22

A Memorable High

A HIT.

The phrase carries significance both in pot parlance and in Hollywood, and in 1978, by some small miracle the two crossed paths and I happened to be at the intersection.

When Cheech Marin and Tommy Chong offered me a role as Sergeant Stedenko in their stoner movie *Up in Smoke*, I grabbed it immediately—I've

Sergeant Stedenko viewed these guys (through his beady eyes) as mortal enemies but I was always grateful to Cheech and Chong for handing me such a memorable part.

always loved comedy but have spent much of my life cast in dramas. That sly duo naturally saw a chance to subvert my well-established authority figure image by making me an obsessive Javert who is also the ultimate Keystone Kop. As Stedenko I lived in a perpetual slow burn as my subordinates—the "supreme idiots" whom I regularly berate—got us into one fine mess after another. The fault was not always with my underlings, as demonstrated by the scene in which Cheech pees on my leg in a men's room and strolls out without Stedenko realizing who he was.

The dialogue in that scene—as in many scenes in the movie—was largely improvised. Despite the loose approach and the movie's shambling tone, everyone was totally professional on set—always on time, knowing what had to be done. After a long day's work? Well, that's another story.

Unlikely as it may have seemed at the time, *Up in Smoke* was the biggest commercial hit of my career, finishing in the top fifteen at the box office in 1978; that earned the green light for a sequel, *Nice Dreams*.

My character was hugely popular and in the sequel I was given an even bigger, stranger role. Instead of merely being consumed by his chase, Stedenko has been seduced by the same form of relaxation favored by Cheech and Chong. When we first see him, he's sitting in his office, in a Hawaiian shirt, with long scraggly hair, smoking pot and watching a porno movie. He zealously confiscates marijuana brought in as evidence, smoking it through an ingenious bong shaped like a gun. The comedy becomes surreal when he starts turning into a lizard as one of the marijuana's side effects. In one scene my hands are turning green and scaly—you see them after I tell a large iguana it has "such beautiful eyes" and then offer it some pot (which it smokes, thanks to the magic of movies). Eventually I sprout a tail and start chasing bugs, which was one of the most physically challenging scenes I ever filmed. As a lizard on the hunt I needed to be up on the wall, so I was attached via braces on my hands and feet, which meant all my weight was putting pressure on my wrists. By the fifth take I felt like my hands were just going to snap off, and I got a crick in my neck from having to keep my head in fly-catching mode. It's the kind of sacrifice that, as artists, we must make, of course. At least it was well worthwhile—even decades later I'm remembered almost as much for Stedenko as I am for Mike Hammer . . . though by a very different demographic.

I've always tried to develop my range and there is no sharper contrast than between Stedenko and Killer Kane, the mysterious, nearly catatonic yet Christ-like figure at the center of *The Ninth Configuration*, also known as *Twinkle Twinkle, Killer Kane*.

William Peter Blatty's deeply philosophical and even religious film takes place during the Vietnam War. It is largely set in an insane asylum for soldiers who may or may not be faking their psychosis. Kane is sent in as a psychiatrist to solve the conundrum but the audience eventually learns he is not a savior but a Marine in need of saving. Having snapped after too much killing, he is now in denial about his own identity.

Bill was most famous for *The Exorcist*, from which I had been bumped. This time I expressed interest in the riveting role of Cutshaw, a manic astronaut who bailed on his launch, but my *New Centurions* colleague Scott Wilson got the part. I didn't enter the picture until the cast was already in Budapest, ready to start filming and the man who was set to play Killer Kane had a fit worthy of one of the movie's inmates. Nicol Williamson was infamous for his temper, and in this case he allegedly took offense at something the hotel operator said and heaved his phone

Awaiting my crucifixion in a *Ninth Configuration* dream sequence

With Jason Miller, Robert Loggia, and the rest of the bocce players, I mean cast, of *Ninth Configuration*

through the window. The Communist government was irate, so Williamson was fired and I was called in as a last-second replacement.

I clicked with the cast instantly, including Jason Miller, the man who had been given the role of Father Karras in *The Exorcist*. We quickly became good friends, and I would hang out with him, Scott, Robert Loggia, and some of the rest of the cast after hours. We put a lot of time and energy into sports and competition, playing basketball and softball and even setting up bocce courts outside the hotel and inside our hallway. Beyond the exercise, several of my castmates also exorcised their demons with some pretty serious partying. I never could keep up with Jason and the others once they really started drinking, but I loved hanging out.

It was an unusual role and one that demanded emotional distance, as if I was preoccupied with something mysterious and deep—Bill Blatty kept asking me to take the spin off my line readings, to flatten them, to make them less expressive, almost monotonic. He wanted me to save all expression for the eyes. It took me almost halfway through the shoot to find just the right tone. One thing that helped was that Bill had Barry de Vorzon's music recorded prior to the filming and he played it for us to set the mood and inspire us. It was innovative and because music speaks deeply to me, it helped me find my way.

However, while Bill had figured out the music beforehand, he didn't resolve the ending until after we were finished. This movie is the antithesis of *The Exorcist*, serving up a vision that good (and therefore God) does exist. At the end Kane dies to show Cutshaw that at least one man would make the supreme sacrifice for another human and that he should therefore retain his faith.

Bill wanted Killer Kane to commit suicide—after Cutshaw leaves the room following their final conversation, the audience sees a knife slowly drop from Kane's hand.

I wasn't crazy about it. Suicide didn't seem like a noble gesture, but a selfish one, especially if Bill thought of Kane as Christ, dying for our sins—in this case the mayhem and destruction of the Vietnam War. I asked Bill if we could try it another way. The previous scene is one of the great barroom fight scenes in movie history, one where Killer Kane's self-denial finally cracks and he saves Cutshaw from a biker gang, killing them off in a murderous outburst. The scene took three days to choreograph and we did much of it in one take. The build-up, along with Kane's and Cutshaw's suffering, is agonizingly long and the action is stunningly violent yet over quickly. I thought Kane's death should stem from an injury he suffered during the fight—we see the gang leader (played by Steve Sandor) come at Kane with a blade though the camera cuts away before the audience sees Kane get cut. In my view, Kane didn't call attention to his injuries because he'd rather die then face the legal and psychological consequences of killing all those people. At my behest, Bill filmed a take where my hand slowly opens and is empty—the blood dripping down is from wounds suffered in the fight. So which version ended up in the movie? Well, it depended on when you saw it. The movie has been released with two titles in at least three different edits of wildly different lengths—Bill kept going back and making changes. My version is out there somewhere, though in the current DVD release Bill restored the knife to my hand.

It was a film I had high hopes for, though the all-male cast, daring approach, and dark subject matter left this serious drama to become a cult favorite while my stoner films found mainstream success.

CHAPTER 23

The Long Ride

THE HORSE TENTATIVELY ENTERED THE RUSHING WATER, THE RIDER SAT on him, tall and confident. Less than a minute later, with the cameras rolling, the powerful currents of the Chattahoochee River pulled the horse under. The rider vanished from sight.

My brother James and I spent nine years trying to get this movie together and it was almost completely undone in the opening shot. *The Long Riders* was born out of the fun we had working together on *The Wright Brothers* television movie back in 1971, but it took a circuitous journey to the screen. James wrote a musical for the stage about Jesse James and his brother Frank called *The Bandit Kings*, and then we started thinking about how we could re-imagine the tale as a movie. It evolved into a story about the James and Younger gang and eventually included the Millers, who were also in the gang, and the Fords, with Robert being the notorious killer of Jesse James. Later we rewrote it, blending our ideas with those of Bill Bryden, who had his own Jesse James script. Another writer named Steven Smith came in to pull all the threads together. The script was done. We still needed a producer and a studio to front the money.

We met with several producers who never could get a studio's light to go from red to green. Then my brother met Tim Zinnemann, who was moving from assistant director to producer. He would help us guide *Long Riders* to the screen. Then came our stroke of inspiration: real-life brothers would play each set of brothers. I pitched the idea to director George Roy Hill who scoffed at the notion. United Artists thought it was great,

Jeff and Beau Bridges joined with the Keaches and the Carradines for this picture to show the studio our idea for *The Long Riders.*

but they didn't believe we could pull it off. So I arranged to get sets of brothers together for a photograph, and that's what finally sold them on the movie. The photo includes the Keach boys as Frank and Jesse; Keith, Robert, and David Carradine as the Youngers; and Jeff and Beau Bridges as the Millers. United Artists paired us with Walter Hill, who had written *The Getaway* and directed *The Driver, Hard Times,* and *Warriors.*

By the time Hill became involved, the Bridges were no longer available, so we replaced them with Randy and Dennis Quaid and then added Christopher Guest and his brother Nicholas as the Fords. Finally, in the summer of 1979, we were ready to shoot. And that's when our stuntman, Cliff Happy, went down in the river on my first day as a movie producer.

Cliff's saddle was loose and started sliding toward the rear of the horse, taking Cliff with him, just as the horse was losing its footing in the stiff currents. Somehow, a wrangler on shore had both the presence of mind and the skill to lasso the horse's head as the horse was bobbing up and down. Cliff and the horse—and the movie—pulled through fine, though we were all a little frightened.

We endured other minor catastrophes. To film a robbery scene in Parrott, Georgia, that was supposed to take place in Northfield, Minnesota, we trucked in red dirt from up north. After we spread it out over the paved streets a massive storm hit, washing the dirt away. We suspended shooting that scene for a few days while waiting for another truckload to arrive.

The producer job produced headaches, but acting in this movie was a special experience. We became a band of brothers, bonding over our love of music. We jammed almost every night. I played piano and the rest of the guys slung guitars. (The Guests never mingled as much and would often sit separately at dinner, I think because their characters were outsiders and, ultimately, villains.) Several of us also went on golf outings together, and Randy and I used to play chess on an electronic chess set. One day we were playing a game while awaiting a setup for a barroom scene and forgot to shut off the game; during the middle of our scene, we suddenly heard a robotic voice announce, "Pawn to Queen 4." Walter had to yell, "Cut," and gave us dirty looks as Randy and I scrambled over to turn off the chess game.

The relationships we forged transformed us into something like the real James-Younger gang. That became apparent on the day a newly hired cameraman yelled at us for coming into the scene too fast on our horses. First of all, you don't scream like that around horses. Second, he had no authority to talk to the cast in that manner, especially since two of the stars were also his bosses. David Carradine shot me a look—we didn't even need to speak—and all seven of us charged at him on our rides.

"Get the fuck out of here," David snarled; then, I, switching to my producer hat (though I was still wearing my cowboy hat), proclaimed, "You're fired."

The guy got off easy. If he decided to hang around, one of the gang probably would have mauled him.

James and I were constantly shifting from actor to producer and back to writer again, doing rewrites regularly on the set, though one of my favorite lines was ad-libbed by David Carradine. We're riding a train and his character, Cole Younger says, "When this is all over, I'm goin' to write a book, make myself more famous than I already am."

My character, Frank James, says, "I trust you'll give me a copy."

At that point David came up with the perfect retort, a wry statement that summed up the ethos of these men. "Nope. You gotta pay, Frank; you gotta pay."

Walter Hill did a great job of imposing his vision on our script without undermining its essence; unfortunately, none of us had enough clout with the studio to prevent them from lopping off some great footage that would have better developed my Frank James character and Randy's Clell Miller. They just wanted to keep the story moving and focus on the action and not the personal relationships.

The studio let us down by doing a mediocre job of publicizing the movie, and I believe to this day that the movie made money even though the studio claimed it only broke even. (It also reportedly did extremely well in VHS rentals and sales, though we never saw a cent from that.) Still, James and I did get our movie made and you can only imagine how proud our parents were to see their boys taking a movie they'd written, produced, and starred in off to the Cannes Film Festival. I arranged for the James and Younger gang to enjoy one final ride—wearing hats and dusters over our tuxes, we went on horseback (with our ladies following in horse-drawn carriage) from the hotel to the theater. A grand entrance, a great memory.

CHAPTER 24

The Butterfly Effect

WHEN 1982 BEGAN, I HAD BEEN STARRING IN MOVIES FOR OVER A decade without becoming a movie star. This year would mark the end of that journey and, thanks to the transformed television landscape, the beginning of a new one.

My last time out as a leading man in movies was my most notorious, but for all the wrong reasons. *Butterfly* puts the lie in the cliché that any publicity is good publicity.

My twenty-six-year-old co-star Pia Zadora took home a Golden Globe as New Star of the Year, beating out Kathleen Turner, Elizabeth McGovern, and Howard Rollins. Somehow she did that before the movie had been released in America. It seemed like quite a feat until people realized that her husband, millionaire fifty-eight-year-old Meshulam Riklis, had financed the entire movie then wined and dined Golden Globe voters, bringing them to his Las Vegas hotel to see Pia sing and later providing a private movie screening.

When the movie was released here, the critics were not so kind. Nor were the Razzies, the mischievous PR concoction that had just started two years earlier as the anti-Oscars, handing out Worst of awards. Pia won Worst New Star and Worst Actress, while the film "earned" eight other nominations, including Worst Picture (losing to a complete bomb called *Inchon*, which starred Laurence Olivier and was financed by the messianic religious leader Sun Myung Moon). Fortunately, my name was not among the nominees.

I took the lead role in *Butterfly* because I was a tremendous fan of James M. Cain, and this twisted tale filled with murder, greed, and incest promised a great character for me to delve into. The screenplay was strong but the director, Matt Cimber, was more skilled as an editor than a director. He had directed forgettable films like *The Candy Tangerine Man* and *The Witch Who Came from the Sea* and wasn't used to coaxing out serious dramatic performances, so he had a difficult time making Pia feel comfortable. We all wanted her to succeed, especially me since acting in tense or sensual scenes opposite an inexperienced and awkward co-star was not easy, even if she was sexy and sweet. Pia often turned to me for help, which was tricky because the director was standing right there while her husband was looming in the background.

At the other end of the acting spectrum was Orson Welles, who had a few scenes as a judge in the movie. At first, Riklis was reluctant to hire Orson because of his price tag, but before I signed on I worked hard to persuade Matt Cimber to make it happen. Working with Orson was a thrill, although the great man was riddled by insecurities, and he had grown absolutely enormous. Arriving on set before anybody else, already in his judge's robes, he'd get situated in a special oversized chair, then he'd be the last one out so people wouldn't stare. The set built for the trial scenes was in a warehouse across from the Las Vegas airport, which was so noisy that we had to shoot at night. Orson would sit in his special chair with a bottle of vodka neatly tucked under his robes. Between takes he'd discreetly nip at the bottle; when there was a longer break he'd light up one of his beloved cigars. One night, as we were setting up the next shot, I suddenly noticed smoke surrounding Orson. Somehow the cigar—possibly aided by the alcohol—had set his judge's robe on fire.

"Will somebody please put me out!" Orson shouted. People rushed over with water and even a fire extinguisher, but before they turned that loose on him, he yelled, "Enough, already, I'm out!"

Orson's insecurities played out in other unusual ways. He requested a fake nose as part of his makeup, yet the one he had created was an exact replica of his real nose. It was as if he was trying to find something to hide behind. He also hired Barney McNulty, cue card holder to the stars, whose biggest clients were Bob Hope, Milton Berle, and Frank Sinatra. Orson would get a bit crotchety, saying, "Closer to the camera, Barney, move a little more. No, try the other side of the camera," only to have the director move Barney back so Orson was looking in the right direction. Once the cameras rolled it turned out Barney was just another crutch, like the fake nose—Orson knew all his lines cold.

My favorite memory of the film was having dinner with Orson at the MGM Grand Hotel—just the two of us. He didn't want to talk about himself or his films; he seemed more interested in me. I was surprised that he was so familiar with my work, and he was incredibly gracious, asking me questions about my acting and about working with John Huston. We talked about Shakespeare, of course, and I told him how deeply influenced I was by his Falstaff in his film, *Chimes at Midnight*, and this clearly pleased him.

He definitely took his eating seriously, albeit with some unusual contradictions. That night he ordered not one, but two of the restaurant's roast beef entrees, though he told the waiter, in all seriousness, "but I want the potatoes baked because I'm on a diet."

A little old lady came up for his autograph during dinner but he calmly dispatched her without looking up, saying, "Not while I'm eating dear." At the end of the meal, however, he sent the maitre d' over to her with his autograph.

That Championship Season could have been a contender. It had a remarkable story and a phenomenal cast. Based on Jason Miller's play, the movie tells the story of four old basketball teammates and their coach, who gather to celebrate their past glory but find that the present and the future are creating divisions among them.

Robert Mitchum had been Jason Miller's third choice for the role of the old coach after George C. Scott and Bill Holden (who died around that time) but I thought he was a perfect fit, as a larger-than-life character with an air of authority. That's who he was off-screen too, although I think that detracted from people's appreciation of his acting chops. He had trouble remembering lines in his long speeches, but everyone was patient with him and he still at this point had the spark in his performance. I learned so much by just watching him react to the other actors. It has been said that the best acting is "reacting," and Mitchum certainly personified that. He allowed his thought process to register in his eyes before he came back with his response.

The other three ex-jocks besides myself were Bruce Dern, Paul Sorvino, and Martin Sheen. Bruce and I were the two biggest sports fanatics and we became good friends—even in 2012 when we reunited on the set of *Nebraska* we were as apt to be discussing football lines as script lines. Paul and I bonded over tennis, which we played fairly regularly. We were about even—I had a big serve but a weaker backhand than Paul so I'd torment him with plenty of lobs. Paul would get back at me in restaurants— at some point in the meal he would spontaneously burst forth singing Italian opera at full volume. And boy, he could project. I was deeply embarrassed the first time, but our fellow diners actually applauded when he was done.

Marty and I played brothers. We'd been friends for years in Malibu but on the set, Marty made it seem as if we really were siblings—the kind that were always at each other's throat. He maximized our performances by pushing my buttons, going beyond the script to needle me and provoke me. One day, he took his belligerent drunk character far enough that I got pissed off and shoved him up against the wall. I was genuinely annoyed, but it really helped create dramatic tension between our characters. My character, a reticent milquetoast man, was a stretch for me, and I always felt slightly dissatisfied with my performance, like I had gone too far to the wimpy side. (Of course, I'm always hard on myself, which is why I have a hard time revisiting my work.)

Jason, who had adapted his play into the movie and was directing too, gathered us together at Marty's house for the first reading. It seemed as if, despite some disparate acting styles, the film had strong potential. Unfortunately, the production was done in by economics. Jason had opened up his play with flashbacks to the team's championship game, which we were going to film on location in Scranton, Pennsylvania. After we started shooting, however, Cannon Films said we couldn't afford it. We'd have to talk about the game, rather than show it—essentially making it seem like a play stuck in a proscenium instead of a movie. It was a crushing blow to us and to the movie.

Still, at our opening night party, everybody had, shall we say, a few celebratory drinks. Then the cast had to pose for press pictures, so the four of us younger actors flanked Robert, who held a basketball. One ornery photographer was a particular pest, endlessly shouting, "Mitchum, over here. Over here, Mitchum, over here." Robert finally grew fed up and purposely misinterpreted the shout: He snapped off a crisp pass—bull's-eye—right into the lens, sending the guy toppling over. All four of us, on instinct, swiveled our heads away. Not long after, we found out the photographer was trying to sue Mitchum. Every time the lawyers or the press inquired about what happened, each of us had the same response: "I didn't see a thing."

Maybe if *That Championship Season* had lived up to its potential, my movie career would have continued chugging along. But after working with larger-than-life stars like Mitchum and Welles, and seeing the wild ups and downs they endured, I was ready to take a chance in another medium, in a more intimate environment.

CHAPTER 25

Just Wear the Hat, Kid

AT THE MOVIES IN 1982, *BUTTERFLY* WAS UNDONE BY AN INEXPERIENCED director and a novice actress, while *That Championship Season* was under-mined by budgetary restrictions that hampered the storytelling. On tele-vision that same year, I starred in an epic Civil War miniseries, *The Blue and the Gray*: Director Andrew V. McLaglen was a venerated old hand, having spent years at the helm of *Have Gun Will Travel* and *Gunsmoke*, and having made multiple westerns and war movies with legends like James Stewart and John Wayne. This helped him attract an all-star cast, and CBS spared no expense, shelling out more than sixteen million dol-lars (back when each million meant something) to re-create authentic uniforms and large-scale battle scenes. The contrast between my movie and TV careers could not have been more obvious.

The golden age of the television miniseries and movies for TV had really kicked off back in 1977 when *Roots* and *Jesus of Nazareth* aired within months of each other. I didn't cash in immediately—after my time with *Caribe*, I preferred staying focused on movies and, starting in 1978, returning to the theater. In 1980, I did carve out some time for a secondary role as an army major in the miniseries *A Rumor of War*. The cast included my good friend Keith Carradine and Brian Dennehy, whom I later became close with, and the talented but troubled Brad Davis. In the elevator each morning he seemed so out of it you'd wonder if he'd make it through the day, but he always rose to the occasion once the cameras started rolling; it made the fact that he cleaned himself up the following year such a relief and then his later death from AIDS such a tragedy.

Rumor of War led to CBS casting me in the lead role as Jonas Steele in *The Blue and the Gray*. I felt at first like I'd wandered into an episode of *This Is Your Life*: Unit manager Jon Anderson was a childhood friend; the cast included Robin Gammell, who had sublet me his New York apartment when we both appeared in *Hamlet* in Central Park back in 1964; Robert Symonds, who directed me in *The Country Wife* the following year; Lloyd Bridges, whom I had met after working with his son Jeff on *Fat City*; and Colleen Dewhurst from my 1972 *Hamlet* (I'm happy to report we got along fine this time around). The rest of the roster was star-studded, with Paul Winfield, Robert Vaughn, Geraldine Page, her husband Rip Torn (who always had his fishing gear with him), and Sterling Hayden, who was powerful as John Brown. Sterling struggled with alcohol throughout his life, and during our time together on the set in Arkansas, he'd call me up in the middle of the night and say, "Let's talk," because having company would keep him away from the bottle.

Many of my scenes were with Julia Duffy and John Hammond. My character, Jonas Steele, married Julia's Mary. Julia was a delight to work with; she was sweet and sexy and had a light touch—she was also light enough for me to carry across the threshold and up the stairs on our wedding day. John played a young illustrator but he never seemed fully comfortable in his role, even though he gave a convincing performance. He later gave up acting and became a lawyer and appeared much happier for the transition.

Our director, Andrew McLaglen, not only regaled us with stories about John Wayne and Jimmy Stewart but also knew everything about filming action sequences, from where to put the camera to how to talk around horses. That was something I'd come to appreciate on *Long Riders*—movie horses were not only well trained but also smart, so you never said "Action" because they'd get antsy, and you never said "Cut" because they would think they were done and head for the barn. Instead you would use different phrases each time, like "Any time now" instead of "Action" and "We've got it" for "Cut." (During the miniseries I persuaded the wranglers to let me go riding each morning before the shoot started.)

Andrew also assembled a remarkable troupe of Civil War re-enactors. I'd never really experienced anything like that before. Talk about taking your role seriously. These men lived in tents during the entire shoot, and they knew endless details about each battle. Their knowledge of tactics was a history lesson unto itself, and they truly helped make the movie more realistic.

The highlight, however, was working with Gregory Peck. He played Abraham Lincoln, which was perfect casting. Greg was exactly what you'd expect of the man many folks remember as Atticus Finch—courtly and kind, an old-school gentleman of the highest caliber. He was, by far, the biggest star on the set, but he treated everyone as an equal, extending himself to me for discussions before our scenes together. In his consummate professionalism and graciousness, he reminded me of Henry Fonda. In one crucial scene, Steele and Lincoln were testing the innovative new Spencer repeating rifle, which proved critical to the Union cause. That particular morning was so cold that neither of us could cock the rifle. Even as our hands grew numb and I grew frustrated, Greg remained patient and calm, which set the tone for the rest of us.

Greg brought more than just natural grace and charm to the role, he also gave a great deal of thought to every line. His finest moment was in his delivery of the Gettysburg Address, reshaping the delivery of the climactic line, "that government of the people, by the people, for the people, shall not perish from the earth."

Most readings stress "of," "by," and "for," but Greg, a passionate and politically active Democrat who had been on Nixon's enemies list, instead shifted the emphasis in each phrase to the word "people." This imaginative touch beautifully underscored Lincoln's point about the bonds shared by all Americans.

We hoped to work together again and Greg later wrote a letter to me, offering me a role in a project that, unfortunately, didn't come to pass. Instead, when he started a fund-raising series for the library in Los Angeles, he invited me to take part. I did several readings there, including one with Kathy Bates in which we read some of Lincoln's letters and a scene from *Our American Cousin*, the play performed at Ford's Theatre the night Lincoln was assassinated.

The Blue and the Gray had been a big deal in Arkansas—I was invited to a football game at the university and to meet legendary coach Lou Holtz. Later, John Tyson, son of the chicken tycoon, gave me a tour of his family's chicken farm. When the show aired in 1982, it was a big deal with all Americans, with nearly 40 percent of all households watching TV tuned in to our show. Even today it remains the seventeenth highest-rated miniseries ever. CBS was pleased. That would change my life.

—◆—

"Are you reading that trash again?" my mother would ask in dismay whenever she caught me with the paperbacks of *I, the Jury* or *Kiss Me Deadly* and *Vengeance Is Mine* that my teenage friends were all passing around on the sly. Even though I coveted my mother's approval, I was always seduced back into Mike Hammer's world of cold stone violence and hot and heavy sex. My parents thought Mickey Spillane was cranking out soft-core pornography. They weren't the only ones—everyone from book critics to protective politicians fretted about Spillane's popularity; Frederic Wertham, who infamously attacked comic books as a corrupting force, also went after Spillane. As a kid, however, I wasn't thinking about literature or about politics, I was thinking about tough guys and beautiful women. I fantasized about being part of the world Mickey Spillane had created. It only took me thirty years to finally get that chance.

In 1981, CBS had revived the Mike Hammer franchise with Kevin Dobson in *Margin for Murder;* the movie scored good ratings and the following year Armand Assante played Hammer in a theatrical remake of *I, the Jury.* Ronald Reagan's America was clearly in the mood for a throwback, a tough guy who knew how to dispense justice, no matter what the bureaucrats in Washington said. CBS wanted another Mike Hammer movie, but Kevin, whose cop series *Shannon* had just flopped, was now stepping into a starring role on *Knots Landing.* Lucky for him, but also, lucky for me.

Thanks to the popularity of *The Blue and the Gray*, CBS was pushing me for the role. I was ecstatic about the thought of playing Mike Hammer and impressed by the solid script. All I had to do was win over the executive producer, Jay Bernstein.

Jay was one of those guys that you read about—he moved out to California from Oklahoma and started in the mailroom at William Morris; his heady mix of ambition, imagination, and brazenness (Jay might prefer the word chutzpah) catapulted him to the top of the Hollywood PR game. As a press agent and then a manager, he represented performers across the spectrum, from Sammy Davis Jr. to Sally Field, from William Holden to Farrah Fawcett. He drew attention to Suzanne Somers by having her mince around the Central Park skating rink in the middle of winter in a mink, high heels . . . and a bikini. A few years after we met, Jay was the guy with the inspiration to insure Mary Hart's legs for a million dollars, a sweet publicity grab if ever there was one.

Jay had wanted to make the move into producing, and one day while flying to New York for a meeting with producer Dino De Laurentiis, he found himself sitting next to Mickey Spillane on the airplane. At that time, Mickey had written seven of the top fifteen all-time best-selling fiction titles in the United States, but he was wary of outsiders, especially Hollywood types. Jay sat down next to him and quoted a line from Mike Hammer, "She walked toward me, her hips waving a happy hello." He reeled off line after line and charmed Mickey so thoroughly that by the time they landed Mickey had handed over the rights to Mike Hammer for one dollar. Mickey's only rules were that Hammer wear a snap brim hat, have short hair, and, Jay later wrote, "carry a .45, not a sissy .38."

After his success with *Margin for Murder* and a few other projects, Jay wanted to move from being a packager to a hands-on producer, so he returned to Mike Hammer, looking for a star with whom he could work closely. Jay had heard of me, of course, but just enough to make him suspicious. Jay was an arch-conservative (at least by the standards of those innocent days) and from what he knew of me—I'd starred in *Indians* on Broadway and *Up in Smoke* in the movies, and I'd lived with Judy Collins—he was convinced that I was nothing but a long-haired screaming liberal.

Fortunately, Jay also knew another Stacy Keach—he had met my dad and knew he had a Republican voting record Jay could get behind. That nudged the door open a little for me. I didn't go into my meeting with him to pretend I was someone I wasn't, or even to assuage his fears; I just wanted to convince him that I could play Mike Hammer better than anyone else. Once we were in the room together, instead of circling each other like opponents, we began talking about my dad and immediately eased into natural friendship. I didn't do a screen test; Jay just hired me on the spot. He put me on the phone with Mickey Spillane. Oh, what a moment, what a thrill and honor.

"Do you have any advice, Mr. Spillane?"

"Just wear the hat, kid."

CHAPTER 26

I, Mike Hammer

MICKEY GAVE ME THE HAT. THEN JAY GAVE ME THE COAT.

After being cast as Mike Hammer, I re-read Mickey's books. The character had a larger-than-life quality, which was not surprising since Mickey had written for Superman, Batman, Captain America, and Captain Marvel. He initially conceived his creation as a comic book hero called Mike Danger. Yet Mike Hammer became more complicated than that: He was a vigilante—an Old Testament kind of guy, far more angry and violent than Sam Spade or Phillip Marlowe—but a champion of and for the common man. He filtered the world through a dark, cynical lens and shredded what he disliked either with his fists, a gun, or a droll, acerbic wit. He was based in part on an ex-Marine and ex-cop named Jack Stang (who had a cameo in the original *I, the Jury* movie) and in part on the Texas Ranger Frank Hamer who famously took down Bonnie and Clyde. (This connection to the Texas Rangers represented some kind of synchronicity for me.)

I also revisited the numerous screen versions, taking notes on them all, especially Ralph Meeker's explosiveness and indignation and Darren McGavin's lighter touch. Jay and I agreed we wanted Mike Hammer to play as a cross between James Bond and Dirty Harry; Ian Fleming had cited Mickey as an influence and, well, with *Dirty Harry* the connection was unmistakable. The visual image in my mind, however, was closer to Steve McQueen in *Bullitt*, with a tweed jacket and a turtleneck sweater. Jay, ever the visionary, trashed my outfits as soon as the wardrobe person and I returned from our shopping expedition.

"Just wear the hat, kid": Mickey Spillane's advice on playing Mike Hammer GENE
TRINDL/MPTV IMAGES

Mike represented old-fashioned values, so he should look like he stepped out of a bygone era, like he'd just been tossing back drinks with Spade and Marlowe. So Hammer needed a trench coat, and since he had no vanity and stood up for all the downtrodden people in the world, Jay decided that Mike's clothes should reflect that mentality. Jay would do whatever he could to make the trench coat and Mike's suit look as rumpled as possible. He'd personally take the clothes, roll them up in a ball, and then stomp on them. He had wardrobe store my spare suit in the desk drawer of Hammer's office. If there was an Emmy for wrinkles—perhaps the "Columbo Award for Achievement in Dishevelment"—the statue would have been mine.

Jay cared about clothes, but he was also concerned about the body wearing them—he was planning on beefcake shots of me, but since I was in my forties and getting beefier, he talked me into a strenuous workout regiment until I lost twenty pounds and looked buff enough for the role.

～～

Mike Hammer wasn't the kind of guy who exercised much—punching out bad guys was enough of a workout—but it's easier to imagine him in a gym than on a polo field. Yet during *Murder Me, Murder You*, I'd leave the Warner Bros. lot after work and zip over to the Burbank Equestrian Center to train in my new favorite sport.

My dad was always drawn to horses, but he grew up poor on Chicago's North Side and had no opportunity to ride. Maybe that explains his affinity for westerns; it certainly explains why he transferred his love of horses to me. Anyway, he'd take me to local stables in Griffith Park to ride during my childhood, feeding my own fantasies of becoming Roy Rogers or Gene Autry. When I was twelve years old, my maternal grandfather, William H. Peckham, a wealthy Texas oilman, took the family to a dude ranch in Wyoming. The wranglers taught the children there to rope and hogtie calves, to gallop, and even to change horses in the middle of a race. Then they staged a Junior Rodeo. My team won the relay and I earned blue ribbons for calf roping and the horse-changing race. Naturally I grew cocky, and then careless, and shortly after the rodeo I mishandled my steed on a narrow path above the North Platte River; the horse threw me but my right foot got stuck in the stirrup, and I was dragged along the trail for what seemed like an eternity. I was fortunate that I didn't break any bones, though I lost a layer of skin on my backside. I did have the presence of mind to calm my horse afterward and get right back on.

I've ridden in a number of movies: *Doc*, James Michener's *Dynasty*, *Judge Roy Bean*, *The Killer Inside Me*, *The Long Riders*, and *The Blue and the Gray*, and in the late 1970s, after I settled in Malibu, I bought a small Arab mare and a quarter-horse gelding and rode them regularly.

Polo was a new twist. When Bill Holden died in 1981, Stefanie Powers honored his memory by creating the William Holden Wildlife Foundation—Bill may have been a classic creature of Hollywood, but he felt more at home in Africa, working on conservation issues. To raise money, Stefanie, an avid polo player, decided to form a celebrity polo team and hold fund-raising matches. Stefanie invited me to join the team, promising to hire professionals to teach those of us who had never played polo the fundamentals. In addition to Stefanie, my teammates included actors Alex Cord, Geoffrey Lewis, Pamela Sue Martin, and my former *MacBird!* co-star William Devane.

Combining my love of horses with a highly competitive and strategic sport was a great new thrill—I learned how to "ride off" a foe and how to hit forehands and backhands. We became quite a good team. Bill Devane became so enamored with the sport that he went into the business of buying and selling polo ponies. We fared quite well, both in terms of fund-raising (bringing in $130,000 at the second annual event) and competitively. After one tournament triumph, Muhammad Ali came out to present our trophies—as a man used to large, even gaudy, championship belts, Ali glanced at the small plastic bauble and muttered to me, "Kind of chintzy, don't you think?"

It wasn't the quality of the trophies that brought my polo career to an abrupt halt but the abrupt halt of my polo pony. One day I was riding a horse I'd never been on, and when he sensed that my knees were not braced against his body, he decided a sudden stop was in order. I flew through the air and landed on the shoulder I had broken during high school football. Embarrassed, and in pain, I re-mounted and finished the game but I never played again.

Before that, however, I was offered a role in a soapy TV movie, *Princess Daisy*, based on a Judith Krantz novel. The *Mike Hammer* movie had been a hit—Jay had been relentless in promoting it, even corralling Mickey and me for a multi-city tour—and we were to shoot a second movie and the series in the fall, but first I had a little open time.

I took the role of troubled Prince Stash Valensky because I knew my character died early on and before he bit the dust, he was scripted to play polo. I was excited to get back on a horse. Before the film wrapped, I enjoyed another special treat. I'd worked with great stars like George C. Scott and Roger Moore, but this time I had the unique pleasure of having an ex-Beatle as a castmate. Ringo Starr was warm, funny, and quite generous. One weekend he invited the cast out to his estate. It was amazing. He had a magnificent compound, with pasture land and even a small zoo. I think one reason he needed such a sprawling space was that going out in public didn't come easy. This was not long after John Lennon was killed, but beyond safety concerns, Ringo had reached a level of celebrity that I could never fathom, and really didn't aspire to. Among the cast, Ringo was able to relax and be himself.

The other highlight was having the former *Bionic Woman* Lindsay Wagner play my wife. Of all the women I've shared romantic scenes with on stage and screen, Lindsay was, without a doubt, the best kisser.

—•—

"I snapped the side of the rod across his jaw and laid the flesh open to the bone. I pounded his teeth back into his mouth with the end of the barrel . . . and I took my own damn time about kicking him in the face. He smashed into the door and lay there bubbling. So I kicked him again and he stopped bubbling."

One glance at a Mickey Spillane novel and you'd immediately realize we had to soften up Mike Hammer to make him a palatable presence in people's living rooms each week. Everyone involved agreed on that. The trick was finding the right balance. When the violence occasionally started feeling gratuitous, I'd point out that we were tilting in the wrong direction, and both the network and the writing staff would honor my position.

I wanted to emphasize the humor, the street poetry in Spillane's writing—I always feel that when done right (meaning not jokey or too broad), humor is the best way of revealing a character's humanity. If my gun was quick, I wanted my wit to be quicker. Jay and some of the suits were concerned that the humor would diminish Mike Hammer and his perpetual revenge quest. In a show that would quickly be criticized as both too violent and sexist, I knew humor added much-needed texture, so I kept pushing the writers to add more, always add more—using metaphors as if this were poetry or jazz, which was always preferable to bluntly saying, "Get your ass over here" or "Call this guy an ambulance." And I'd do it on my own, using an inflection or an eyebrow, tilting the meaning of what might otherwise play as pure aggression.

While we thought of Hammer as a cross between James Bond and Dirty Harry, I also made sure he was different in one, well, two crucial ways: Mike Hammer bleeds, both literally and metaphorically. He absorbs his share of hard knocks but I also emphasized what Jay would have thought of as the more liberal side of Hammer's persona. Mickey had created an avid Commie-hater but we moved Hammer from the Korean conflict to a more complicated era, making him a Vietnam vet who had fought only because he had to—there he learned, more than anything else, how to survive and not to trust anyone. Hammer could be a vengeful vigilante who stood outside the law, but unlike so many conservatives, he was not an elitist. I played him as a populist, serving the underdog, someone who didn't work for money but who stood up for the innocent and the dispossessed (the 99 percent in today's parlance) against the oft-corrupt powers that be. This didn't water down Mike Hammer; it simply layered his character and broadened his appeal. I strived to ensure that Mike always had an emotional investment with the victim—that pathos and justice were his partners on each case.

<hr/>

Mickey gave me the hat and Jay gave me the coat but, frankly, I didn't love either of the ones chosen for *Murder Me, Murder You*. For the series I went to wardrobe and found a fedora and a green trench coat as a reminder of Hammer's military past.

Those were minor details, however. Nearly everything else had clicked into place from the start, beginning with Earle Hagen's noirish classic, "Harlem Nocturne," as our theme song. Earle had been a prodigy, playing trombone for Tommy Dorsey and Benny Goodman while still in his teens and writing "Harlem Nocturne" at the age of twenty back in 1939. He moved to Hollywood and arranged scores for movies like *Gentlemen Prefer Blondes*, before becoming one of television's most prolific songwriters in the 1960s, writing a fresh *I, Spy* score each week (winning an Emmy for his efforts) while also penning themes for everything from *The Dick Van Dyke Show* to *Eight Is Enough* to *The Mod Squad*. Watching Earle and his band jam during the recording sessions was always one of my favorite parts of *Hammer*. I especially loved listening to trombonist J. J. Johnson, who also did some scoring for the show. Shortly before Earle's death in 2006, he was honored by the Television Academy for his illustrious career, and I had the privilege of playing "Harlem Nocturne" on piano at the ceremony; I wore my Mike Hammer fedora for the occasion.

Jay and producer Lew Gallo did an impeccable job of casting, starting with Don Stroud as Pat Chambers, Hammer's ally in the police force. Don and I had become fast friends while shooting *The Killer Inside Me*, during which we'd go drinking and carousing. Jay also gave small parts to up-and-coming actors like Delta Burke, Sharon Stone, Ray Liotta, and Jim Carrey. Jim appeared alongside former NFL defensive star Lyle Alzado, an utterly incongruous pairing. Lyle was so strong that when he poked you in the chest you thought your lung had collapsed. Jim left you doubled over too but with his antics. On camera he played it straight in this role but between takes you could tell he had something special, the way his clowning kept everyone on the set (with the notable exception of the director) laughing.

The one part that had to be recast from the first movie to the series was that of Velda, Mike's loyal assistant, who quietly adores him. This was one area where we departed from Mickey's original concept. He had Hammer in love with Velda, but that wouldn't work on a weekly series, especially if Hammer was going to be falling into bed with a parade of beautiful women. Instead, we had Velda silently pining for Hammer. Tanya Roberts, a former *Charlie's Angel*, who was absolutely gorgeous and quite good in the first movie, was no longer available; she was off showing her stuff as *Sheena, Queen of the Jungle*. Lindsay Bloom, who had a more sisterly look that better fit our vision of Velda, replaced Tanya. When she first auditioned, she was blonde, with a southern accent and, according to Jay, a few excess pounds. So he rejected her. Casting director Tim Flack thought he saw the right qualities, however, so he had her lose weight and her accent, then he dyed her hair and brought her back in without telling Jay he'd already seen her. This time Jay thought she was perfect for the part. And she was.

With Mickey's blessing, Jay and I also expanded Hammer's circle of associates. Most important was Kent Williams as the politically ambitious district attorney prosecutor Lawrence Barrington, a bureaucratic foil designed to drive Hammer to distraction. Their verbal sparring always gave Hammer a chance to stick in a shiv made of barbed wit or to argue with passionate conviction for his ideals. Hammer couldn't always be going exclusively through Pat Chambers, so our writers created a coterie of Runyon-esque characters like computer geek Ozzie the Answer, Jenny the barmaid, and streetwise guys like Moochie. Jay also conceived of "The Face," the mystery woman who always appeared tantalizingly just out of reach of Hammer. I thought that was a great touch, adding a romantic tension to the series.

The mystery woman was unattainable, but each week there were plenty of women who dropped into Mike's life, if not his lap. They were dubbed the Hammerettes and from the beginning they were a focal point—they aroused enthusiasm in our male viewers but antagonized many women, including studio and network executives. These women found Mike's lifestyle an exercise in old-fashioned sexism. I thought that critique unfair. Mike wasn't a misogynist or an abuser. He was single and loved beautiful women. If the women loved him back, there was nothing wrong with that. There was, however, a problem with Jay's casting tactics. Many Hammerettes were former Miss This or Miss That, but to land this gig they had to pass a most unusual test.

Jay was a huge believer in cleavage, natural, robust, and firm. He developed what he called "the pencil test." He'd drop a pencil down an actress's shirt, and if it didn't slide through the actress had the part. It was better than the casting couch but not by much. Jay, who was defiantly anti-feminist, was charming and chaste during the process, but he still alienated plenty of people including top executives. The one time I walked into his office as he was about to perform a pencil test I was so embarrassed I just turned and walked right back out. I pretended not to notice. Imagine if men had to come in and do a test with their. . . .

～

The most temperamental of my co-stars was Hammer's 1966 Ford Mustang. I loved the idea of it—another symbol of Hammer as a man displaced in time—but it constantly cried out for attention. It wouldn't start up consistently, so whenever we filmed chase scenes, we had to have the engine already running before Hammer jumped in.

As always, I loved the driving scenes and the fight sequences. I stopped doing some of the bigger falls, but I participated in close to two hundred fights. We mapped out a formula where each episode had three action sequences: The first would be almost comical, the second would be more straightforward but with some light moments thrown in, and the third would be deadly serious. We'd occasionally run into problems with guest actors who didn't know how to throw a staged punch. It wasn't just that it took extra time to choreograph the action; it was also that actors who are nervous about performing during fight scenes tend to be dangerous. I tried to stay on my guard and simultaneously to put the other actors at ease, but I still got clipped a few times.

I wanted to make sure I didn't get caught off-guard by sloppy writing, which was a definite danger, given the grueling pace of a weekly series. Jay arranged for writer Ed Scharlach to come to my trailer every day so we could punch up the next day's dialogue. Ed was the perfect choice since his background was actually in comedic writing—he'd written for *That Girl*, *The Odd Couple*, and *Mork and Mindy*. I trusted Ed to nail the Mike Hammer voice. He also wrote all of Hammer's narrative voiceovers, which were a crucial part of the series. They personalized the drama, capturing Mike's thoughts and his worldview, but they also served a pragmatic purpose. We recorded those after completing an episode because they could cover up a multitude of screenwriting sins by filling in the gaps. "What I didn't know then but would soon learn . . ." Mike would say, explaining action that happened off camera, which could be essential in a show that prided itself on plot twists but that sometimes took one sharp turn too many. (I also used those monologues to lighten the tone a bit.)

As I wore down from the demands of being in every scene, I argued for the idea of broadening the show's scope, of cutting away from Hammer to show the bad guys in action. The writers liked that idea since it would open up more options, but Jay and the network insisted that we see everything from Mike's perspective. It was tough for me but it did keep the show true to Mickey's original narrative structure.

Until the show hit the air, I didn't know how it would be received. I certainly didn't realize that this role was a game changer for me. But the ratings and the amount of press—along with the word from the network that they wanted a second season—quickly transformed me into something new, a television star. In fact, later that year, as a response to a *TV Guide* list of the medium's sexiest women, Scripps-Howard News Service did a list of TV's sexiest men. I made the cut. This was the kind of exposure Burt Reynolds had in mind when he recommended I do a television series all those years ago.

Beyond my physique and mustache, the media zoomed in on one question: How did it feel to go from Hamlet to Hammer? I was asked variations on that again and again. I won't pretend that Mike Hammer was Shakespeare. That doesn't mean I had sold out. I was working hard in a rewarding role. Hammer remains one of my favorite characters of all time—he's athletic and romantic, he's funny but a tough guy. And he's the hero. Hammer was the best thing that had happened to my career since Joe Papp put me center stage in Central Park, and I hoped the money and fame would provide new opportunities for me to stretch myself as an actor.

The series had already given me something I craved the most: true love.

CHAPTER 27

A Soul in Pain

LOVE. IT'S NEARLY IMPOSSIBLE TO PROPERLY PIN DOWN WITH WORDS. Love can be delicate or unshakably solid; it can create dizzying cravings or lasting contentment. Love is human nature at its most perfect and most mysterious, so elemental yet so damn complicated.

I have been married to an amazing woman, Malgosia, for more than a quarter of a century, and I revel in the life we've created with our two children. It would be easy enough now to lean back on a rocking chair on the porch (if we had a rocking chair, and a porch) and recount our life together through a golden-hued haze. The truth, as everyone knows, is that any relationship requires tremendous effort. And our early days together were the most painful and challenging of my life. If not for Malgosia's love, along with her trust, tenacity, and patience, I don't know how I would have survived my sea of troubles, much less righted my ship.

Malgosia had developed those virtues living under Communist rule in Poland. It was, obviously, a tougher and less forgiving climate than anything I had experienced. When she was working as a television hostess in the 1980s, government officials ordered her to sign a loyalty oath. She refused, knowing what it would cost her. Fortunately, before she suffered the consequences, a friend on the inside warned her that she was on a blacklist and helped her to leave the country.

I met Malgosia on the set of *Mike Hammer* while I was married to another woman, Jill Donohue. Jill was wonderful and we had great times together. I cared for her, but she didn't want children and the idea of being

Mike Hammer brought me fame and glory, but more importantly, it was on the set that I met Malgosia.

a couple, but not a family, was unsettling. I felt as if I was staring into, and drifting into, a void.

I had started using cocaine because it felt good, like a blanket to smother my insecurities, helping me fit into a world where I was an outsider. I began using it regularly because I deluded myself into thinking I could do it in a controlled way, making myself a better, more durable actor. I fell into abusing cocaine because it was the easiest way to handle the brutal pace of my work, which required me to be in every scene of a TV series. It took my arrest and my time in Reading Jail to wake me up long enough for a close, hard look at what I was doing. That would not have been enough, however. It was Malgosia who made me want to leap off the path where cocaine was leading me and onto one I had always dreamed about; it was with her I could see the porch, the rocking chair, and the family. I cleaned myself up and stayed clean on my own, but it was really Malgosia who gave me the hope, and the tomorrow worth seeing with clear eyes and a clean soul.

~ ~

When I first met Malgosia, she didn't know about my drug problem. I hid it from her, just like I was hiding it from Jay Bernstein and everyone around me. I'd have hid it from myself if that were possible. Deception was consuming too much of my time and energy. Then I got arrested.

After being freed on bail, I returned to France to resume work on *Mistral's Daughter*, and I was a changed and chastened man. I knew I had to face myself. I could no longer look away from the shame I had brought to the people I worked for and those who loved me, not to mention the harm I had done to myself. Being clean meant being open and honest, so I brought my relationship with Malgosia out of the shadows and, that June, Jill and I formally separated.

I did not enter a 12-step program, feeling I should break the habit on my own. I did lose my way once or twice in the months leading up to my trial, but I never touched cocaine again after I went to prison. I never expected to go to prison at all. The mantra—repeated endlessly by my agent, manager, American lawyer, English barrister—was "A fine, a slap on the wrist." During the months between the arrest and the trial I was pressured by Jay, the studio, and the network to downplay the extent of my addiction. In other words, Jay wanted me to lie, to protect the future of the show. I wanted to be done with dishonesty, so I usually told reporters I wasn't comfortable talking about the subject while my fate was undecided, which was true. Only once did I cave; while doing a press junket for *Mistral's Daughter*, I told a reporter that I hadn't done drugs and would be exonerated. I felt guilty as hell saying that and felt I got what I deserved when she later wrote me a letter filled with bitter disappointment.

Most days, that summer and fall, I felt great. My lawyer assured me I'd get off lightly; I was clean, I had Malgosia by my side, and I was back at work on a new season of *Mike Hammer*.

But just a few days before I was to leave for England, I threw out my back during a chase scene. The studio sent a doctor over to my trailer with a cortisone needle that was the medical equivalent of a .357. The doctor shoved the needle into the base of my spine. I couldn't run away, both because I couldn't move and because I wanted to keep working, so we didn't fall behind while I was in London for my trial. Nobody had any idea how far I was about to fall.

I tried maintaining an aura of optimism, but it weakened on the plane to England, when the combination of jangled nerves and a long flight caused my back to spasm and seize. I spent the next four days horizontal, lying flat on my back during meetings with my lawyers and barristers. Their news was not the kind to encourage me to get up and dance. I had decided to plead guilty and hoped to settle the matter without having to take the stand, and without going to jail. I was supposed to be back on the set of *Hammer* the following Monday. We had a dossier of letters from Columbia and CBS arguing that the headlines had already sufficiently damaged my career and were punishment enough, while actors like Robert Wagner and Lee Remick pitched in with character references.

It wouldn't do a bit of good. A Greek millionaire playboy named Taki—another glamorous foreigner—had received a four-month sentence though he had less cocaine on him than I did when he was apprehended at Heathrow Airport; an actual dealer had just been sentenced to four years on a cocaine charge. The tabloids were filled with utterly hysterical stories about the drug scourge invading England. I was part of the problem.

—◆—

December 7 was a day that would bring me infamy. I was awake before my wake-up call but was in too much pain to even tie my shoes. I went to my court date on a gurney in an ambulance, which I'd hoped to avoid since the press would interpret it as a ploy for sympathy.

My trial was essentially over the moment it began. The customs officer testified that he thought I'd brought in the drugs for personal use, not trafficking, a fact my defense hammered home. I testified about the humiliation I felt, about kicking my destructive habit. The judge was unmoved by any and all of it. He had bought into the competing narrative—that anyone toting more than thirty grams was smuggling with intent to distribute. He had decided to make an example of me. I would not be going home, the judge informed the court. I would be spending this Christmas with Her Majesty. Well, I wouldn't be dining at a palace exactly. I was heading to Reading Gaol, best known as the place where Oscar Wilde was incarcerated for "the love that dare not speak its name."

As my sentence was read—nine months in prison—I felt like someone had kicked me in the groin with lead cleats. My knees buckled and my stomach shot up somewhere around the back of my throat. It was the lowest moment of my life. I was put in handcuffs and taken out to a van (though not before one officer asked me to autograph a copy of the book of *The Blue and the Gray* for his wife). Eventually the van deposited me at what looked like a medieval fortress. This was my new home.

—◆—

Just the sight of the orange plastic bucket made me want to weep. My cell, the size of a closet, was sparsely furnished, but the bucket stood out as the symbol of how far I had fallen. It was my toilet for the night. Morning brought a trip across the hall where everyone dumped their contents. You can't imagine the stench, and I wouldn't recommend trying.

I was in the hospital wing, which entitled me to a wooden plank under my mushy mattress and a brief visit from the doctor. That was about it. I had eleven days until my appeal, which seemed an impossibly long time. How then, would I survive nine months, if I lost on appeal? An officer asked if I wanted to see my mug splashed across all the papers. The headlines were going to be variations on "Hammer in the Slammer." It seemed likely only to carve out another chunk of my soul to allow more space for shame and humiliation. I said, "No thanks."

The inmates watched a Clint Eastwood movie that morning. I skipped it to do some writing, but in the throes of a deepening depression I slept instead, waking occasionally to the sound of Clint's gunshots. The next day I was permitted to walk in the yard. I gazed at a construction crane on the outside. "Not even close," said the guard. I was not the first inmate to fantasize of a dramatic escape. "It falls short of the wall by about fifty feet. Believe me, we checked."

This visual reminder of my physical isolation left me drained. I had permanently stained my reputation, personally and professionally. Worse was the knowledge that if I lost my appeal on December 18, I'd have let down everyone on the series—two hundred people would be out of work at the holidays because of my stupidity. I sat pouring salt on my self-inflicted wound, finally understanding how destructive my addiction really was.

That afternoon I received a telegram from Malgosia, telling me to hold on, not to lose faith, that she was there for me no matter what. I fell to my knees and let out a sob of relief, thankful for her unselfish love and support.

Others reached out as well. Timothy Dalton, who had become a good pal on *Mistral's Daughter*, tried visiting but was turned away, though the guards passed on the Shakespeare plays and paperbacks he had brought for me. An officer gave another book to me, saying I should turn it into a movie. *The Springing of George Blake* told the saga of the British spy turned double agent, who was arrested, then escaped and fled to the Soviet Union. The book was quite absorbing, though Blake's story had already been loosely adapted into John Huston's *The Mackintosh Man*. While I was reading, three prisoners in the yard called through my window, asking for autographs, "for our girlfriends." Willing to do anything to boost my self-worth at that point, I was happy to oblige. As I was handing the papers through my window, an officer chased them away, the papers scattering in the breeze. The officer informed me he'd been told to discourage this—in fact, until my appeal, officials were trying to keep me separated from the rest of the prison population as much as possible.

The incident became an odd side note at my appeal, which, not surprisingly, I lost. My barrister mentioned what had happened, saying my time in prison was "not without incident." The *National Enquirer* translated that for American readers as "Keach Terrorized By Cons."

The reporting on my prison experience was rarely hampered by the truth. Salacious tabloid journalists cooked up some fantastical stories (the England press alleged a red carpet treatment in which I had guests for parties) as did ex-inmates looking for a payday (they claimed contraband pot use and dealing). Other tales bore the distinct fingerprints of Jay Bernstein. He was desperate to keep my name in the spotlight, to make me a figure worthy of sympathy. When Jason Miller called the prison but was not allowed to speak to me, Jay turned it into a story about officials trying to hide something. Jay loved referring to my "Midnight Express" situation after the notorious 1978 Turkish prison movie; any stories about me being beaten up in Reading were figments of Jay's fertile imagination. The reality is that prison and Malgosia saved my life.

When a child misbehaves and a parent calls for a "time out," it can sound silly, almost trivial, but there's definitely logic there. I think I'm actually fortunate I lost my appeal. I was heartbroken at the time, but having my tomorrows creep along at such a petty pace was just what I needed. (I was released after six months for good behavior.) It was a shock to the system and a chance to put my obligations and temptations on hold in order to reflect and find myself again. The slap on the wrist that I had been foolishly anticipating would have put me right back on the *Mike Hammer* set; free of consequences for my actions, I'd have been far more likely to falter again.

The prison chaplain organized a few group discussions with fellow inmates about the nature of addiction and how to spend productive time while being incarcerated. I wrote myself a letter, telling myself that I should think of this experience as being no different than being on the set of a long movie shoot in a lousy location, and I should make the best of my time. As I started piecing together a new me, I realized that while I was responsible for my own behavior, I couldn't go it alone.

The number of actual letters I was allowed to write and the number of visits I could have were extremely limited, so I had to make each one count. My parents flew over, and their hugs and reassurances mattered more than their news that I had received a Golden Globe nomination for *Mike Hammer*. My agent, Ron Meyer, also paid a visit. Some "friends" distanced themselves from me but others extended a hand. I received warm and encouraging letters from numerous actors, including Gregory Peck, Burt Reynolds, and Roger Moore. Al Pacino provided a much-needed laugh with his wonderful lack of false sentimentality: "Sometimes a bunch of us sit around and talk about you, and sometimes we just sit around and talk."

My fans reacted similarly—a few felt I had betrayed their trust, which I understood (though the "rot in hell" letters implied that the writers had other issues), but the vast majority rallied to my side. One woman named Sussi wrote regularly, and each time she included a beautiful miniature painting. The very nature of fandom is sometimes hard to fathom, but at that moment in my life I wasn't looking for answers; I was simply thankful for their compassion.

One person whose support and understanding became crucial to my recovery was the warden, Governor Brian Hayday (with whom I still exchange Christmas cards). He didn't regard me as a criminal, but as someone who had made a costly mistake and was now trying to set things right. He was the one who generously allowed me to receive my fan mail, typically three hundred to five hundred letters per week (after prison guards read it first). More important, he appointed me librarian and allowed me to keep a typewriter in my cell. I was also responsible for taking inventory of new inmates and inmates who were leaving, as well as handing out books to remand prisoners (those still awaiting trial), young offenders, and the rest of the prison population. This gave me something to occupy my time, a responsibility, and it also allowed me some small measure of freedom. As a trustee, I was one of the few who was allowed to interact with both the convicts and remand prisoners. Most convicts at Reading were doing time for drug-related offenses—smuggling and dealing—but the prison also held local vagrants who were being held largely because they were homeless. We were an international bunch, with many Turks, Spaniards, Australians, and Africans, most of whom had been nabbed at Heathrow or Gatwick airport.

Some inmates were starved for books and I'd recommend titles and procure new ones. Many inmates, however, were largely illiterate. I'd read their letters to them and help them write their own. It gave me a sense of purpose, a reason for being there beyond my own circumstances, and it helped me to feel useful and fulfilled in some small way. I was also put in charge of showing a movie one Sunday per month; action flicks were the order of the day and once I chose *The Long Riders*. (The British inmates knew me more from *Conduct Unbecoming* and *The Squeeze* than *Mike Hammer* though, not surprisingly, many recognized me as Sergeant Stedenko from the Cheech and Chong movies.) As a trustee I was allowed out of my cell more than most inmates, but even so, being in this place—in the immortal words of my celebrated predecessor, Oscar Wilde, "Where every day is like a year, a year whose days are long"—was extremely difficult. I started writing a book—*Xmas with Her Majesty*—and even though I only wrote a treatment, it was a purgative experience, another step in putting the negatives of my past behind me and getting ready to start over.

A new beginning, of course, was only possible because of one person: Malgosia. I placed her photo by my bed and read her letters dozens of times. She stayed with a friend in a basement flat, sleeping on their kitchen table, so she could be nearby for our rare visits. On one visit, she brought her elegant mother, Wanda Tomassi, to meet me, and I told her that I wanted to marry her daughter. "Not while you're in jail," she said with a smile. I could wait. Malgosia's faith in me allowed me to see past the prison walls, restoring my desire to create a future.

CHAPTER 28

Meet the Press

Jay Bernstein was a multi-faceted man. He could be:

a) Full of himself. He carried a cane as an affectation and called his memoir *Starmaker*.

b) Difficult and demanding. Producers came and went on *Mike Hammer* more quickly than Hammerettes.

c) Defiantly old-fashioned. Two words: pencil test.

d) Shameless. He was happy to fabricate stories and manipulate the press if it served his purposes.

And yet:

Jay Bernstein was more than a slick promotional genius. He was a loyal friend, who defined the term "above and beyond the call of duty."

Think about it. Jay gives an actor a fantastic role and turns him into a TV star. The actor repays him by doing drugs while working, lying to him, and getting arrested, essentially one thing after another to undermine Jay's career-defining moment as a producer. If Jay had ditched me when I was in prison I would have understood. I disrupted his show, throwing lives into chaos, and hurting Jay's reputation with CBS, a network with whom Jay needed to maintain good relations.

Jay was no sentimentalist, nor was he a moral relativist. He didn't make excuses for me. As with the Reading warden, Jay saw me as a good guy who had harmed myself more than anyone else, and was now, justifiably, being punished for my wrongdoing. When my debt was paid, Jay believed, I shouldn't have to continue suffering for my mistakes.

When CBS said they were canceling *Mike Hammer* while I was behind bars, Jay took out ads in the trades contradicting them, saying the show was merely on hold and might be revived. Then he shelled out forty thousand dollars of his own money (according to Jay, though he was probably exaggerating for the sake of the story) to fund a fifteen-city, thirty-seven-day one-man crusade, going on every television and radio talk show that would have him. On his pilgrimage, Jay was careful to portray me as neither hero nor victim. I was simply a man seeking a chance at redemption. He pointed out that I could have refused to return to England for my trial, since it was unlikely they'd go to the trouble of extraditing me. (I never would have done that, though if I'd known about the prison time I'd have delayed going until after shooting the entire season.)

Jay was savvy, handing out I LOVE MIKE HAMMER buttons and T-shirts. (After I was released, he made more, declaring, HAMMER IS BACK.) He did his best not to turn his mission into a showdown with CBS, though he could never resist a good ploy. After network executive Harvey Shephard essentially said only rerun ratings would matter, and that the letters flooding CBS would be dumped without being read, Jay went on the air with Shephard's home address and asked viewers to write him there about my personal rehabilitation. Supposedly, four hundred thousand pieces of mail showed up at Shephard's front door. Again, that number came from Jay, so take it with a pound of salt, but gradually, CBS did start talking about how I should not be punished twice. Maybe they believed in redemption or maybe they were hooked by Jay's other point—my arrest and prison sentence had made me a bigger celebrity than ever before.

Everyone, from my lawyer to my press agent, had his own plan for my escape from prison, each one more elaborate—and unrealistic—than the last. They weren't literally orchestrating an escape scheme; they were plotting how to elude the press barrage that would await me on the day of my release in June 1985.

"Enough," I finally decreed. "This is crazy. The press won't simply disappear if we evade them this one time. And my fans have earned the right to see and hear from me. I'll just face them."

I ran the gauntlet of paparazzi outside the prison and then talked to reporters before getting on the Concorde to fly to New York where I met with another flock of journalists. I would continue dealing with this situation head on, accepting responsibility for what I had done and making myself available to anyone who wanted me to speak about the perils of drug use and the potential for rehabilitation. Even though I had served my time, I viewed this as part of my penance. It was occasionally uncomfortable, but I reminded myself that I had the chance to help others struggling with addiction and that gave me the incentive and the courage to keep going.

My first job after prison was narrating a television documentary called *High on the Job*, about the problems of cocaine abuse in the workplace. I testified before Congress, alongside former Minnesota Vikings star Carl Eller, and I spoke at rehab centers and on college campuses. I talked about the drug's seductive qualities but also how recovery includes the difficult task of recovering from self-loathing, of feeling so low for having allowed the drug to control you. The only invitation I turned down was from David Letterman—I needed more distance before I felt I could joke about the topic, and I was wary about appearing to trivialize the issue.

My most memorable event was one where I didn't have to say a word. I had signed on with Nancy Reagan's "Just Say No" campaign. Malgosia and I met Mrs. Reagan and the president at a White House reception. Soon afterward, we were invited to a Hollywood event honoring the first lady. I bought an ad in the program thanking her for her support and her work on this issue. I thought that would be the end of it. In the middle of the evening, the emcee called attention to the ad, and then to me. I had never met the man but I knew who he was, as did everyone in the room, as well as everyone in America. The man with the microphone was none other than Frank Sinatra. When he mentioned my name, I slid down in my seat, thinking he was about to take me to task for my arrest. Instead he lavished praise on me for how I had publicly accepted responsibility, made no excuses, dealt with my problem, and reached out to others. Any

To Malgosia Tomassi and Stacy Keach
With our best wishes & congratulations!
Nancy & Ronald Reagan

Joining forces with Nancy Reagan's "Just Say No" campaign was one way for me to give back after my stint in Reading Gaol.

concern that I was an outcast in Hollywood ended when he finished, by saying, "Stacy, if you ever need anything, just give me a call. My name is Sinatra, S-i-n-a-t-r-a. Stand up and take a bow, Stacy."

When I was in Reading, famed bookmaker Jimmy the Greek ranked the chances against *Mike Hammer* returning to CBS as 1,000–1. Jay and I beat the odds, but we paid a steep price.

If you gave Angela Lansbury a trench coat, a fedora, and a mustache, it wouldn't make her into Mike Hammer, yet somehow CBS executives thought they could transform my series into another *Murder, She Wrote*. It wasn't just that they were de-emphasizing action in favor of whodunit plotting. The entire tone of the series was changed, or gutted, violating the integrity of Mickey Spillane's vision.

Barbara Corday had become president of Columbia Television and, no surprise here, the *Cagney & Lacey* co-creator clashed with Jay over everything about *Mike Hammer*. She had backup too—CBS wanted the series to draw in more women. (The network had also put me in a soapy TV movie with Teri Garr called *Intimate Strangers* that scored big in the ratings.) The show would kick off with a two-hour movie in which Hammer would swoon for a movie star played by Lauren Hutton, while the Hammerettes would largely be relegated to the sidelines. We'd also be on during the more sedate 8:00 p.m. time slot.

Corday was quoted as saying she was "pleased that we're not seeing so many women with their clothes cut down to their waist that have no reason to be in the show. That was part of the book that didn't translate well to the screen."

She acknowledged there were risks involved in toning down the sex and violence, but I think she miscalculated the balance. I didn't mind making Hammer more vulnerable and compassionate, but since our series had debuted, a growing number of copycats had filled the airwaves: *Hunter*, *The Equalizer*, *Spenser For Hire*. With Hammer neutered, our traditional audience had plenty of other options, and women were never going to turn out in enough numbers to make up the difference. At the end of the season, the series went off to the big sleep.

I was no longer the star of a hit series. Instead, I was unemployed. Acting is a tricky business, filled with uncertainty and rejection. It is inherently competitive—when someone else gets the part, you "lose out"—and that can make it lonely. I had learned, however, that my career was what it was, and I should be happy with it. I couldn't constantly compete or worry about unfulfilled expectations. I couldn't live as if each success validated my career, and any failure or rejection marked a condemnation. No one should buy into that poisonous thinking, but it is particularly destructive for those in the arts, who are constantly subjected to the subjective opinions of others. While I was obviously not happy with the series' demise, I finally knew not to take it personally. I would go on. I had the role of a lifetime to look forward to: family man.

CHAPTER 29

Family Guy

IN JULY 1986, MY DEAR MOTHER, NEARING HER SEVENTY-SECOND BIRTH-
day, was leaning on the arm of my good friend, actor Peter Jason. She
looked up at Peter as they walked down the aisle of St. Michael and All
Angels Episcopal Church, on Coldwater Canyon Avenue, the church I'd
attended as a child. "I can't do this again," she quipped. "This better be his
last time."

Mom needn't have worried. The fourth time was the charm. With
Malgosia, I finally got it right . . . after one final obstacle. Fifteen minutes before the ceremony, there was no bride in sight. Malgosia's car had
broken down. She finally arrived in her maid of honor's car, racing into
the church, wedding dress in hand. After she changed, I finally achieved
my moment of bliss, a mere thirty-five minutes late. The reception was at
Malibu Lake, and we dressed in all white. Not only was it the last time
my mom and dad had to come to one of my weddings, but also within
two years, Malgosia and I gave them a grandson, Shannon, and two years
later, a granddaughter, Karolina.

When I was filming *The Ninth Configuration*, Ed Flanders, who played
my brother, showed me a photo of his kids and said, "Don't go through
your life without this experience; you'll be sorry if you do."

Malgosia and I are blessed with two great kids: Shannon, now twenty-
five, is a graduate student at NYU, studying public relations; Karolina,
now twenty-three, is studying theater at Pepperdine University.

Acting is a peripatetic existence, but I desperately wanted to avoid
being a long-distance dad when the kids were young. I had wanted

I waited my whole life for this day.

children for so long; now I wanted to be with them. Malgosia and I decided early in our parenting adventure together that whenever I would be called away to a distant location, we would take the kids with us. We were able to do this until school obligations interfered and even then if I was going to be gone long enough, we'd pack as a family—when I starred in *Art* in the West End of London in 1998, we enrolled them in The American School in London for the length of the run.

Children are eminently adaptable and ours took to being nomads. Occasionally, things would go awry—when I was in Egypt filming *Legends of the Lost Tomb*, Karolina got severely ill, her fever reaching the upper end of the thermometer. The hotel sent a doctor who provided something to break the fever, but once she was stable Malgosia wanted to bring her back to California to recuperate, leaving the Pyramids for another day. Still, we were able to share many memorable experiences as a family instead of running up long-distance phone bills.

Malgosia, of course, spent even more time with the kids than I did, and she taught them Polish. There were practical and philosophical reasons—we wanted them to be able to converse naturally with Malgosia's parents and we believe knowing a second language is a great life benefit—but the kids also used it to their advantage. I don't speak Polish, so when they wanted to ask for something they knew I might say no to, they'd speak to Malgosia in the mother tongue . . . and get the yes they wanted. I've learned enough over the years now to understand a request to borrow the car, or a trip to the shopping mall. Now they know that I know so they have "codified" their Polish to avoid detection. If I can find a portable translator maybe I'll invest in one.

When I was at home, I threw myself into being a normal dad, though I was fortunate that, where we lived in Malibu, normal meant hiking to waterfalls in the valley behind our property or taking Karolina for horseback rides on the beach. Still, parenting is a role that requires constant improvisation. One crucial trick is figuring out how to share your enthusiasms with your kids without imposing yourself onto them. I've always been athletic, and like many other dads I know, I harbored that secret fantasy that my son would be the next John Elway or Babe Ruth. I signed Shannon up for T-ball when he was five, and soon after—probably too

My favorite roles: husband to Malgosia, father to Shannon and Karolina

soon—promoted him to Little League. Even though he never really demonstrated any special talent for the game, I was determined to maximize whatever potential might be locked away. On the first day of practice, Shannon was asked to play catch with the coach. As the ball arrived, he extended his mitt palm up; the ball skipped over the mitt and hit Shannon square in the face. I ran over to my little boy, who was trying so hard not to cry, despite the mix of pain, fear, and failure. A cloud of guilt consumed me—I should have practiced with him more in the backyard; no, I shouldn't have pushed him so hard.

Several years later I'd play one of the most memorable fathers in television history on *Titus*—Papa Titus would have made his son feel even smaller in that moment, and while the show earned big laughs out of my bullying character, I know that in real life Christopher Titus swallowed a lot of pain and anger dealing with a dad like that. I was no Papa Titus, and after that day I let Shannon find his own path. The good news is that Shannon shares my love for baseball, and we developed enough mutual respect for each other that our bond has been able to survive the fact that

I root for the Giants and he chose the Dodgers. (It's my fault, of course, for raising him in Southern California.) He did join me in cheering for the Giants in 2010 when I had the thrill of taking him to a World Series game to watch Matt Cain shut down the Texas Rangers. It was a great game but also a memorable father-son moment.

As parents, Malgosia and I wanted our kids to find their own niche in life, and while I would not be a stage dad, I was particularly determined to avoid my parents' edict of "Be a Lawyer, Be a Doctor, Don't Be an Actor." There'd be no Walter Pidgeon lecture in my household. Shannon played my son in an episode of the second *Mike Hammer* series when he was about eleven, but when he decided his interests were in international business and public relations I was proud, and a little relieved. When Karolina expressed a desire to pursue acting we encouraged her; she's quite good at it and she has the passion for it so she'll be able to handle those challenges. She even bounced right back after a classmate accidentally smashed her nose during a stage fighting lesson, so I know she has the toughness she'll need. I know that every time she goes for an audition, however, I'll shuffle into my "Dad" shoes, assuming the protective posture that my parents did. And I know that Karolina will go out and handle it fine on her own.

Malgosia is a strong-willed woman. She has inner strength to spare, and it was she who gave me the courage to finally stand up to my parents and to face the world honestly on the most delicate of topics: my hair.

I've always prided myself on going my own way, doing what I believed in. Yet when it came to hair I totally capitulated to pressure from my parents and from the Hollywood system. My dad went bald early and always believed it cost him roles in TV and movies, so when I started shedding strands at an early age, my parents were not subtle in their advice. In my twenties, my parents shelled out twenty-five thousand dollars for a hair transplant but back then the technology was still kind of primitive. The doctors harvested hair from the back of my head and it worked, but only a little bit. It was also exquisitely painful and ruined my shaved head look, which had worked well in *The Country Wife* and *The Traveling Executioner*.

Karolina, appearing here in *The Cherry Orchard,* may be following her father's footsteps.

Playing Shannon's father on screen COURTESY POSITRON PRODUCTIONS

Years later when I shaved my head for *Art* in London, I had a grid in the back of my head that looked like a tattoo gone bad.

When the transplant didn't work my parents switched to rugs. "Wear your hairpiece," was a common refrain. Mom would nag me, saying I should not leave the house naked. "Burt Reynolds never takes his off," Dad would add. "Neither does William Shatner."

I understood the need to project an image, but these follicle follies made me feel like I wasn't being myself. I was always playing someone else. (My brother felt the same way.) My parents had allies, of course. Publicity guru Jay Bernstein, who wore a series of (often terrible) toupees, pushed me to maintain my public face at all times. Malgosia, however, took an instant dislike to the very concept of rug-wearing. "Are you going to wear that *czapka*?" she asked, her tone and the Polish word itself underscoring how ridiculous it all was. Our wedding became a rite of passage, and it was a few years after that when I told my parents that my fake hair and I were parting ways.

What I do on my days off is one thing. On the set, however, I still willingly commit to whatever the role demands—it's no different than makeup or a prop. If you see a gallery of my acting work, you'll see quite the array of hairpieces. *New Centurions* and my original Mike Hammer hairpieces were carefully sculpted and looked impressively realistic; in *Hemingway*, they struggled to make the younger me look right, but the middle-aged and older Papa were right on. For some parts, I have also filled in with the help of a soft pencil and a makeup tool that sends tiny particles of color out of an atomizer to stick to the scalp.

Among the most outrageous wigs I wore were as 120-year-old Abraham Wright in *Brewster McCloud* (with makeup designed by the legendary John Chambers, now made famous by *Argo*) and Bad Bob in *Judge Roy Bean*. Those were meant to be over the top, but on some productions, when the budget was lower or the shoot was rushed, well, let's just say that some of my 'dos don't look so great, ranking up—or down—there with the worst of Howard Cosell.

In *Mountain of the Cannibal God*, it was hard to tell the difference between my wig and a rat's nest. In *Mistral's Daughter*, I had so much material it looked like I was wearing a Medusa hair-hat. Occasionally, of course, my hairpiece is bad on purpose—in Oliver Stone's *W*, I played the Reverend Earle Hudd, a composite of numerous charismatic preachers, a group of men known to sport toupees that are a bit much. When I look at myself in that film I am even more thankful that Malgosia taught me how to feel comfortable in my own skin . . . even when there's no hair covering it.

CHAPTER 30

The Bell Never Tolls for Mike Hammer

MIKE HAMMER IS CANCELED. LONG LIVE MIKE HAMMER.

After the series was dropped, I devoted an increasing amount of time to theater: *Idiot's Delight* at the Kennedy Center in Washington, in which I played a vaudevillian, Harry Van, who, coincidentally, had issues with cocaine; *Sleuth*, on a national tour, in which I made a new lifelong friend in co-star Maxwell Caulfield (his wife, actress Juliet Mills, is Karolina's god-mother); and *The King and I*, which toured in Japan with Mary Beth Piel, who had played Anna with Yul Brynner—and where the signs translating each line of English into Japanese operated on a slight delay, always leaving the audience's reaction slightly behind, which made for a surreal experience in timing. We would get laughs and gasps in the middle of our next line.

Yet I had also made myself into a bankable television actor and did not want to fritter that away. From 1988 through 1997, I appeared in fourteen TV movies, as well as guest spots on a couple of series. My TV tough guy persona was not going gently into the good night.

It started with Ernest Hemingway. I had read Hemingway in college, and he was the first American author to awaken my sense of the power of prose in our times. The literary master also shared many characteristics with a certain macho, pugnacious, irresistible-to-women detective I had played. I went to CBS during my *Mike Hammer* stint and proposed a Hemingway miniseries, only to discover that there were already plans for a syndicated production. Fortunately, the producer's lawyer and my lawyer were one and the same, Sidney Feinberg, and Sidney had recommended me for the part.

Even though I drew on Hammer for aspects of my role, two real-life models were of greater influence: John Huston, and my maternal grandfather, William H. Peckham. Both shared many traits with Hemingway. My grandfather was an outspoken and hedonistic Texan with a huge laugh, who loved fly fishing and hunting—his house was adorned with trophies of lions and polar bears, some shot while Aydaddy (as I called him) was on the prowl with his buddy Theodore Roosevelt.

For *Hemingway*, we traveled all over the world for six months. I toted a trunk load full of books by, and about, Hemingway with me everywhere we filmed. A collection of his letters served as my bible for the project, since the depth of feelings revealed in them is often deeper than even his fiction. Our journeys followed Hemingway's footsteps fairly closely. In Spain, we re-created the running of the bulls in Pamplona. Professional runners pulled off the dangerous parts, but I got close enough for a taste of the adrenaline rush that comes from putting yourself in a situation like that. I never knew I could run that fast. In Kenya, we spent twelve days camping in the bush. One night Malgosia and I heard a low growl and something scratching at the tent . . . no fool, I never ventured outside to see what it was—but we think it was a lion or a cheetah.

Unfortunately, the project suffered because our director, Bernhard Sinkel, was a German who had chosen to do this project because he viewed Hemingway as the embodiment of the "ugly American." Sinkel was making a pronouncement about the essence of his personality that I fundamentally disagreed with and I had to waste time and energy defending Hemingway's moral structure. Also, Sinkel was a bully toward many of our crew, and one afternoon, I finally lost my cool while filming in Hemingway's Key West home. We were shooting a scene where Hemingway was showing his then wife, Pauline, the gun that his father had used to commit suicide. The prop director thought that the gun was close enough to the .38 Smith and Wesson the father had used, but Sinkel did not, calling the prop man a "stupid fool" in front of everyone, yelling, "You don't know what you're doing." I was tired of his hurtful grandstanding and, without thinking, I grabbed Sinkel and started to shove him up against the wall. I was ready to go all Papa on him—which undoubtedly would have been disastrous for my career—when Malgosia intervened and stepped in to calm me down.

There are aspects of that performance of which I'm very proud, especially in Hemingway's later years, but while I won a Golden Globe and earned an Emmy nomination for my performance, I look back with some regret. Too often I gave in to Sinkel rather than fight him, overacting and portraying Hemingway as too brutish, depriving him of the nuance he deserved. Both Hemingway's son Jack, with whom I corresponded, and his granddaughter Margaux, with whom I became friends until her tragic suicide, thought I'd captured his spirit. The project left me

In my Hemingway mode, showing Malgosia how to handle a gun

wanting more: I have since narrated Hemingway's short stories for audiobooks, and I'm putting together a one-man show with Jim McGrath, a former *Mike Hammer* writer.

━◆━

"So, eleven hundred men went in the water; 316 men come out and the sharks took the rest, June the 29th, 1945. Anyway, we delivered the bomb."

Like most Americans, the little I knew about the tragic story of the USS *Indianapolis*, the boat that delivered the materials for the atomic bomb and then was sunk by the Japanese, came from Robert Shaw's monologue as Quint near the end of *Jaws*. The entirety of the story, which we told in *Mission of the Shark*, was even more complicated and upsetting than what Quint taught us.

I played Captain Charles McVay, who was at the helm of the *Indianapolis*. McVay became the only captain ever court-martialed for allowing his ship to be sunk or for "hazarding his ship by failing to zig-zag." McVay was relieved of active command, given a desk job, and later committed suicide, although I don't think this was entirely the cause. (He had been suffering marital problems and bad health as well.) In researching my role, I learned that the Navy had covered up its own ineptitude, both in the orders it gave McVay on his historic delivery mission, and in failing to rescue the survivors, because nobody knew they were out there. There was overwhelming evidence that the Navy itself had placed the ship in harm's way as well as testimony from the Japanese submarine commander that zigzagging would not have saved the ship.

It was one of those roles that touched and haunted me for years to come. I had the privilege of meeting some of the survivors, as well as McVay's son, Kimo, and listening to their stories inspired me to join the campaign that in 2000 finally persuaded Congress and the Navy to fully exonerate Captain McVay.

There was a role for McVay's father, a Navy admiral, and to bring a certain veracity to the role, both in terms of family resemblance and inspiring filial devotion, we hired my father. Dad and I had never worked together and even though we loved being on the set with each other (and my brother James, who had a small part that was edited out), it was not an easy experience. It was a bittersweet irony that the man who had taught me so much about acting now felt intimidated working with his famous son. Nervous, he had difficulty with his lines—once he'd blow one, he became frustrated and embarrassed, creating a bit of a downward spiral. So we printed up cue cards, which gave him security and confidence, and he came through with flying colors. I really felt for him. He wanted so much to turn in a first-rate performance, and he finally did, but not without a few battle scars.

The shoot itself had challenges that made me think of Quint on his boat. We filmed the scenes depicting the USS *Indianapolis* aboard the USS *Alabama*, stationed in Mobile, Alabama. Then we moved to the Bahamas where the water was warm and beautiful and the presence of sharks was quite real. The crew spread nets across the area where we were shooting for protection but sharks are not easily deterred and they like to chew stuff . . . like nets. So we knew the waters might become shark infested. While I obviously could never imagine the paralyzing fear the real crew felt, this was plenty terrifying for me. We had to spend what felt like hours in the water, holding on to debris. At one point I was so cold and tired that I started to nod off. As I snapped back into consciousness I spotted a fin slashing through the water in my direction. I nearly panicked before realizing it was a stunt man swimming with a shark fin attached to his back.

I have been and always shall be Mike Hammer.

Certain roles stick to you, and I'm happy that Hammer is mine. After the TV movie in 1989, I did a few audiobooks of Mickey's novels like *I, the Jury* and *Vengeance Is Mine*. I still find the stories riveting, so in 1997 when a couple of producers approached me about creating a syndicated version of the series, I was intrigued. Jay was wary but Mickey needed the money, so they agreed, asking me to be an executive producer, to protect Hammer's integrity. I did my best. We had good stories but the backers never came up with enough money, and we wound up living hand-to-mouth, shooting during the day and working on rewrites all night. We had to cut down on the number of stunts and fights to save money, limitations which hindered any chance of success. I did particularly enjoy scenes with Hammer's next door neighbor, the yoga teacher who served as a comic foil. She was quite beautiful, but I didn't have to worry about my wife being jealous, because it was Malgosia who played the part. We also cast my good friend, Peter Jason, as Skip Gleason, my NYPD connection (Peter and I had worked on *Cheech and Chong*, *The Blue and the Gray*, and *The Long Riders* and would later reunite on *Titus*.) In addition to Malgosia's and Shannon's appearances, my dad played a judge on one episode, sailing through the dialogue without any problem. I was relieved. He was no longer intimidated working with his son, and it gave me real pleasure to witness his performance.

That production was bumped off after twenty-two episodes, but Hammer lives on, and not just because I bought the Mustang I drove in the series, which Malgosia and I gave to Shannon for his sixteenth birthday. In addition to the traditional audiobooks like *Complex 90*, producer Carl Amari and I created a new genre that we call "radio novels." We've used short stories by English radio playwright M. J. Elliott and by award-winning writer Max Allan Collins, a close friend of Mickey's, whom Mickey entrusted to complete his unfinished novels after his death in 2006. These productions feature full casts, sound effects,

Shannon with his old man and his new, old car—the Mike Hammer Mustang

and music (written and arranged by yours truly). For the first time, we have stepped outside Hammer's perspective to broaden the action, even though the narration still brings everything back to Hammer's point of view. We won an Audie Award in 2011 for Best Original Work, and I'm as proud of these efforts as I am of the original series. Working in this format also makes me nostalgic, taking me back to my days in the studio watching my dad create *Tales of the Texas Rangers*.

Nothing pleased me more than when both Stacy Keaches appeared on screen together as we did in *Mike Hammer*.

CHAPTER 31

Speak the Speech

NOBODY LIKES THE WAY THEY SOUND WHEN THEY FIRST HEAR THEIR voice on a recording. A cleft lip and cleft palate, however, are often enough to make one truly self-conscious. I had only partial clefts so I never had trouble making myself understood the way children with more extreme clefts sometimes do, but I did speak with a telltale nasal voice. As a boy, I set out to reinvent how I sounded, my first lesson in how flexible an instrument a voice can be. My dad, perhaps because of his radio background, was always after me to speak more clearly too—he'd have me do sight readings of newspaper articles, emphasizing the need for both clarity and accuracy so the words came out, as Hamlet would have it, trippingly on the tongue. Having a birth defect may have started me off at a disadvantage, but striving to develop a good voice paid dividends and today my flourishing side career doing voiceover work provides particular satisfaction.

I've continued improving my instrument along the way. I learned a great deal while studying in London, as I've mentioned, but my education never ended. Judy Collins introduced me to a voice teacher named Max Margulies who worked with both actors and musicians. I'd read a line and he'd say, "Can you pitch that just a little bit higher and be a little bit clearer without forcing it?" He wanted me to strive for what he called "a head voice" instead of a chest voice, where the sound gets trapped in your throat. Another great voice teacher, Seth Riggs, who has worked with many stars including Michael Jackson, had me visualize getting my voice unstuck from my larynx. Age and cigarettes have deepened my voice from a tenor to a baritone, which helps me to resonate with even greater authority.

Voice work has given me a way to supplement my income, but it also allows me to stretch in many different directions as an actor, and to explore the other passions of my life, be it science or religion, history or theater. I started auditioning for voiceover work in the late 1970s when my movie career was dwindling. I learned that voiceover performers get pigeonholed just as actors do—you can be an ANNOUNCER in a voice filled with EXCLAMATION POINTS!!! Or you can be a narrator. There is also often a split between documentaries and commercials. I would not have turned my nose up at commercials to help pay the bills but was glad to find my way as a documentary narrator. (Today, the rise of animated movies plus video and computer games offers a whole new set of opportunities for voice work.) I began listening with greater intensity to other voiceover actors. Morgan Freeman hadn't emerged yet, but I picked up ideas on technique from hearing James Earl Jones, Alex Scourby, and Richard Kiley, among others.

Over the years, I've gotten much better at finding the nuances, the little colorings that bring specific meanings to each word. I've learned to avoid the temptation to "put a spin" on something that doesn't warrant it and I've discovered that simply by thinking a specific thought, you can express it fully and clearly. It's only taken me some fifty years of performing to learn all this. I think just as the acting helped my voice work, the voice work has also made me a better actor. It's a symbiotic relationship.

My first gig was *The Search for Solutions*, a multi-part science documentary, which was perfect because I was already reading about science on my own. A new friend, Gary Greenberg, was involved with a group called Environmental Communications, which provided art- and science-based slide series and videos to colleges and libraries. I joined EC's board of directors, nurturing my interests in science and teaching. Gary hosted weekly gatherings where we'd discuss articles from *Scientific American* to better understand complicated notions like black holes and string theory. I was a layman, but I was dedicated to learning and eager to keep up.

Gary has since invented three-dimensional microscopes, and together we wrote *Mary's Magic Microscope*, a children's book devoted to an exploration of the microworld, and began developing two film projects. *The Universe in a Grain of Sand* artfully depicts sand grains from all the beaches in the world in a way people have never before seen—this is designed for planetarium domes and IMAX theaters. *The Art of Science* explores the historical and contemporary parallels between art and science. I'm co-producing and narrating both films, and I also do the musical scoring.

My studies with Gary gave me the informed perspective that enabled me to become the voice of the PBS series *NOVA*, which I narrated for over a decade. I learned so much it felt like I was getting paid and getting an education simultaneously. *NOVA*'s goal was to bring science to ordinary people in a way that was entertaining and provocative, that was easy to understand without ever talking down to the viewers. The writing was so phenomenally clear that all I had to do was narrate in a way that made the topics sound comfortable, even familiar. (The *Secrets of Making Money* episode on counterfeiting was so well explained I expected to see new $50s and $100s flooding the streets.) For *NOVA*, and for other science and history documentaries that I've done for National Geographic and American Experience, I've tried to treat my narrator as a character—he's me, but a more refined, intelligent version. I think this has helped me find the right balance in sounding authoritative while remaining welcoming and accessible.

My favorite *NOVA* episode examined the disappearance of the Mayans and the Aztecs; part of its appeal—along with documentaries I've narrated on subjects ranging from war planes to Nikola Tesla—was that it blended science with history, which also fascinates me. (I was enough of a Tesla freak that I read everything I could find on him and even tried developing a movie about him when I was younger.)

I'm always amazed, though not surprised, at how in our polarized society science and religion often seem to exist in mutually exclusive spheres. I am a believer in science, but I believe in God, too. God to me is Nature, the Creative Force, that which started everything. I am a spiritual person. I dug deeply into roles like Martin Luther, Barabbas, and the Christ-like Killer

Kane. I do not, however, proselytize. I hold a profound respect for people who believe in Buddha or Mohammad or Krishna, or the "Dream Time" of the aborigines. I also respect atheists and agnostics with equanimity. I find it difficult to accept the people who preach that "I'm right and you're not. My God is the real one." (One thing that affirms my faith is synchronicity, a force that is outside of us and beyond our perceptions. This led me not further into religion but into the writings of Carl Jung.)

I was raised Episcopalian. On my mother's side I have a distant relative, John Peckham, who was the Archbishop of Canterbury in the thirteenth century and debated Thomas of Aquinas. Having been brought up a Christian, I welcomed the chance to participate in two different audiobooks of the Bible. In one I read the Book of Job, which was a great acting exercise because the story is just a hair this side of the line of melodrama, and you want to play it for all it's worth without crossing over that line. The story itself always baffled me: Why would God go to such extremes with Job, allowing the Devil such latitude? But reading it for this job crystallized my belief that the Bible is not to be taken literally; it should be interpreted metaphorically and as parables. On the other project, I read Paul, in his many wonderful letters—it's a text that is full of contradictions, which appeals to the historian in me, but it's also an immense undertaking, since it comprises nearly one third of the New Testament.

I've always been catholic in my tastes and interests, but when I married Malgosia, I also became Catholic, because she feels so deeply connected to her faith. I came to appreciate that bond when Shannon was two, and we were in France at the Cannes Film Festival. Malgosia decided we should fly to Rome to have him blessed by the Pope. I thought she was kidding. You can't just call up and get the big guy on the phone. Can you? Well, John Paul II was Polish, and when Malgosia informed the Vatican that she had attended the same academy of theology in Poland as him and mentioned a professor as a common bond, we were in.

"When would you like to come to the Vatican?"

Malgosia said, "How's Tuesday at noon?"

No problem.

That night we realized that we had obligations on Tuesday, so Malgosia called back and asked if we could see the Pope on Wednesday. That was fine; he could accommodate our schedule. It was a valuable lesson in how strongly John Paul felt tied to his heritage, and also how tenacious and determined my dear wife could be.

~

File this under "If at first. . . ." In the 1990s I hosted a mystery docudrama series called *Missing: Reward*. I thought it would be a chance to make some extra money, and also do some good, but it turned out to be a bit of an embarrassment—the scripts barely distinguished between the importance of offering rewards for a missing child and a missing collectible item in your attic, like rare coins, or figurines of the Seven Dwarfs. Not what I had in mind.

American Greed more than makes up for that. Along with *NOVA*, it is the voiceover project with which I am most associated and of which I am most proud. I feel a bit like Mike Hammer, going after the bad guys, exposing those who prey on the vulnerable, particularly people like the doctors who take advantage of cancer patients. (The Ponzi schemers often

Malgosia and I brought Shannon to be blessed by Pope John Paul II.

seem more sad and deluded, as if they really will be able to make it all work out if they can just get one more score. They remind me of gambling addicts.) A spinoff show, *American Greed: The Fugitives*, focuses on stories where the criminals are still at large and enlists the audience's help in bringing them to justice.

Both shows are cautionary tales, and I know too well how vulnerable people are, and how easily they can be seduced by opportunities that seem too good to be true. When I was eleven, my grandfather, Clifford Williams, made a modest living as manager of the Ford Motor Company in Taft, Texas. He and my grandmother, Artie Pat Williams (whom I called "Mammy"), lived in a small house, and he wanted to give her the dream vacation she never had. A "friend" convinced Clifford to invest a couple of thousand dollars in an oil drum up in Sinton, a small town ten miles away. Clifford would "double his money in two weeks." And he did.

When the four-thousand-dollar check arrived, it came with a letter imploring him to reinvest with another one thousand—this time he would triple his money in three weeks. Clifford really believed he was on the road to riches (and he was doing it in oil, the field that had made Mammy's ex-husband a wealthy man). One Sunday afternoon, Clifford asked me to hop in the car and join him for a trip to Sinton to take a look at the oil drum he had purchased. We parked the car on the side of the road, walked on over, and he said, "Climb up there, Stacy, and tell me how much oil we got." I climbed the ladder running up the side of the drum, and looked down. "There's nothing here, Grandpa," I yelled.

He was stunned, to say the least; climbing up to see for himself made it all too real. "Son of a bitch!" he muttered. We drove to a house in Sinton where my grandfather rang the bell. There was no answer. Then a neighbor told him, "There's nobody there. They moved two weeks ago."

Clifford was crestfallen. The realization that he had been taken had sunk in. I will always remember the painful look on his face as he turned to me and said, "Don't you dare tell Mammy!"

So it's no surprise that I find a certain joy in busting the bad guys. Yet while my producer always wants me to really hit the word, "Guilty," I can't exult too much during my readings or I might undercut the seriousness of these crimes. In the recording booth I sometimes like to go over the top intentionally, as a joke, deepening my voice to a growl and stretching the word "Guilty" out till I sound like a hanging judge out of a Wild West parody.

The show's slogan is "Some people will do anything for money" and one day while sitting at my synthesizer, I noodled a blues riff and started laying out a lyric that began: "Some people think it's funny, they'll do anything for money." Within an hour, I had written a song, "Anything for Money." I recorded it and our producer, Chuck Schaeffer, decided it would work on the show itself. My success made me think back to my parents deciding I should take piano lessons. My piano teacher, Miss Gohl, was an elegant woman in her early forties; once a promising concert pianist, she wore floral dresses and heavy perfume and a denture that she would click when she wasn't talking. She was a great teacher but my parents had to force me to practice, since I'd always choose football in the streets over the piano. I was glad they made me stick with it. I still don't practice as much as I would like to, but playing "Rhapsody in Blue" or "Clair de Lune" brings me a sense of serenity, and I love having a different outlet in which I can be creative.

I've also written scores for the Mike Hammer "radio novels," which are more ambitious and perhaps even more satisfying than a single song like "Anything for Money." Of course, my favorite part of the Mike Hammer audiobooks is the chance to pour myself into a dramatic role, even if it's only with my voice. My producer, Carl Amari, also expanded our horizons with radio adaptations of all the classic *Twilight Zone* episodes; I handle the narration, trying to find my own voice yet also paying tribute to the great Rod Serling with a bit of clipped diction.

These weren't my first forays into dramatic audio fare. Back in the 1980s I was among a bunch of actors who helped co-found a group called L.A. Theatre Works (LATW), with our producer, Susan Loewenberg. The goal was to create a venue for actors who lived in California and wanted to do theater without having to go to New York. We couldn't raise the money for a traditional theater, but Richard Dreyfuss came up with the idea of doing radio plays. We started with an adaptation of Sinclair Lewis's *Babbitt*, which featured thirty-four actors including all of the original crew— Edward Asner, Richard Dreyfuss, Hector Elizondo, Harry Hamlin, Julie Harris, Amy Irving, John Lithgow, Marsha Mason, JoBeth Williams, and me. We've also added live performances over the years.

Radio plays have significantly expanded my opportunities for playing great roles, especially since your age and appearance don't limit you. I got a chance to work with actors with whom I'd never previously crossed paths. Richard Dreyfuss and I co-starred in Arthur Miller's *The Crucible* (I played John Proctor); I was proud when that became one of LATW's all-time best-sellers. I've had a chance to flesh out my Shakespearean canon further, playing everyone from Bottom in *A Midsummer Night's Dream* to the Ghost in *Hamlet*. Richard and I starred together in *Julius Caesar;* he was Antony, and I was Brutus, the role that was a watershed moment for me decades earlier when I was studying at LAMDA. That show, like so many others, had a fantastic cast, which included a cameo by Kelsey Grammer plus JoBeth, Harold Gould, Paul Winfield, and John Randolph. John had been the gravedigger in 1964's *Hamlet* in the Park and had been one of the veteran actors who really welcomed me to New York and to the profession. He was so supportive and giving to all the young actors. He made us feel secure. We kept in touch and I was happy to work with him. As we get older we have been in so many casts that reunions become more common. They become more cherished, too.

Another classic that eluded me onstage was *Death of a Salesman.* I had been invited to play Willy Loman several times when I was not available. In 1999 I was approached about stepping into Brian Dennehy's shoes on Broadway if he left for the Los Angeles production. Those would be big shoes to fill, and not just because Brian has a good three inches on me—he was brilliant in the role. Still, I'd have jumped at the chance but Brian managed to finish out the Broadway run and do Los Angeles, too so I welcomed the chance to finally play Willy Loman at LATW. Harris Yulin had just played the role in Europe and he was brilliant in it as well, so we discussed the play's tone, how to balance the humor and the tragedy in Loman's failures and self-delusions. It was a gratifying experience, and, fortunately, a well-liked performance.

～

There are the classics by Shakespeare and by Arthur Miller, and then there is Homer. Not the ancient Greek guy. I'm talking about the fat, balding one who loves doughnuts and Duff beer. Matt Groening and the

Radio plays have given me a new shot at great works: I performed *Glengarry Glen Ross* with a stellar cast that featured Alfred Molina, Hector Elizondo, and Bruce Davison.

staff at *The Simpsons* have bestowed upon us a modern American classic. I have done animation voiceovers for the paycheck (*Rugrats, Scooby-Doo*) but when *The Simpsons* came calling I was truly honored to be asked to join their legendary pantheon of guest voices. I played beer magnate Howard Duff on three episodes and going into the room for my first day was my most exciting table reading ever. I was giddy, like a fan, getting to hear all the voices I'd laughed at for so long coming out of the mouths of this talented troupe. The audience was made up of the show's writers and producers, an equally impressive bunch and making them laugh (admittedly, at their own handiwork) was a delight.

I had also tried for years to break into Disney, auditioning for numerous movies there to no avail, but I finally got my big break, riding on the coattails of my documentary work. Leslie Iwerks is the granddaughter of Ub Iwerks, who co-created Mickey Mouse with Walt Disney and figured out how to blend live action and animation for *Song of the South*. She is also the daughter of Don Iwerks, who was a legend for his technological innovations at Disney. Leslie is a talent in her own right, earning an Oscar nomination for her short documentary *Recycled Life*, and I was happy to narrate her documentary *The Pixar Story* in 2007. *The Pixar Story* garnered an Emmy nomination, but it also introduced my work to John Lasseter. I had the chance to meet John at the movie's screening at the Marin Film Festival. John had just taken on responsibilities at Disney too, and I think it was this connection that led to me getting cast in *Planes*, which was supposed to go straight to DVD but turned out so well that Disney gave it a theatrical release in the summer of 2013.

Animated movies require a different type of performance—you usually are recording solo instead of acting opposite your co-stars, so the director wants at least three, if not more, different readings of each line: I luuuuve you. I LOVE you. I luv ya. I love YOU. The more choices they have in the editing room the better—it's a treat for an actor since you get to play with the material, kneading it in one direction then the other, stretching your imagination to its limits. It is also a definitive reminder that a movie actor must exist in the moment, not knowing which take or which scene will be in the final cut—this was the lesson I first learned on *End of the Road*, four decades earlier, and it is, I would guess, the only thing anyone will ever find in common between *End of the Road* and *Planes*.

CHAPTER 32

Thine Own Self

I SAT IN THE DARKENED THEATER IN BERKELEY, CALIFORNIA, MY LIFE changing before my very eyes. I was eighteen and for several years had yearned to become the next Marlon Brando or James Dean. Suddenly, these symbols of rebellious youth had been swept away, replaced by a proper British actor a quarter of a century older. I now wanted to be Laurence Olivier. Mesmerized by his performance in *Richard III*, I hoped the day would come when I would some day step into that role.

In my early career, from 1961 through 1974, I'd never strayed too far for too long from the classics. Then I'd shifted focus to movies, television, and more commercial theater. I'd had some great showy stage roles in the 1980s—*Barnum, The King and I, Sleuth*—but I had tackled no serious theater since *Hughie* in 1980, no classical work since *Cyrano* two years prior, and no Shakespeare since 1972. Post-Hammer, my agent and manager wanted me to resist the theater's siren call, telling me I'd lose money if I passed up this TV part or that movie role. I now had young children to provide for. It didn't matter. It was time.

When Michael Kahn, the artistic director of the Shakespeare Theatre Company in Washington, DC, offered me *Richard III* in 1990, I think I said yes before he finished the sentence. I had known Michael since the 1960s and admired his tremendous theatrical sensibility, which extends to every aspect of a performance, from lighting to costumes. Then there was Richard himself. It wasn't just Olivier; Richard is one of Shakespeare's greatest creations, a richly textured character who is wildly funny in one sentence, murderous in the next, and both in the one after that.

I've always loved characters that offer the dichotomy of a public and private persona—Richard has much in common with Buffalo Bill, another consummate showman wracked by internal pain. Richard also resonated with me personally more than most other roles—having been teased as a child because of my cleft lip, I identified with Richard's drive and his desire to achieve. The intensity of his need for vengeance was not something I had to work hard to summon up.

I wanted to tip the crown to Antony Sher, who had done a wonderful Richard with the Royal Shakespeare Company—his Richard was completely encased in braces on both legs and arms. I used the idea of the leg braces but then added my own touch. My Richard was, despite his deformities, agile and athletic. (I worked out ninety minutes a day to get in shape for the part.)

It did take me a little while to shake the Olivier from my readings. I've stolen from him—we all have—in small doses, but here it was difficult not to imitate him. He was so transparently brilliant, the way he disdainfully extended his hand to Buckingham to kiss the ring. What I did was perform an all-out impression all the way through one day and that got it out of my system, enabling me to find my own voice, my own theatrically showy moves.

When my Richard finally ascends to the throne, he pulls off his brace, as if attaining power finally allowed him to shed everything that had held him back. Then when the throne is slipping from his grasp at the end, he again reaches for the brace, a literal and metaphorical crutch. In the end, Richard is alone—without even a horse, as everyone knows—and nearly helpless. Yet he remains defiant, using his brace as a weapon to try and stave off the inevitable.

While I obviously greatly admired Olivier's movie, from what I've read, my dirtier, grittier Richard was probably more in line with the man who had previously been considered the greatest Richard III of the twentieth century, John Barrymore, back in 1920. Barrymore had always fascinated me, both for his boundless talent and his monumental personality. Shortly before Michael Kahn invited me to play Richard, I had decided to bring Barrymore to life in a one-man play. I sought out playwright William Luce, who had written one-woman plays about Emily Dickinson,

Making glorious summers as Richard III in Washington at the Shakespeare
Theatre Company CAROL ROSEGG/SHAKESPEARE THEATRE COMPANY

Charlotte Bronte (both played by Julie Harris), Zelda Fitzgerald, and Lillian Hellman. He'd come out to my place in Malibu and we'd go back and forth on developing the storyline and the anecdotes we wanted to use.

As an actor, you learn to loathe the downtime—you want to relax and to be with your family, of course, but you don't want too many nights of wondering when the next part might come along. Busy is better. At that moment in time I was blessed with busy-ness. First came *Richard III*, followed by a series of roles in TV and movies, some to pay the bills (*Class of 1999*), some that were genuinely exciting (*False Identity*, a chance to act with my father and be directed by my brother, who was happy to boss me around) or intriguing (*Milena*). As a result, before William and I could finish readying the Barrymore project for production, our option expired. Other producers took the idea to other actors—there was even an announcement in the *New York Times* in 1993 saying John Lithgow would be starring in the show on Broadway. When Luce finally got the rights back, he showed it to producer Robert Whitehead, who gave the script to Chris Plummer. Suddenly the project I had initiated was heading for the boards with another actor in the spotlight. It was a great disappointment for me not to initiate that role, but at least my idea hadn't gone to waste, and I knew Barrymore was in capable hands.

In fact, he was in multiple hands in the mid-'90s: Nicol Williamson brought his own one-man Barrymore show to Broadway and my old pal Jason Miller wrote *Barrymore's Ghost*, apparently with me in mind—I was still jumping from one role to another so Jason played Barrymore himself. I was flattered to read an article in which he said, "Sometimes the writer [in me] said, 'Get me Stacy Keach! You stink!'"

Who knows, maybe one of these days, someone will say "Get me Stacy Keach" and I will finally get to play Barrymore.

We all have our guilty pleasures. As much as I consider myself a devotee of the classics, there's nothing I love more than a good old-fashioned mystery, entertainment for its own sake. I devour books by John Grisham and James Patterson and reveled in my parts in slick commercial shows like *Deathtrap* and *Sleuth* for the twists and turns they give an audience.

My favorite in the genre is definitely Rupert Holmes's *Solitary Confinement*, in which I played the wealthy recluse Richard Jannings ... as well as Fillip, Eldridge, Conroy, Girard, Fleischer, and even Miss Davis. I filmed those parts—the lowly help Jannings regularly abused—ahead of time, going through a makeup process as extensive as many movies. We made multiple masks of my head as impressions used to create distinct faces and identities for each person. Working out the timing was a bit tricky because we filmed those parts without accounting for audience reactions, so as Jannings I had to adjust on the fly. I also played one other character live, the masked villain—to pull that off I'd slip behind a suit of armor that Jannings owned; a double could pretend to be me while I sneaked backstage, donned a gorilla mask, climbed through a dumbwaiter, and came onstage and removed the mask to the astonishment of the audience.

I relished every moment of it, but there was nothing more satisfying than the big reveal at the end of the evening. We had made up fake biographies for the playbills; someone named Jane Rollins played Miss Davis

For *Solitary Confinement,* I became a man of many faces.

and Art Calvin was Conroy. Only during the curtain calls did we finally end the deception, letting the audience in on our secret. Each night the audience was shocked then delighted at having been tricked. They loved it. The show broke box office records when we played at the Kennedy Center in Washington.

The show came to Broadway, and while the audiences who came out still loved the show, the critics killed it. They bashed it as a gimmick—they wanted the play to be about something more. To me, that missed the point. It was a uniquely theatrical experience. Isn't that enough for any play to deliver?

The next production that brought me to Broadway arrived with the Pulitzer Prize for drama after a successful run in Washington, which earned me my first Helen Hayes Award (I had been nominated for *Richard III*). I thought *The Kentucky Cycle* would redeem me commercially and critically in New York, but while I earned a Drama Desk nomination, the play suffered the opposite problem from *Solitary Confinement*. It was definitely about something, but maybe it was about too many things—it was really two plays, or, one play over two evenings. The first part started as a deeply felt family drama, and then shifted its focus to America's labor movement in Part Two. The power of Part One dissipated in the second half and New York critics and audiences did not appreciate the scope of the experience. I still admired the work for its boldness, for Warner Shook's inspired direction, and for reaching for the stars and nearly getting there.

Most of my film and TV work in the 1990s was aiming far lower, but projects like *Escape from L.A.* and *The Sea Wolf* enabled me to perform regularly in the theater, in productions ranging from *Camelot* to *An Inspector Calls* to *Love Letters* (in which I co-starred with quite the diverse parade of women—Diana Rigg, Michael Learned, Linda Purl, and Joan Collins). I also starred in a wonderful two-hander with Margot Kidder, *Stieglitz Loves O'Keeffe*. This was Margot's first role after her very public nervous breakdown and, having grown fond of her when we co-starred in *The Dion Brothers* twenty years earlier, I was pleased to see her in such good health. We opened in Winston-Salem, North Carolina, and took the play to Baltimore; features started touting the show as Broadway-bound but we never attracted the investors we needed.

Nevertheless, I couldn't be too disappointed. Washington, DC, may be a swampy cesspool when it comes to politics, but it has a vibrant and welcoming theatrical community. Early in my career, I'd been especially appreciative of the atmosphere I'd found at Williamstown, Yale Rep, and the Long Wharf, but I'd also loved my stint with *Indians* at Washington's Arena Theatre. Sometimes, away from the star-making buzz of New York City, it's easier for creativity to flourish—it's one reason why Chicago births so many great new plays. Once you stop worrying about what happens on Broadway, you start appreciating how good you have it where you are—in Washington, I'd been on a roll, with *Richard III*, *Solitary Confinement*, and *Kentucky Cycle*.

Then Michael Kahn called with an offer I almost could refuse. I couldn't quibble with the director, Joe Dowling, who took over that year as artistic director of Minneapolis's Guthrie Theater, nor with the playwright, a guy by the name of Shakespeare, and I knew Michael would provide top-flight production values. Still, *Macbeth*—the play in question—was one I had avoided since *MacBird!*, in part because they felt similar but also because MacBird was someone with whom the audience could empathize, while Macbeth is one of the most difficult of Shakespeare's major protagonists. The play works brilliantly on an intellectual and a poetic level, but it's hard to work up emotion for a guy who listens to his wife and kills the king who had been so generous to him. Richard, at least, seduces the audience, who can eventually feel and maybe even weep for him. Macbeth is a tougher nut to crack.

I said yes in the end. I'm glad I did. Joe and I came up with a new opening—a bloody battle scene that leaves the stage littered with corpses, three of whom then emerge from the dead as the witches who see into the future and stir up all that trouble. Joe took the entire company to see *Braveheart*, which had just opened, so we could feel the energy he wanted for the battle scene.

I found a way to make Macbeth work for me—I played him as insecure and vulnerable until he killed the king, then his guilt flipped a switch and he became crazy. (Upon encountering Banquo's ghost I leapt onto the banquet table, a bit I borrowed from Olivier.) As I took Macbeth around

In the Scottish play, as we supertitious actors call it CAROL PRATT/SHAKESPEARE
THEATRE COMPANY

the bend, I gave the audience reason to care for him, creating stakes that invested the play with an emotional drive to match its relentless action.

⚊ ⚊

Washington felt like home in a way that London once had. But after I got out of prison I found out I was persona non grata in the United Kingdom. Actually, I didn't realize it until the late 1980s when I was offered the part of Magwitch in a miniseries version of Charles Dickens's *Great Expectations*. I was ready to fly to London when Britain's Home Office issued a last-minute decree declaring that there was an unwritten law about ex–drug offenders, and I was not allowed back in the country to work for a period of ten years after my release. It was particularly ironic since Magwitch is a British ex-con with a long memory. The part went to Anthony Hopkins, who followed that with an even more memorable part, as Hannibal Lecter in *Silence of the Lambs*.

In 1998, my invisible prison door finally swung open when I was invited to be part of the first American cast to perform Yasmina Reza's hit *Art* on the West End in London. Starring with George Wendt and David Dukes was a satisfying way to close the chapter on the saga of my arrest. We rehearsed at the Old Vic, where you could feel the ghosts of all the great British actors who had worked there over nearly two centuries. I had seen Alan Alda perform the lead role of Marc on Broadway and watched Richard Griffiths, whom I'd be replacing in London. (Richard was sweet and generous, sharing pointers about the part.) Alan and Richard had such different takes on the part that I knew I had plenty of room to find my own way.

On the first day of rehearsal, director Matthew Warchus took George, David, and me to the British Museum, and told us to pick out a painting we liked. I don't remember what the others chose, but it was clear we definitely had different tastes, which helped set the stage for our respective roles. I narrowed it down to three, one of which was by Hieronymus Bosch, whose magnificently detailed paintings were the polar opposite of the white canvas that was the centerpiece of our play.

Art provided one of my favorite moments in my acting career. It happens near the end, when the friends are at each other's throats and Serge deflates the tension by handing my character Marc a felt-tip pen, offering up the white canvas for him to deface. I'd take the pen but then pause, dramatically, allowing the audience time to realize what was about to happen. The gasps and the nervous laughter started to build, and then reached a crescendo, as I very slowly and deliberately drew a straight line down the painting at a diagonal. I quickly filled in a stick-figure downhill skier in a stocking cap as the audience erupted with a mix of emotions, often depending on each individual's taste in art. It is as satisfying a moment as an actor can have—and then Reza undercuts it brilliantly when Marc and the audience learn Serge had used washable ink and Marc and Serge soon restore the painting to a clean slate.

It was hard to imagine that my life could get any more fulfilling—I was finishing my ninth noteworthy play in as many years. The family was with me in London, the kids going to school there. Yet with my sixtieth birthday in sight, I was about to find that I could remain a leading man onstage and also finally get great character parts in film and television. I just had to be able to play a hateful bigot . . . or two.

CHAPTER 33

The Knack

RICHARD III IS ONE OF THE MOST FASCINATING CHARACTERS IN LIT-erature, created by the world's greatest playwright. Dr. Bob Forrest is a cheesy villain in what would charitably be called a campy B movie. The link between these disparate men that I brought to life in 1990 was that each died a vivid and flamboyant death.

"Nobody at Warner's died like me. It's the one thing I had a knack for." Jon Robbie Baitz wrote that line for Lyman Wyeth, my character in the play, *Other Desert Cities*, but he could have written it for me. From *Strange Reflections*, the film I made in high school in 1958, to *King Lear*, a half-century later in Washington, DC, my life on stage and screen has often ended in an untimely fashion. *Class of 1999* (in which I played Dr. Forrest) was a particularly original demise, since it's not every day you get your heart pulled out through your chest by a giant robot, but I've also been electrocuted (*Children of the Corn*), stabbed through the eye (*Ooga Booga*) and, as the old gangster movie dialogue goes, shot full of enough lead to start a pencil factory.

And so, ladies and gentlemen, macabre though it may be, for your entertainment and pleasure, I now present my top ten most memorable death scenes, five each from stage and screen.

STAGE
#5 *Deathtrap*
The most challenging part of Sidney Bruhl's death by axe was that as the life rushed out of him, his arm jerked and he flung the telephone handset so it flew up and the cord (remember when phones had cords?) wrapped around

a beam above his desk. I worked hard in rehearsal to master the phone toss, and while there was one night where I aimed too low and the phone smashed into the beam and nearly ricocheted into the audience, I think if the phone toss had become an Olympic event I'd have had a shot at a medal.

#4 *Kentucky Cycle*

I played a villain in the first part of this play, murderous to those around me and bullying at home. My son, a half-Indian whom I treated badly, finally provides my comeuppance, giving me the Agamemnon treatment by stabbing me in the bathtub. It was a fittingly gruesome ending that we made work with a tray of blood capsules stashed in the tub so that when I arched back I released a rush of red that flooded the soapy water. It was a heavy moment.

#3 *Hamlet*

Hamlet's duel with Laertes at the end of the play needs to be a breathtaking action scene. The catch is that Hamlet ends up dead—the breath literally taken from him, which is tricky after an athletic sword fight onstage that leaves you panting. I remember during my first run as Hamlet, at the Long Wharf, hearing a boy in the front row saying, "Look Mommy, he's still breathing."

I worked hard after that to be in good enough shape, to learn to conserve my breath, and to learn how to "breathe dead"—long, slow inhales through the nose.

My best Hamlet death scene was in New York, where I grabbed Laertes's sword before the fight and when he pulls it back the audience sees blood—he has cut my hand, poisoning me. I was flattered two decades later when I went backstage after Kevin Kline played Hamlet to tell him how wonderful he had been and he told me that this moment had stayed with him ever since. Sam Waterston was Laertes, and we worked diligently to choreograph a dynamic duel. That's one thing about dying onstage or in the movies; you don't really want to create something moving and powerful—you want to create something natural, something real, and then let the audience feel those emotions on their own. To do that, you must carefully plot out all the moves—the more complicated the death, the longer it takes to rehearse. Getting that right is often what makes for an extraordinary scene, more than emotional acting.

#2 *MacBird!*

I mentioned this one earlier. The script called for me to cry out, "My heart, my heart," but I wanted to finish the show with a bang and came up with the forward fall on my own. It was worth the pain to jolt the audience like that every night.

#1 *Richard III*

After Richard's desperate and angry cry, "a horse, a horse, my kingdom for a horse" in the final battle he is totally disarmed. Yet he remains defiant and resourceful. In my production I ripped the metal brace off my leg, using it as the final weapon in his arsenal, forcing Richmond to really earn his victory with that final thrust of his sword.

SCREEN
#5 *The New Centurions*

This was my most realistic and tragic death scene, getting gunned down as a police officer. We filmed on a back staircase in one of the deadlier sections of Los Angeles. I had to do the classic movie reaction in which you clutch the wound and go down in pain. I think what helped it avoid falling into the cliché trap is that my character—who had already been shot and survived—initially reacts as if this was another hard knock to endure, when in reality, his life was quickly bleeding out of him.

#4 *The Life and Times of Judge Roy Bean*

I made this movie right after *New Centurions*. I didn't have to do much beyond a forward fall for this one—it was in post-production that John Huston made it seem as if Paul Newman's shot had created that giant hole straight through my body. It still makes me laugh every time I see it. Movie magic.

#3 *Hair*

This was my segment of a delightfully gruesome John Carpenter anthology called *Body Bags*. My character gets a hair transplant—something I can attest to being both painful and foolish—but these hairs help aliens put microscopic worms inside me to feed on my brain. It was a devilishly fun way to die on camera but was actually quite uncomfortable to film, since my excessively hairy face was perpetually itchy and I couldn't scratch without ruining the makeup. It was a true exercise in self-discipline.

2 *Cold as Ice*

In 1978, *Saturday Night Live* was at the peak of its creativity and popularity. In addition to the brilliance of the Not Ready for Prime Time Players, the show's mastermind Lorne Michaels made room for other, even quirkier, sensibilities on the air, filmmakers like Albert Brooks and my friend Gary Weis.

Gary's film had no dialogue. It was really a pre-MTV video set to the tune of Foreigner's hit single, "Cold as Ice," featuring a severe looking blonde woman dispassionately dispatching me. She starts with scissors, plunged deep in the center of my back, just beyond the reach of my flailing hands. Then she pops me with a handgun—I flinch and quiver as each bullet punctures my body, almost as if the pain of betrayal hurt more than the bullets themselves. Before she does me in, I ham it up with facial expressions similar to a child who just had his puppy stolen. In the final scene she blasts a shotgun, from point blank range, to an area just below the waist. This time, as I sink to my knees and then pitch forward, I take it in the other direction, a stone-faced, dead-eyed glazed look conveying my disbelief at this cold-hearted killer. Dying has never been so fun. Or so funny.

#1 *Hemingway*

Without question, this was the most memorable death scene for me, especially since I had spent months living inside the mind of the titanic personality and American icon. Hemingway's granddaughter Margaux came to the family home in Ketchum, Idaho, the day before we filmed this scene but the set—which had letters bearing 1961 postmarks on his desk—felt so real she could not bring herself to be there for this scene. It was chilling for me as well, especially as I walked through his steps that day, lying down on his bed, walking into the kitchen to get keys, going out to the garage for the gun. Then I came back to the vestibule, closed the door and, finally, with my own nerves completely frayed by this experience, stuck the gun in my mouth.

Dying is easy; surviving stunts and stage fights is hard.

I always loved stage fights, especially the swordplay in classical theater, and I've prided myself on my ability and willingness to do my own driving and as many of my own stunts as possible. Those scenes have been some of my favorite moments in acting—seeing the sparks fly off the swords in my duel with Harris Yulin in *Coriolanus*, or taking my Mustang hard and tight around a corner in a *Mike Hammer* chase scene.

Sometimes, however, even the most perfectly choreographed stunt can go awry, and on many low-budget movies they're not all that well planned. The result can leave the actor embarrassed, in pain, or, potentially near death.

My first real stage fight came while I was Mercutio in *Romeo and Juliet* at the Oregon Shakespeare Festival. One night during the sword fight, the actor playing Tybalt missed my parry and crashed the hilt of his dagger into my left ear. I said, "A plague on both your houses" more times than Shakespeare intended because I couldn't hear my cues or anything else for that matter . . . except the ringing in my head.

Sometimes we don't get hurt when things go wrong; we just look silly. While playing Edmund in *King Lear* at Lincoln Center, I faced off with Edgar using broadswords and shields, but once the handle on my shield broke and I was forced to fend off the blows with only my sword. The actor playing Edgar didn't quite know how to proceed, and when he finally got around to stabbing me, I was in the midst of trying to get my shield back together. On that night Edmund's death was more comic than tragic. That's better than really getting hurt. Normally, we want audiences to think fake blood is the real thing, but on my final night of *Macbeth* in Washington in 1995, audiences thought my actual blood was a bit of stagecraft when MacDuff sliced me right under the eye with his broadsword.

In TV and movies, you can get hurt doing fight scenes—John Stamos got so caught up in his own performance during an *ER* episode where he had to pounce on me (as his drunken dad) that he cracked two of my ribs— but the greatest danger comes during stunts, explosions, and special effects.

At the end of *Traveling Executioner*, the water tower in the Kilby Prison yard was going to be detonated. When it blew up, we were about

150 yards away, well out of range, or so we thought. With the cameras rolling we heard a large blast and a millisecond later felt pieces of metal whizzing past our heads.

One of the main reasons *Gravy Train* (*The Dion Brothers*) got made is that the producer loved the idea of a chase scene and shootout in a building being hammered by a wrecking ball. It was a great concept, but while our wrecking ball was made of plaster of paris, it was still massive and dangerous. It was mounted on a spring, and then launched through a wall—Frederic Forrest and I were on the other side and the ball bashed through much harder than anticipated, taking the wall down and us down with it.

The closest I ever came to really dying on a movie was during *The Greatest Battle* (*The Mareth Line*)—twice. Hunkered down in a foxhole, I was supposed to come up for air just in time to witness an armored tank going by. Because it was late in the day and we were losing the light, the director never bothered rehearsing the scene. The tank didn't have its course properly mapped and it came straight for me. I dove out of the way, knocking the camera and the cameraman down, saving both of our lives.

Then we had to shoot a scene in the desert where a low-flying plane was shooting down at my jeep. I was supposed to leap out of the jeep and run for cover—in the desert, mind you, where there's minimal protection—and the plane then blows up the jeep in the background. I went to the special effects expert, a little gnome of a man with a withered arm and, I think, some missing fingers. I said, "I'm very concerned about this shot."

Soon after this picture was taken, the special effects wizards on *The Mareth Line* blew up the jeep . . . and almost got me.

"You should be," he replied.

"When the car explodes, I could get hit by a flying piece of shrapnel."

"Yes," he agreed, nodding his head. "It could happen. We have to get lucky," he said as he limped away on his one good leg.

We had only one take to do it. I ran for my life. The jeep exploded. *Whoosh. Thud.* The jeep's metal door stabbed into the sand, just a few feet away from me. It was in the shot. I was safe. We got lucky.

CHAPTER 34

Daddy Dearest

"WATCH IT, BE CAREFUL," I SNARLED, READYING MYSELF FOR A FIGHT. "Remember where you are."

Edward Norton knew perfectly well where we were—we were at a turning point in a crucial scene, at the heart of *American History X.* That's precisely why he had decided to ditch the words on the page, calling me a "chickenhawk" and a "fucking snake," stepping on my lines, getting in my face, all while the cameras rolled.

Edward's improvisations were brilliant, but so was his tactic—we had already done a few takes of this moment in which his character, Derek Vinyard, finally has it out with my character, his former neo-Nazi mentor, Cameron Alexander.

American History X is a film about white supremacists in America, but rather than a Hollywood movie with cartoony violence, it shows how vicious that world can be, and the film digs below the surface to examine how these ideas take hold with America's youth. I was nervous about taking on the role of this scheming leader—a composite of several figures—because I didn't want neo-Nazis coming after my family. I could not, however, turn down a movie like this. It wasn't just that my part was good, it was that I felt the movie had potential to have a genuine impact, hopefully prompting honest discussions about race in America, a topic that so few people are ever really willing to approach from outside their own perspective.

Getting a call back to the big leagues was also rewarding, because most of my other film work (including TV movies) at that particular moment in my journey, could have filled a chapter called The Forgotten Movies of Stacy Keach. The list is too long: Anybody remember *Amanda and the Alien, Prey of the Jaguar, Trust in Me, Raw Justice, Legend of the Lost Tomb, Future Fear, Sea Devils, Unshackled, Fear Runs Silent, Icebreaker, Militia, Mercy Streets, Sunstorm, Birds of Passage,* or *Against Their Will: Women in Prison*? (And can anyone figure out the point of that title—would there have been women willingly going to prison?) Not to worry, I'm not insulted if no one remembers—some of these made *Mountain of the Cannibal God* look like a David Lean epic. I'm not complaining about the parts; these movies kept me working and paid the bills so I could act in plays like *Macbeth* and *Art*.

In *American History X,* Edward Norton was a revelation. He's a searcher, the quintessential perfectionist, always seeking something better. Edward's dedication to his work, and the demands he makes on himself and those around him were intimidating at first—and I confess I was sometimes thrown by the level of his intensity and his spontaneity—but once we got to know each other, and trust one another, I found acting with him an extremely rewarding experience. I know it takes tremendous patience to act opposite him—he wants to nail his part perfectly based on what is in his head—and it can drive some actors nuts, but I really appreciate and respect the way he works himself into those moments. As an actor you have to be malleable and adjust your process. I learned to work off of Edward. Once I realized he'd never accept just one take even if he nailed it, I'd keep something in reserve, saving my best for after I saw where he was going with a scene.

Maybe he saw that I had made this adjustment and decided to provoke me. It was a masterful maneuver. You can see my temper rising on screen and I'm not really acting anymore—I'm reacting, to Edward. Soon I too was creating dialogue out of the emotions of the moment. I yelled, "This is not some fucking country club . . ." and then he was interrupting me and we were spitting verbal daggers at each other. When I said his brother is "not some whiny pussy like you," I was genuinely trying to get under his skin. The fight that ensued felt like a totally natural outcome. After he had beaten me up, it was easy to find the rage and sense of shaken dignity that prompted me to snarl, "You're fucking dead now, Vinyard."

There was another improvised fight scene on *American History X*, but it happened after the filming was finished. Director Tony Kaye was making his first feature film after building his reputation on music videos. Tony's a great guy and we got along well. He got along with Edward during the filming too, even though Tony said he didn't even think he was right for the role and the studio pushed Edward on him. Tony hadn't loved the original script and appreciated Edward's constant desire to improve it, both in writing and in the improvisation during multiple takes that Tony encouraged.

Everything fell apart in post-production when the two men clashed over competing visions for cutting down the two hundred hours of film. New Line eventually brought in an editor to work with Edward and to finish the project. Tony, who wanted a much shorter, even rawer film, made the dispute public with dozens of bitter ads in *Variety* and *The Hollywood Reporter*, boasting ("the greatest British filmmaker since Hitchcock") and quoting John Lennon or Shakespeare. At one point New Line mimicked him with an ad that quoted Dr. Seuss.

Tony turned nasty, calling Edward a "narcissistic dilettante," saying New Line had "raped" his movie, and getting the film pulled from the Toronto Film Festival. In the midst of this he called me up asking for support. I felt trapped. I liked Tony and generally think the director should make the call, but New Line gave Tony two months to prepare a new cut and he didn't come through. The way I understood it Edward had the studio's backing and was trying for the best possible movie, not merely throwing his weight around. Normally I don't shy away from choosing sides, but in this case I told Tony I was going to remain neutral. (Without backing down from his views about how he was treated or what the film should have looked like, Tony later admitted that he had lost control emotionally and gone too far, calling himself an "immature idiot" in one public apology.) The finished version of *American History X* makes for a pretty damn powerful film—even if a couple of my best scenes were cut—and I give both men tremendous credit.

The role became a touchstone for me, helping a new generation of fans discover me, even if sometimes that felt a little scary. Several years after the film, I was walking through O'Hare Airport in Chicago, when a formidable-looking skinhead walked straight for me. Leather vested, shaved head, mustache and goatee, nose and ear piercings, exposed Nazi swastika tattoos on both arms, everything about him made me nervous. I knew what was coming.

"Hey," he shouted out as he approached. "Weren't you in *American History X?*"

"I was," I replied, and my heart was in my throat.

He gave me a hard look like he was going to throttle me, then totally threw me off guard: "Great job, man, great!"

"Thanks," I said, as relief washed over me. I kept walking, not wanting to sign an autograph for the wrong reason but realizing that something I had learned in prison continued to hold true: Recognition is the highest form of respect among criminals.

Bigoted? Check. A master manipulator? Check. A domineering father figure? Check. Scary as hell? Check.

It's amazing that my next big role after *American History X* could share so many traits yet be so totally different. Playing the dad on *Titus* probably earned me more laughs than all my previous acting roles combined. Ken Titus was as selfish and irascible as Al Bundy and as narrow-minded and behind the times as Archie Bunker. He was also the catalyst for many of the show's plots and often got the best lines. I've never had so much fun.

Here's Papa Titus giving his son some bad news: "I got a little story I wanna tell you. Once upon a time, your dog got hit by a truck this morning!"

When young Christopher asked, "Dad, what's gay?" my reply was straightforward:

"Son ... gay ... is when, two men ... make God cry!"

Papa Titus's philosophy on women was no more enlightened:

"I don't go straight for the ten. I go for the six and drink 'til she's an eight!"

"You don't drag a woman out of a strip club. You put a twenty in your zipper and back out slowly."

Papa Ken Titus, always with a beer in his hand and a snarling quip at the ready

This was, amazingly enough, based on a real person. Christopher Titus was a successful stand-up who was getting tired of his own jokes when he decided to wring the humor from his dysfunctional childhood. He had been raised by his father, who was a heavy drinker (allegedly always with a beer in his hand: "water skiing, funerals, parent-teacher conferences, intensive care"), a womanizer (married six times), and verbally abusive ("wussy" seems to have been a favorite word). Yet Ken Titus never missed work or car or home payments and taught Titus plenty. His mother, on the other hand, was a violent paranoid schizophrenic who was in and out of institutions. In his stand-up act, Titus's first family-based comedy bit was about how when he was in kindergarten he was gluing macaroni on paper plates, and his mom was in therapy gluing macaroni on paper plates, and he put his mom's artwork on his refrigerator. (This later became a scene on the show.)

He developed all that into a stand-up show called "Norman Rockwell Is Bleeding" and then that evolved into *Titus*. The show was innovative in its format—monologues and flashbacks—and edgy in its content, which was dark and intensely real. The scripts were fantastic. Christopher was a comic genius for his ability to take the tragic events of his life and find the humor in it for everyone to share.

I thought the show was too original and twisted to become a hit, but I wanted the part anyway. I was going up against old friends like Ken Howard and Len Cariou, who I'd run into at auditions, but fortunately for me, those guys are just too nice. Christopher later told me that I got the part because I "scared the shit" out of him—I guess he saw how my Mike Hammer and Cameron Alexander traits could translate to comedy.

Christopher and I came from different performing backgrounds, but we melded together well. I learned from Christopher about how important it is to ground comedy in the truth, no matter how outrageous it is; while I played much of it straight, Christopher and the producers always encouraged me to go for more when it was appropriate. If you've ever seen me singing, "I can see clearly now, the rain has gone" into a spatula while sashaying around in my underwear, you'll know I held nothing back.

To play a character like this (or Cameron Alexander), you have to get into his skin and not make value judgments. I met the real Ken Titus, who, despite (or because of) his utter lack of political correctness, was quite charming. He was also proud and loving, even if he could never show his son that directly. When I asked how he felt about becoming this buffoon on TV, he said, he was fine, "as long as people are laughing." Then he gave me notes about how I could be funnier. And they were good notes. I also found it quite moving that when he died, at only fifty-eight, in 2001, all his living ex-wives came to his funeral and seemed genuinely fond of him.

We'd shoot the main scenes in front of a live audience (the flashbacks were filmed like mini-movies two days earlier), but instead of the typical sitcom one scene at a time approach, we'd go straight through, like a play. It was invigorating and I loved playing off Christopher, though it was often difficult to keep a straight face around co-stars Zack Ward and David Shatraw, both of whom must have been class cut-ups as kids.

Actors often want to make dialogue their own, and there is a time and place for that (like in an indie movie or with a director who likes improvisation), but I come from Shakespeare and always felt that my job was to bring life to the words on the page. Not that I'm necessarily putting this show on par with *Hamlet*, but *Titus* really reminded me of how important that is, especially in comedy. The writers had crafted every word of every sentence. I was not there to rewrite; I was responsible for finding the level of intensity and the context, since small adjustments could make a huge difference.

The writing grew more refined and even darker as we went on, tackling subjects like suicide and homophobia, with Papa Titus surprising everyone by pushing his son to take a stand against homophobia—it became personal once someone he knew was beaten up—and Christopher referencing Matthew Shepard in his monologue. It was not preachy and it was not simple satire; we showed people how they really are and let the audience decide what was right and what was wrong . . . while we were cracking them up. ("Dad, I want a gun," the young version of Christopher pleaded while watching a guy with a large weapon in his hands. My response: "You don't need one of those, son. The men in our family have penises.")

Fox started pushing back, the new network president asking for changes that Christopher thought would damage the integrity of the show. He's a guy without a filter and so he said to her—in front of all her underlings—"Do you even watch the show? Let me explain to you how this works. . . ."

I was heartbroken when the show was canceled. Still, it changed my life. I found a whole new, younger, audience—look at the hundreds of thousands of hits on the numerous collections fans have made on YouTube of Ken Titus's greatest moments—but the show also made me realize that I needed to always make time for comedy. I made appearances in nine comedies in the years since the show ended in 2002. Some of them are wonderfully funny, but I've never found another series like *Titus*.

CHAPTER 35

Hitting My Stride

WHEN I WAS A YOUNG MAN ...

Not to worry, this is not a chapter yearning for the good ol' days, about the joys of youth. Au contraire. Back then, I was full of dreams and ambitions, some of which I fulfilled, some of which were waylaid by the other plans life had in store for me. I could not have imagined, however, how important endurance and perseverance are—when you're twenty-five you think life is a sprint, but when you hit fifty you appreciate that it truly is a marathon. I surprised myself when I turned sixty not long after one of my best movie roles in *American History X* and in the middle of making the TV series *Titus*.

Yet what is most satisfying, looking back from my seventies, is that I was able to maintain that momentum for another decade . . . and then reach another level. I feel fortunate, because the new millennium brought me rewarding roles in television and movies, while I was still able to hold the stage in some great theatrical roles, new and classic.

That's not to say I didn't need to take on some work for financial responsibilities, but even some of my B movies have been more memorable: Bruce Campbell, a beloved master of the genre since his *Evil Dead* days (we'd both been in *Escape from L.A.* and *Icebreaker*), invited me to play Dr. Ivanov in *Man with the Screaming Brain*, which he wrote and directed. I enjoyed traveling to Bulgaria, working with Bruce, and putting on a deliciously hammy accent.

W. was everything *Man with the Screaming Brain* wasn't. Sure, playing a Texas preacher in an Oliver Stone movie about a right-wing politician might sound like it's heading over the top, but everything—from my accent to the camera angles and close-ups Oliver chose—were about nuance and detail. I played Reverend Earle Hudd, an Evangelical minister who helped George W. Bush stop drinking. He was a composite character, so Oliver arranged for me to meet with two totally different ministers in Baton Rouge, to give me ideas about building an interior life for Earle. One was a real firebrand, who headed a congregation of some fifteen thousand people, and was also the coach of the local high school football team; the other was soft-spoken and self-effacing, bordering on meek. To construct a layered character I pulled bits of behavior from both men, as well as the many other Texans and religious figures I've known throughout my life.

On the set, Oliver was fascinating. He was extremely attuned to the delivery of each line. Every morning he'd bark impatiently at us, demanding more—like a coach, he refused to let us rest on the previous day's accomplishments, pushing us to dig deeper to gut level feelings. Every afternoon, he'd be easygoing and complimentary, building us back up again so we left the set feeling we had achieved our goals. I consider my brief performance in *W.* to be one of my best, and I owe much of that to Oliver.

An Oliver Stone movie always captures headlines, but a few years earlier, I landed in a TV series, *Prison Break*, which generated more buzz than anything I'd been in—it was my first time being in something that became an "event."

I made the jump off the short list into the cast as Warden Henry Pope, in part, I think, because the unit manager, Garry Brown, had been assistant director on a forgettable trucker movie I'd done called *Revenge on the Highway*. Garry helped persuade Brett Ratner to hire me, and then he also made my time on the set manageable: Malgosia and I were living with the kids in Warsaw for the year, so I'd fly in to shoot my scenes; Garry arranged for me to shoot on the last day of one episode and the first of the next one, so I could then return home for two weeks. (Fortunately, Chicago has a big Polish population and, thus, Polish Lot flies direct to Warsaw.) It was exhausting but I loved being a part of such a high-quality show.

The scripts were dynamic and engaging, really differentiating the voices of each character in a way most shows don't. I was able to draw on my experience in Reading, the compassion of my warden, Governor Brian Hayday, to add even more texture. The series was such a hit that I'd fly back to Poland to discover that my children's friends (both Shannon and Karolina attended the American School in Warsaw) were watching it online. My one disappointment was that because the main characters actually broke out of prison at the end of that first year, I played Warden Pope for only one season. If only they had been held behind bars for another season, I would have gladly continued racking up the frequent flyer miles.

Anger Management, Neighbors, 1600 Penn, and *Malibu Country* were ratings rivals in 2012–2013, yet they shared one common bond: me. I appeared in at least one episode of each, with *1600 Penn* giving me one of the funniest character names of my career: I played a twisted homage to the late segregationist senator Strom Thurmond, a wheelchair-bound, egomaniacal, bigoted senator named Frohm Thuroughgood.

This may seem like a lot of sitcoms for one season, but since *Titus,* I have gone out of my way to seek comedy roles. I've gotten to appear on some of the best, reuniting with my former Yale classmate James Burroughs on *Will & Grace,* playing an accidental father of sorts on *Bored to Death,* and doing those whacked out commercials for *30 Rock.* My favorite was a recurring character on *Two and a Half Men,* in which I played the father of Charlie's fiancée. What made it so great was that my character, Tom, was in a long-term relationship . . . that was interracial . . . and with another man. I had never met former *Good Times* star John Amos, but we fell right into our parts and enjoyed cracking each other up on the set.

The characterizations were original—we were not swishy or stereotypes, just two older men who happened to love each other, and who acted like any other couple, bickering and then making up. The writing crackled, and the relationship felt completely fresh, unlike any others I'd played or even seen in TV or the movies: "Two grown men should be able to pick out a club chair without it turning into Iwo Freaking Jima," I snapped during one argument.

With Charlie Sheen, the second generation of
Sheens I've had the pleasure of performing with

We loved tweaking our delivery to play to the audience's reaction. When we made up at the end of that episode, John said, "Let's watch SportsCenter and fool around a little."

"Do you need to take a Viagra?" I asked, raising my eyebrows.

"You're my Viagra, baby."

"Ohhh, you're so sweeeet," I cooed. "Just for that you can hold the remote." And the scene ended with us cuddled on the couch.

We were a great counterpoint to Charlie's character on the show. Whatever was going on behind the scenes—and there was obviously plenty—Charlie was a complete professional on the set, generous with the cast and the crew. I've known Charlie and his brother Emilio since they were boys, and I can see Marty's gestures and inflections in Charlie (especially when I worked with both of them on *Anger Management*), yet he has his own distinctive style too, with impeccable comedic timing. It's too bad Charlie left, because I likely would have been back for more scenes of domestic bliss with John. The same unfortunate fate befell me in the quirky HBO series *Bored to Death*, where the show's creator Jonathan Ames was just getting my story arc going as the show was canceled.

Those stung, but more like pinpricks—the real heavy blow was the rapid demise of *Lights Out*, the FX boxing series in which I was a co-star, playing the father and trainer of the former heavyweight champion, Lights Leary. This was not your typical television series. The show runner, Warren Leight, had plenty of TV experience, but he also had a Tony Award and Pulitzer Prize for Drama, something most TV writers can't put on their resume. Filming in New York, he assembled a cast of veteran theater actors—my other son, the manager with loose morals, was played by Pablo Schreiber, and my daughter was played by Liz Marvel, while supporting roles were filled by actors with their own impressive collection of theater awards: Bill Irwin, Ben Shenkman, and David Morse.

All that theater experience, from Warren down, helped layer the show with pathos and tragedy—theater actors have an ability to find a deeper means of expression, to vary the intensity of the character's emotions. Yet this also put extra pressure on our star, Holt McCallany, whose experience was in film and television. Holt more than held his own with all of us; he gave a strong performance that anchored the show. (Perhaps it's because he has the-atrical roots: His mom, Julie Wilson, is not only a great cabaret singer, she's also a Tony-nominated actress, while his late dad, Michael McAloney, pro-duced the Tony Award winner *Borstal Boy*.) We quickly developed a genuine father-son bond, occasionally going out to a bar to watch some real fights.

The entire experience was like that—great writing, rich characters, a cast that bonded—and we had the full support of FX, which spent a small fortune promoting the show. But nobody watched. Maybe we were on the wrong channel—despite the boxing and the depiction of the dirty fight world, this was a more subtle sophisticated family drama (kind of closer to an off-Broadway play) than shows like *Sons of Anarchy* or *It's Always Sunny in Philadelphia*, which are great but which play big and broad.

Holt McCallany played Lights Leary; I played his father and trainer. I really thought this series coulda been a contender. PHOTO COURTESY OF FX NETWORKS, LLC

Still, everyone remained blithely confident despite the ratings—FX was not the sort of network to abandon a critically acclaimed series after just one season. We'd have time to grow, and Warren had great ideas for the second season. Even I got caught up in the optimism, despite the residue of skepticism that has stuck to me from my years in the industry. So while the decision was logical we were blindsided when the knockout blow landed. And down we went.

The ability to handle disappointment is obviously a running theme in my life, and I think it's an underrated trait—it's something you usually learn the hard way, but I've found that it's crucial to navigating your way through life's inevitable storms. I wasn't good at it in the early days, and it helped fuel my drug problems. I've come to understand how vital it is to pick yourself up off the mat, to shake off the pain, and get back into the ring of life.

In many jobs, turning sixty-five means mandatory retirement. In theater, it means you're old enough to plunge into one of the most intellectually, emotionally, and physically demanding roles ever written: *King Lear*. So in 2006, months after my sixty-fifth birthday, I began to ascend this craggy and difficult mountain at Chicago's Goodman Theatre.

As King Lear, with one of my favorite Shakespearean companions, Ed Gero as Gloucester CAROL ROSEGG/SHAKESPEARE THEATRE COMPANY

There was no better Sherpa for this task than the Goodman's artistic director, Robert Falls, who has a vivid imagination and a precise eye. I had worked with him two years earlier on Arthur Miller's final play, *Finishing the Picture*, which had looked back at Marilyn Monroe's disastrous experience in *The Misfits*, her last movie. Bob had perfectly cast each role in that play—Linda Lavin, Stephen Lang, Scott Glenn, Frances Fisher (who had played Titus's crazy mom in the series), Matthew Modine, and my old pal, Harris Yulin—and then masterfully blended our disparate acting styles. (Unfortunately, the New York critics were invited to this out-of-town opening—I think the play still needed a few more tweaks, and when the *New York Times* panned the show, our hopes of reaching Broadway dimmed. They went out forever when Arthur died a few months later.)

For *Lear*, Bob and I discussed his concept, the set, and costume designs, all well in advance of the first rehearsal. (We met quite often while I was in Chicago shooting *Prison Break*.) So, as I did my months of research—starting with a book called *The Masks of King Lear*, written by my old Berkeley professor Marvin Rosenberg, who revealed how different actors have interpreted different moments throughout the play—I wasn't just studying the role in isolation; I was learning it in the context that Bob had planned.

I had always seen myself playing Lear in the period the play depicted, with Stonehenge on a revolving stage for a set. Bob persuaded me to do a modern production, placed in the 1970s regime of Romanian Nicolae Ceausescu's brutal dictatorship, replete with cars and guns, rather than horses and swords. Bob unraveled much of the traditional approach to the play, giving Edgar a drug problem, making Oswald a rapper, and portraying Kent as a military man who later disguises himself as a skinhead, wielding a tire iron. When the cast first assembled, we spent the better part of a week watching films and discussing the play with questions about our respective characters. Then we went full bore into rehearsals, and no one was tentative.

Bob's concept was incisive, his execution brilliant, though some audience members walked out because of the changes he made and the gritty realism the drugs and violence brought to the show. Chicago's schools were ambivalent about sending their students, though I felt that young people would connect with this production better than with a traditional Shakespearean production.

The role is exhausting to play, particularly up through the storm scene on the heath. Bob set a pace that literally made it feel like climbing a mountain. I presumed we'd have two intermissions like most versions of *King Lear*, since the play runs well over three hours. Bob wanted to maintain the reality and the momentum of Lear's downfall, so he limited us to one, nearly two hours into the show. I swore I'd never do anything like that again . . . right up until the moment Bob decided to re-stage the show in Washington at Michael Kahn's Shakespeare Theatre Company in 2009.

People often wonder if Shakespeare can be relevant in a rapidly changing world. Well, *King Lear* is about a complex and petty political leader, egomaniacal and blind to his own flaws, which sparks his own downfall; then he goes wandering off, grieving and angry, looking for redemption. The play I starred in right before my second turn with *King Lear* was the national tour of *Frost/Nixon*. Enough said.

The biggest difference for me between Lear and Nixon was that Nixon was a pivotal figure in my lifetime and most of the audience knew him equally well. I went through several wigs—including one bizarre, curly one—fake noses, and contact lenses, trying to find the right look. I don't resemble Nixon at all. Director Michael Grandage told me, "Don't try for a literal interpretation of Nixon" and he was right; the play is good enough that if you capture the essence of Nixon—and I did master some of Nixon's trademark vocal inflections—the script will get you into the character. It's also essential to suspend any value judgment; I needed to become Nixon, not bring my personal feelings about him to the part. (It's no different if you're playing Iago in *Othello*, a truly unredeemable character.)

With Lear, I found it helpful to study my predecessors' takes on the role—generally I encourage comparisons because they help you find your own way—but with Nixon I decided against seeing Frank Langella's extraordinary Broadway performance because I wanted to instead work on capturing the real man, instead studying hours of Frost's actual interviews with the ex-president. (In Washington we played at the Kennedy Center, right next to the Watergate Hotel and some real life participants in the drama—journalist James Reston Jr. and Nixon advisor Frank Gannon—came backstage to meet the cast.)

I also had my own connections to the characters beyond the fact that I watched the Watergate hearings—perhaps the biggest event of my lifetime—like a soap opera. My close friend Howard Kaminsky published Nixon's memoirs and his Manhattan home is adorned with photos of the two men. Howard shared plenty of stories about Nixon. (In the 1970s, Howard had also introduced me to Nixon's literary agent, Swifty Lazar, who is another character in the play, and we became friends. Swifty took us out to dinner and Studio 54 one evening in the 1970s, setting me up with the lovely Diana Ross for the evening.

All of those connections made every moment more personal, which helped inform my performance. I also had a strong link to the actor who played Frost, Alan Cox. Alan's father is Brian Cox, a great Shakespearean actor who is probably better known here for his work in *The Bourne Identity*. Brian and I were at LAMDA together, and in 1970 I was back in London

Richard Nixon's fall from grace feels like a Shakespearean tragedy.

and called him up about going out for a drink. "Sorry Stacy, my wife's about to have a baby. I have to get to the hospital." That baby was Alan.

Most significantly, I had firsthand knowledge of how David Frost worked as an interviewer, how he managed to get people to say things they hadn't intended. David interviewed me back in 1969 just as I was becoming a known entity. *I Dream of Jeannie* star Barbara Eden was also on the show and David chatted with her while I sat nervously trying to figure out how I would project to the television public. I tuned back into what they were saying when David asked her if she was self-conscious about baring her midriff on TV every week. Then he said, "You're sitting next to a Shakespearean actor, would you like to do a play with him?"

Barbara said yes and David pivoted to me, inquiring if I would be interested in co-starring with Barbara.

"Only if I can show my belly button," my mouth said, even as my brain was desperately trying to shut it down.

"Reaaally," David said with a sly grin. "Show us your belly button, Stacy."

And, much to the horror of my dear mother watching at home, I lifted my shirt and revealed it to the world.

CHAPTER 36

The Readiness Is All

My right arm wasn't working properly. It wasn't really working at all, to be honest. It felt as though it was attached to my body by a rubber band. I must have slept on it funny. Fortunately it was Monday; no need to rush and transform myself into Richard Nixon. Anyway, a shower would help. It didn't. Something was wrong.

That something, I found out after the paramedics rushed me to the hospital, was a stroke, or rather, several small strokes. I would not be onstage the next night; I'd be in the hospital with a stent in my neck, encouraging my blood to flow through my entire body. The show must go on, of course, and I was relieved that my understudy Bob Ari was well prepared (he had served the same role on Broadway for Frank Langella)—he filled in so ably that I didn't feel like I had let the show down; it was ten days until I returned. Malgosia, always protective, would have preferred I rested even more but I felt good and was ready to work. (My blood pressure elevated later in the tour but I took medicine for that and kept going.)

Knowing that my smoking had played a role in the strokes, I quit my cigarettes for several months afterward. However, in June, I learned that my close friend David Carradine had died suddenly, and I was so shaken up that I reached for the comfort of a cigarette and picked up the habit again soon after. I smoke much less than I used to, though I'm sure, dear reader, that Malgosia and my kids would encourage you to pester me about quitting should you ever meet me somewhere.

Frost/Nixon and *King Lear* were invigorating for me and I was eager to be part of another serious drama. Oddly enough, I almost turned down the next opportunity, even though the part was written with me in mind. The play was wonderfully written and the production would take me back to my theatrical roots at Lincoln Center.

When I first read *Other Desert Cities* for its off-Broadway run, I was apprehensive, even though I had loved working with Jon Robbie Baitz on a previous play of his, *Ten Unknowns*, and Robbie told me that he had written the character of Lyman Wyeth for me. Naturally, I was flattered, but Lyman is something of a secondary role, with more time offstage than on, and worse, at first, I found Lyman to be a humorless bore. Still, the play sings like Chekhov, and with Joe Mantello directing a cast that included Stockard Channing, Thomas Sadoski, and friends old (Linda Lavin), and new (Liz Marvel), well, I couldn't say no.

The play would earn rave reviews both off and on Broadway; it was a Pulitzer Prize finalist, a Tony nominee for Best Play, and an Outer Critics Circle Award winner. Each of us in the original cast, plus Joe and set designer, John Lee Beatty, earned at least one nomination or award. But it didn't come easy.

Robbie writes wonderfully literate speeches, but they require layers of recognizable behavior to land them properly, and we struggled to find just the right tone, amidst what became a frustrating myriad of possibilities—a wealth of riches, but how to choose? Liz played my daughter Brooke, the writer whose arrival with her memoir at the Wyeth family Palm Springs home is the play's catalyst. During the early days of rehearsal at Lincoln Center, she struggled with the emotional permutations of Brooke's character. I remember her saying to me in the elevator, after a break, "I'm having a terrible time; I just can't seem to find Brooke's pulse."

We didn't click together right away as a cast, but we gradually shaped a family, while discovering the play's themes, and Joe Mantello, an accomplished actor in his own right, gently steered us there. My part should have come naturally—I was playing an old actor from Southern California (I am one, and we spent many Thanksgivings and Easters in Palm Springs as I was growing up) and a politician (I've played Lyndon Johnson and Richard Nixon); my parents were conservative Republicans who could have been friends and neighbors of the Wyeths.

I was resistant to Joe's guidance early on—he kept me sitting in a chair, where I felt stuck and shackled. Finally, he explained that I have "a big presence" (guilty as charged) whereas he felt that my character "is recessive until he finally explodes."

Joe was right. I finally accepted that concept, but I insisted on adding more humor—not by adding jokes, but in my reactions to Stockard Channing, who played my wife Polly, a wonderfully aggressive and witty bigot, with one-line zingers that elicited gales of laughter from the audience. Stockard played her to a T. Her timing and intonation, her sense of how to gauge an audience, place Stockard in the highest echelon of great comedic stage actresses. By playing a doting husband, I could color Lyman with more humor than I had originally thought possible. For the serious moments, I learned to invoke my parents and how much I missed them, because the play is not just about deception and self-deception but also about loss.

We gradually became a cohesive team, and before each performance the cast would assemble in the wings and perform our pre-show ritual of touching tennis rackets (Linda, as Polly's drug-addled sister Silda, used her pill box) and shouting, "One-two-three, fuck 'em!" We were referring to the audience, but not in a mean-spirited way. I had actually learned this ritual from Christopher Titus during the shooting of our series and carried it with me to the theater for *King Lear* and *Other Desert Cities*, among other shows. It relaxed us, and it provided a moment of bonding, giving us reassurance that we would not be intimidated by a wayward audience, and that, as a company, we would always watch each other's backs and be there for one another.

When the show moved to Broadway, Linda was off to star in Nicky Silver's play *The Lyons*, and Liz had film commitments. Judith Light replaced Linda and nimbly found her way, eventually winning a Best Supporting Actress Tony. Rachel Griffiths, an Aussie best known for her work in *Six Feet Under*, took over the part of Brooke. Early on, she seemed somewhat intimidated by Liz's performance, which she had seen. In trying to make the character "her own," she became self-conscious about the reading of certain lines and the thrust of the scene. One day in rehearsal she simply stopped, saying, "I'm sorry, I'm so sorry . . . I just don't have any idea of where I'm going." We took a five-minute respite while she huddled with Joe and Robbie. When we came back something had obviously clicked—we repeated the scene, and Rachel had found new, fresh colors that none of us had seen before. Her performance was lighter, but no less effective, than Liz's—I have often said that Liz was "earth," and Rachel, "air." Their performances were different, but they each found the pulse of the character they were seeking.

We were all naturally disappointed when the Best Play Tony didn't find its way onto Robbie's mantel. *Other Desert Cities* is an extraordinary piece of work, but the cold, hard fact of the matter is that we opened too early in the season for awards consideration—the Tonys are like the Oscars and plays that open in the late spring stand a far better chance of capturing Tony voters' attention (which is not to say that *Clybourne Park*, another amazing play, was not completely deserving of its win). For me, personally, taking part in this play 370 times in New York (off and on Broadway combined), and getting to spend nine months in a Broadway hit without ever missing a performance, was its own reward.

A quarter of a billion dollars. That is a lot of money. I had done many things in my career—taken my clothes off in an experimental performance piece, played *Hamlet* in Central Park, written and produced my own western, become a TV star twice over. I had never, ever been involved in a project that reaped a quarter of a billion dollars in worldwide box office earnings. Until 2012, that is, when I finally wound up onscreen in my first true blockbuster, *The Bourne Legacy*.

Let me tell you, working on an A movie like that is quite different than, say, *Mountain of the Cannibal God*. I played Admiral Turso, one of the military big shots trying to figure out what Jeremy Renner's character is up to, and I spent much of my time in the crisis room, which was as impressive a movie set as I have ever seen. Of course, no matter how huge the budget, how dramatic the sets and the action sequences, you still need a good story and strong acting. I found myself paired with two familiar faces, Scott Glenn and Edward Norton. Scott and I fell into a comfortable place instantly in our scene, but most of my scenes were with

Edward. I could see some of the other actors and crew grow impatient with Edward's perfectionism, and some would look to me—as the elder statesman—to say something, but I knew better than to interfere. Edward's tenacity served a larger purpose and I had learned how to accommodate it—as I mentioned, I learned not to lay everything on the line in my first takes with him but to treat it as a process, to see where he was going with a scene and build from there. I admired the way our writer-director, Tony Gilroy, understood Edward and gave him the chance to check playback to make sure he was hitting the ball straight. The movie was a big enough hit that there is talk of a sequel, and I'd gladly sign up to go through take after take with Edward again.

"Planes" has already taken off, even before the release of the first movie, and there's even a chance that my character will be a ride in Disneyland. Not bad for a seventy-two-year-old kid like myself—I was a believer in the value of perseverance at age sixty; now I'm willing to proselytize about it.

The cheery disposition of *Planes* is wildly different from two of my other recent film projects. I was offered a small part as Wallenquist, the evil crime lord in Robert Rodriguez and Frank Miller's *Sin City: A Dame to Kill For*. I was happy to take part because I had loved the unique look and feel of the original. I only had one day of shooting, but before that I had to spend a day with Robert's imaginative makeup team, as they created the bloated, cartoony face I'd disappear beneath.

The comic book flavor of *Sin City* derives from its graphic novel origins; Alexander Payne, by contrast, aims for a quiet realism. Still, he pays equal attention to the look of each character in the world he is creating in *Nebraska*. In the movie, Bruce Dern plays Woody, who has alienated everyone in his life but now persuades his exasperated son David (Will Forte) to travel to Nebraska to collect a sweepstakes prize. When he comes through his hometown, he encounters Ed (played by me), his former business partner. They ran an automotive garage together.

"Your teeth are too good," Alexander said to me. "We're going to have to dirty them up." So we created dentures with just the right look for my character, but that wouldn't interfere with my ability to talk. The first go-round with the special effects people produced a gritty set of teeth,

Bruce Dern and I are old buddies but in *Nebraska* I do nothing but antagonize him and Will Forte.

one missing, and a gold one in the back. Alexander, with his keen eye for detail was concerned, since Bruce Dern's teeth were to have a significant gap in the early stages of the film, so we elected to fill in my mouth.

Ed is an angry man, bitter about Woody's departure. The part is small, but I invented a backstory for myself to help explain Ed's behavior. I created a scenario that when Woody left, I was alone in the garage and couldn't manage the car jack properly, and my left arm got pinned under the car. I don't make a big thing of it onscreen—I'm not reverting back to Richard III—it just served as a reminder for me that Woody had abandoned and betrayed me, explaining why all my energy was poured into antipathy for him. I did have one scene with a contrasting feel, in which I sang Elvis Presley's song, "In the Ghetto," in a karaoke bar. I'm not going to make anyone forget the King, but I enjoyed showing another side of Ed, not to mention the chance to belt one out.

Alexander Payne is not only one of the finest directors I've ever worked with—he's possibly the nicest.

Alexander is one of the smartest and savviest directors I've ever worked with. He's also one of the nicest people I've known. Maybe there's a connection there—much of his crew has stayed with him for years. He loves getting multiple takes even if you think you nailed it the first time—but he does not come across as demanding; he is merely encouraging you to try taking your character in new directions (also, this gives him more choices in the editing room), and he does it so affably that you trust him and thus feel free to stretch yourself further and take risks. He is truly an inspiration.

By the time *Nebraska*, and this book, comes out, I'll have my head in a very different place—the early fifteenth century to be precise. I've mentioned that I enjoy finding ways to flesh out my oeuvre in ways that my predecessors like Olivier, Gielgud, and Burton never did. Michael Kahn says he is retiring from his role as artistic director at the Shakespeare Theatre in 2014, and he wants his last season to include his favorite plays in the canon, parts I and II of *Henry IV.* I hope he abandons all thoughts of retiring but I was glad he asked me to play Falstaff—I too love these plays and particularly this character, plus it offered me a unique opportunity, since I may now be the only Shakespearean actor who has played this role twice with a gap of more than forty-five years in between. Obviously I was an exceedingly young Falstaff the first time around. I am older and wiser and have suffered more of life's indignities than when I was twenty-eight, and all of that will undoubtedly influence my performance. Now, I don't have to play at being an old man, I just have to be myself. The other change, of course, is that to illuminate Falstaff's girth I no longer need padding.

Immersing myself in the text of such a complex creation is a treat, and when I'm onstage next spring, I'll be completely present in the moment. But offstage, I always try to look ahead. Perhaps we'll bring *Henry IV* to New York. There has also been talk of taking Robert Falls's production of *King Lear* there. I'm game for either, or both. And there's still Iago in *Othello*, the one truly great Shakespearean character I haven't played, on stage, screen, or radio. I hope to inhabit that part or perhaps to direct *Othello*—I've always envisioned having two actors learn both leads and switch each night between Iago and Othello, which would give the audience a different perspective on the play. I'm also co-writing a one-man show about Ernest Hemingway. He, like Falstaff, remains fascinating to me in both his glory and his tragedy.

All in all, I have had an extraordinary life, and a fortunate one. I am blessed with a wonderful wife and two amazing children, and I've had a career filled with challenging and fulfilling roles. As I've said, my favorite role—in movies, television, onstage in New York or Washington, or out on the road—is always the next one. I hope to see you there.

Curtain Call
The Play's the Thing

JOE PAPP WAS RIGHT. JOE PAPP WAS WRONG.

He didn't think I needed to go to London to study Shakespeare, because he wanted to create a new distinctly American classical performer. My journey to England more than justified itself—I learned history, ideas, exercises, and techniques that have stayed with me to this day—yet his instinct that American actors can be great classical performers without aping the British was, as they say over there, spot on.

Training for actors in America is much better today than it was when I was at Yale; yet as a culture, we often de-emphasize the need for incisive and insightful acting, instead suggesting which body parts should go under the knife. In 2012, I was honored to become George Mason University's first Heritage Professor of Stage and Screen. Being a "Heritage Professor" makes me sound old but it also implies a connection to, and understanding of, our past. I think I've learned a great deal about acting in the last half-century—anything I might criticize about a young actor is most likely a mistake I once made myself—and I like sharing my knowledge.

I taught Shakespeare's plays but also skills that often overlooked: how to approach an audition and, perhaps more important, how to handle rejection. No one taught me this at Berkeley, Yale, or LAMDA, and I think being prepared for the cruelties of this industry would have helped me understand and handle it better. I told my students that when we don't get the part, we mope, we get depressed, we think we're no good, we lose confidence. We lose sight of the most important aspect of sustaining the life of the actor, and that is faith in oneself, a firm conviction that whatever happens "I am good enough to make it." Getting rejected is not necessarily a reflection of one's ability. Directors and producers are looking for imprecise intangibles like "chemistry" combinations, and casting decisions often have little or nothing to do with talent. (Economics matters as much as anything.) Remind yourself you are fortunate not to be part of their chemical imbalances, I tell my students. It is okay to express disappointment about not getting the part, but you must keep a cool perspective about the realities of the business, and not let it detract you from continuing to improve your skills. Realize that this is the way things are, and then focus on the need for actors to act, always. If there is no paying job, maybe there are readings, or perhaps you can organize fellow actors to work on a play or a scene. Don't give up, never give up, and keep developing those acting muscles.

I also encouraged my students to read about acting: My favorite books as a student were Michael Chekhov's *To the Actor*, and Robert Edmund Jones's *The Dramatic Imagination*; as a professor I relied on Declan Donnellan's *The Actor and The Target* and Robert Cohen's *Acting Professionally*.

I have my own ideas about how to act, especially in the classics. So, if you'll indulge me a bit, here are some thoughts on classical acting, including a look at five of my Shakespearean roles as well as Shakespeare's sonnets.

The process starts well before the first day of rehearsal. Do your research. Learn your lines cold. Say them out loud again and again. I had a professor at Berkeley who, when asked how to write, quoted Sinclair Lewis's maxim: "Apply the seat of the pants to the seat of the chair." The same holds true in acting. Put in your time. I know some actors don't like memorizing lines until they know the blocking and the relationships. I don't believe that's necessary, especially with Shakespeare. (It's also good training for television, where you need to be ready to go when the director says "action," because the pace is relentless.)

If you know your lines, you have more time to work on finding your voice and creating a nuanced interpretation, and you are ready to play off your fellow actors. If you do your research and learn your technique beforehand, then you can throw it all away and be present in the moment when it's time to go onstage. Remember, something that works in rehearsal might go off during the middle of a show—you can't force it and you must find something new, right then and there.

Find your own voice. But be patient; it takes time. I spent a good portion of my early career imitating those I admired—I pitched my voice a little higher for the "Once More unto the Breach" speech from *Henry V* because of Olivier, while in *Coriolanus* I'd catch myself adapting the rhythms of Burton.

I don't think Americans should adopt a British accent. Instead, we should go for Mid-Atlantic speech, something between British and American, with softer vowels, as if you're Fred Astaire in a genteel movie role. Say "cahn't" instead of "kehn't."

Young actors get caught up trying to get into a flow. When they encounter a line in Shakespeare they don't understand easily, they tighten their bodies and can't let the line flow out of them, preventing them from making sense of the lines for the audience.

One trick I learned at LAMDA is to look for important words to emphasize—this will slow you down in key parts of speeches when the tendency might be to rush, blurring clarity. I also have discovered that in Shakespeare you should invariably stress the verb, not the nouns or adjectives, as the activated part of the sentence.

Olivier said about *Othello* that the key was breath, breath, and more breath, and that holds true throughout the canon, especially in the soliloquies. But there's more: You must also learn where to stop or pause within lines. Don't ignore a mid-line period if it makes sense, running the thoughts together with no caesura, simply because it's one line. It's also important to remember that punctuation was added and tampered with by many others along the way, so explore saying the phrases many different ways in rehearsals till you find what works for you. You and your director can alter them as you develop your character.

Counting beats quickly becomes a drawback if it takes away from being a real person in a real situation. When you count out iambic feet, you may wonder if you should stress words according to meter—is "opposed" pronounced "oppo-sed" and, "banished" now "bani-shed." The British sometimes faithfully follow the meter to an extreme that drives me crazy. If you are thinking of that onstage, then you are too preoccupied with the meter and the words, instead of the human emotions of the moment. If you get inside your character's mind first, the audience will be more aware of the character than the words, and your lines will make more sense to them, even if they might not understand each specific phrase. If you deliver your lines with a robust energy, clarity, and emotional truth, then the dialogue will seem more natural, no matter how archaic it may be.

Finding the right balance is crucial. I was fortunate to have a professor in college who taught me not to grandly declaim Shakespeare, to treat the language as contemporary speech, so I was able to shed most of my hammy tendencies at an early age. Yet, you still need to try to stretch yourself—every musician has played a sour note, you just keep going, move past it. I have an antipathy for actors who choose to underplay everything. Yes, there are times when it's appropriate to be a minimalist, but the whole "don't act, just be" mantra takes things too far and eventually puts audiences to sleep. If you are just "being," you are missing out on the different colors, the subtle dynamics, that make up even the most basic of "real" human interaction. Look at that word, "interaction," and right there in the middle you find the word "act."

FALSTAFF

Falstaff, when performed in both Henrys together, is an enormous undertaking. Part Two is particularly filled with long speeches—Falstaff does tend to go on—and this reinforces my point about learning as many of your lines as possible before rehearsals even begin.

I've always thought of Falstaff as a potent mix of comedy and tragedy, intersecting at his desperate need for the love and attention of young Prince Hal. Some of that is genuine, and some is driven by his notion of being a privileged member of the future king's court. The showmanship comes easily, but finding that emotional state hidden beneath the bravado is the challenge. I try delivering Falstaff's bluster with a touch of self-awareness—he knows he is full of it, that he is endlessly embellishing when he shouldn't, yet being aware of his own flaws doesn't change the nature of his behavior.

We see this clearly in the story he tells of the robbery, which he expands and exaggerates as he goes, pushing forward even as each false step is exposed. The telling always earns big laughs, which is a challenge for an actor trying to maintain his rhythm and pace, but it's also a challenge to not lose sight of the pathos beneath the humor in Shakespeare's writing.

I also want to explore a side of Falstaff that I didn't see clearly my first time around. I want to capture the sense that Falstaff subconsciously knows what is coming: Shakespeare brilliantly presages the moment he is banished in the scene where Falstaff and Hal are playing a game in which Falstaff acts at being Hal and Hal plays his father, Henry, the king. Falstaff naturally plays this for laughs, saying:

"No, my good lord; banish Peto, banish Bardolph, banish Poins: but for sweet Jack Falstaff, kind Jack Falstaff, true Jack Falstaff, valiant Jack Falstaff, and therefore more valiant, being, as he is, old Jack Falstaff, banish not him thy Harry's company, banish not him thy Harry's company: banish plump Jack, and banish all the world."

It's a tricky scene, since he's making a plea to Hal, yet he is unwilling to believe that this is what fate holds in store for him, even if the king should turn against him. Again, Falstaff will charm the audience and get the laughs, yet the actor must reveal how he is clinging to his belief that he will be saved and cherished by Hal. To accomplish this Falstaff must really buy into the idea that this is all a game, that none of this will come to pass. Yet I can only do that if, in that moment, I allow the slightest shadow of doubt to creep into my mind.

HAMLET

Falstaff, like Richard III or Bottom in *A Midsummer Night's Dream*, is great fun to play. Hamlet is more like King Lear—undeniably rewarding but more of a challenge. The early part of the play is especially tough sledding.

Every actor who plays Hamlet confronts that most awkward of moments, where you reach a part in the play where the entire audience is waiting to hear how you deliver a certain line—a line they've known by heart since they were children, probably since before they knew who Hamlet was.

"To be, or not to be, that is the question . . ."

It doesn't matter if the audience knows it is coming. The only way to make the line work is as if the thought of suicide is just occurring to you for the first time in that particular moment. That need to act as if each line is a fresh thought each night is true of all acting, of course, but it is more of a challenge when the audience knows what you are going to say and when it is a soliloquy—moment-to-moment acting is easier when you're responding to another performer, since the slightest variations in his or her delivery alters your response each time out.

The only way to feel truly spontaneous, as I told my students, "is to take chances, to risk making a fool of yourself." This is one reason I did acting exercises with them where they made nonsense sounds, first as a five-year-old, then as a ninety-five-year-old. It harkens back to what Hugh Crutwell taught me at LAMDA, when he criticized my Brutus for being too well spoken, too well thought out. You need that as a foundation from which you can depart—your first obligation as an actor is to be seen and to be heard, but depart you must, into an unpredictable place, free of preconceptions.

One night you might feel tentative and say, "To be" and then pause and then in a questioning way add "or not to be." The next night perhaps you're more confident and you snarl the line with a touch of sarcasm. The changes can be minute, but they are important—and that first line informs how you deliver the next.

There are so many ways to interpret Shakespeare, if you're willing to take risks. I was tired of seeing Hamlet as neurotic and indecisive, paralyzed by thought. I thought the text supported playing him as someone making too many decisions, making active choices, but racing from one to another, driven by his nervous energy. I realized in rehearsal that while I could literally run across the stage during Hamlet's first soliloquy, I could show that his thoughts and feelings were skittering from one place to the next without physically moving.

I also would argue that Hamlet can seem angry and frustrated in his first soliloquy, but he can't yet seem to be "mad" or "crazy." I found that this quality doesn't really come to light until he sees the Ghost.

Again, Hamlet is not timid in his scene with the Ghost; when he cries "Oh, Vengeance," he must mean it. One of the most difficult scenes is when Hamlet comes up with a sword behind Claudius when he's praying, with the full intention of killing him. If Hamlet is weak from the beginning, then we expect him to be unable to execute and the scene is devoid of dramatic tension. But if Hamlet is strong, a man of action, then when he hesitates and ponders the consequences of his action, it creates a tension that gives us a further insight into his character. (In my own mind, trying to be Hamlet born anew each night, I went out thinking each time that I was going to kill him.) An active Hamlet also makes more sense at the end of the play, where it would otherwise seem jarring that he is a great swordsman in his duel with Laertes.

There are other actors who have also pushed themselves to find new life in this centuries-old play. When I saw Jonathan Pryce play Hamlet and do the Ghost as well (in a different voice), as if it were not an actual apparition but Hamlet's inner demons tormenting him, all I could think was, "I wish I'd done that."

RICHARD III

In the Hospital for Overacting, there is a special ward devoted to Richard III, with actors in costume shrieking, "A horse, a horse, my kingdom for a horse."

There is no such hospital—it exists only in a sketch *Monty Python's Flying Circus*—but it points to one of the tricks to playing Richard.

Richard is, by his very nature, a scenery chewer, and you can't hold back in the role—underplay him and you deprive him of the snake-like charm that enables him to slither his way onto the throne. Yet many actors go too far, and, I confess, there were nights when I did so myself. I've seen actors interrupt the line "That dogs bark at me, as I halt by them," by howling and barking. It felt contrived and unnecessary, trying to elicit cheap laughs from the audience. That section of Richard's first soliloquy—"Deform'd, unfinish'd, sent before my time, Into this breathing world, scarce half made up"—needs to express Richard's hurt and anger. It's part of the balance an actor must find with Richard. The script gives you license to ham it up, but you have to earn it by showing how deeply committed Richard is to alleviating the pain inside him. His actions are dressed in a lust for power and desire for vengeance, but that inner hurt is real—he has been rejected by society, and he needs to be able to look at himself with respect—and it enables audiences to feel for Richard even as they find him scary. The audience must always think Richard is dangerous, and not just entertaining.

Make it personal. I say it over and over but it's true—if you make it personal, it's difficult to overact. For me, I drew on how I was teased as a kid because of my cleft lip, but everyone has felt like an outsider or endured the sting of rejection.

As for that infamous horse, it again comes down to existing in the moment. Richard says "A horse, a horse." The first time—if you were saying this as if it were really the first and only time—it is an act of discovery. Look around and realize that your troops are gone, your horse is gone, all your power and your means of defense are gone. You are playing an action. The second one can be more of a cry for help as can the shout of "My kingdom for a horse," though that can also be played as I did it— Richard is down and he is desperate but he believes that if he could just get one thing to latch onto he'd figure out a way to survive. After all, that is the story of his entire life and his rise to power. This time, however, his options have finally run out.

MACBETH

It is difficult for an audience to relate to a murderer, especially one who has just killed his king, a good man who had trusted and promoted him. To create any relationship between Macbeth and the audience, the actor must show his vulnerability, his sense of remorse, and an understanding of what he has done and what he has lost.

We opened our production with a battle scene. Though Shakespeare wrote it as exposition, it is more exciting to see it onstage, and it introduces Macbeth as a great swordsman and courageous warrior, a genuine hero, which will make his fall more tragic.

We begin to see the more human side of Macbeth after he kills Duncan, especially when Banquo's ghost appears—if you capture his guilt and vulnerability there, right as he is cracking up, then the play takes on another dimension that moves it beyond the action and ideas. It's dangerous for the actor to play for sympathy, however, since he really doesn't deserve it.

I wish Shakespeare had written a scene at the end in which Macbeth interacts with Lady Macbeth in her chamber after she has gone mad and before she dies. It would have helped us see another side of his character. Since he doesn't, the actor must remember that one of Shakespeare's most challenging soliloquies—"Tomorrow and tomorrow and tomorrow creeps in this petty pace from day to day"—actually starts with the line, "She should have died hereafter." Many actors forget that and depersonalize this speech; the bleak nihilism of the "sound and the fury signifying nothing" tempts them into making this a grand statement about the world itself, but it can only become that if one remembers to start by connecting it to Macbeth's loss, the death of the woman he loved, the pain and cost of this journey they started together.

KING LEAR

Sir John Gielgud was once asked the key to a great King Lear. "Make sure you have a light Cordelia," he deadpanned.

Yes, it's funny, but there's a truth to that pragmatism—much of theater is about executing blocking in a way that seems effortless and natural, which isn't easy when you're trying to carry Cordelia's limp body onstage. (My Cordelia, Laura Odeh, is a marvelous actress and eminently carryable, if that were a word.)

There are probably as many ways to play Lear as there are lines to memorize.

In my opening scene, I came out exuberant, dancing and celebrating. This was no aged feeble leader. As with Hamlet or Macbeth, I'm not in favor of playing Lear as completely daft from the beginning—it must be a journey as his guilty conscience eats at him and forces him to retreat from a world he no longer understands. I wanted to create an arc so my Lear has farther to fall when his years of egocentricity and self-absorption help him convince himself that Cordelia has betrayed him. I did foreshadow what was to come, however, with a sudden, "Oh," and a clutch of my heart. I'm okay, but I need to sit now, for a moment, to catch my breath. Later, when Lear is screaming at Goneril and Regan, he again has a minor heart incident. The stage is set, so to speak, for his death, when he is grieving for poor Cordelia, and is ready to go, he no longer has any reason for his heart to continue beating.

"Look there," Shakespeare writes and he repeats the phrase. I played it as if I was seeing Cordelia's spirit leave her body and ascend to heaven, leaning back to watch her go. Then my heart gave out and I fell back dead in Kent's arms. The dead fall is as pure a risk as there is onstage and requires complete trust in your fellow actor. Fortunately, my Kent, Steve Pickering (who also appeared in over seven hundred performances of Robert Falls's staging of *Death of a Salesman*) caught me every time.

The most famous scene in *King Lear* is one that often drives actors nuts and leaves them hoarse. The idea of Lear raging against the storm is taken too literally, with crashing thunder that forces actors to bellow in order to be heard. Such competition between man and nature is counterproductive to the show, not to mention the actor's voice. Lear's last line in the scene with Goneril and Regan is "Oh fool, I shall go mad," so when we next encounter him in the storm with the Fool (brilliantly played by Howard Witt in my two productions), Lear has lost his mind and is a child again, embracing the storm, happy to be challenging Nature and singing in the rain. A little thunder goes a long way, and it's best when underplayed—the storm is inside Lear's head, where he is struggling to grasp what has befallen him and what he has done.

The role and the play are extremely complex, and I believe it's always good to understand it in context of Shakespeare's work and of past productions. I researched where Shakespeare drew his story from, studying *Plutarch's Lives* and *Holinshed's Chronicles*, trying to understand how the pagan culture and Christian overtones of forgiveness and redemption mingled. I watched Olivier's and Ian Holm's movie versions of *King Lear*, and I recalled Lee Cobb's interpretation in the Lincoln Center production where I played Edmund years ago. I wanted all of my research to enhance a more detailed performance, but this was orchestrated well in advance of the first preview, so that when I got out onstage, I could throw it all away and just deal with the text, and be in the moment with my fellow actors in a world we were creating anew in each moment, each performance.

ACKNOWLEDGMENTS

There are many wonderful people who have helped me, sustained me, and inspired me in the writing of this book, most notably Stuart Miller. It was Stuart's encouragement and persistence that led to us working as a team writing the story of my life and career.

I am indebted to my good friend and literary maven, Howard Kaminsky, for introducing me to my incisive and insightful literary agent, Alice Martel; and to Alice for her commitment and enthusiasm in finding the right publisher for this book. That publisher is Globe Pequot Press, of course, and I send my heartfelt thanks to Janice Goldklang for giving this project the green light, to Lara Asher for guiding it all the way to the deadline (and a little beyond), and to the entire team that helped put the finished product in your hands in print or electronic form: Meredith Dias, Lauren Brancato, Sharon Kunz, Bret Kerr, Justin Marciano, Joshua Rosenberg, and Anita Oliva.

Thanks to old friends Oliver Stone, Jeff Bridges, Martin Sheen, Edward Norton, and Linda Lavin for their kind words on the book. And I'd like to extend a special thanks to a marvelous actor in his own right, Alec Baldwin, for his eloquence and grace in the penning of a deeply humbling foreword.

Alec is a new friend, but I'm also grateful for those who have been with me for much of this journey. It starts, of course, with family: my wife, Malgosia, and my children, Shannon and Karolina. For love and support I also always know I can look to my brother, James Keach, with Jane Seymour and their family. Forever raising my spirits are dear friends Jo and Kevin Connor; Stephen Kalinich; Rob Nilssen; Harris Yulin and his wife, Kris; Maxwell Caulfield and Juliet Mills; my Texas family and friends, Miles Compton, Mary Compton, Patricia and Tony Hale, Liesl and Kellene Cain, and Jean and Ken Wright; my friend and business partner, Dr. Gary Greenberg, for his illumination on the wonders of science; and my golfing buddies, Lee Blessing, Bob and Leslie Graham, Sam McMurray, Peter Jason, Dan Toohey, and Burning Tree Golf Club for giving me hope that I may one day be able to shoot my age.

On the business front I would have relied heavily upon my publicist, Dick Guttman; my elegant theatrical agent of four decades, Lionel Larner; my late attorney, Sidney Feinberg; my manager, Chuck Binder and Associates; Jean Diamond, my European agent; Ileana McCalip, my personal assistant; Billie Whitman, our financial guru; and Justin and Maren Fromm, for handling my website. Thanks also to Vanessa Gilbert, my commercial agent at TGMD Talent, and Randall Wixen, my music agent, for giving me the chance to share what I've learned along the way.

Of course I must tip the fedora to so many whom I have worked with on stage and screen. I am so happy that Jane Spillane, Max Allan Collins, and Carl Amari have kept the legacy of Mike Hammer alive. Thanks also to Christopher Titus for giving me the chance to really delve into the world of comedy, and to Chuck Schaeffer, Lisa Wernick, and CNBC for providing exciting and rewarding years on *American Greed*.

My theater career through the decades owes much to Gerald Freedman; Michael Kahn and The Shakespeare Theatre in Washington, DC, for bringing me new challenges and opportunities in the world of Shakespeare; Robert Falls and the Goodman Theatre of Chicago; Michael Ritchie and LA Theater Group; Robert Egan and the Ojai Playwrights Conference; and Martin Jarvis, Ros Ayres, Susan Lowenberg, and LA Theatre Works for keeping the art of radio drama alive and well. Thanks also to Robert Brustein, Robert Goldsby, and John Andrews of the Shakespeare Guild.

I am also thankful to Jim McGrath, the Hemingway Foundation; John Lassiter, Ron Meyer, Frank Marshall; also thanks to Jeff Wilson, Arielle Tepper, and 101 Productions; Jeffrey Richards; David Richenthal; Bruce Nash of Nash Entertainment; Chris Carmichael and Ubiquity Studios; Torsten Neumann and the Oldenberg Film Festival; and producer Norman Twain. Thanks also to Dr. Kenneth Salyer of the World Craniofacial Organization and Nancy Smythe of the Cleft Palate Foundation for all they do on an issue very important to me.

Of course, all those people wouldn't be able to put me to much use if it weren't for my physicians, Dr. Edward Hanzelik, Dr. Philip Bauman, Dr. Steve H. Yoon, Dr. Susan O'Donoghue, Dr. Marc D. Connell, Dr. Donald W. Larsen, and Nicole Marque, who keep this ole body going.

I know I have left out names, and I don't mean to slight anybody. I'd love to include everyone who has played a vital role in my career, from Barbara Garson to Warren Leight, from the Carradine clan to Alexander Payne, but there just isn't room. So let me say that I really have cherished the chance to collaborate with every actor, director, producer, writer, cameraman, stage manager, assistant director, costumer, make-up artist, dresser, caterer, driver, wrangler, special effects person, company manger and production assistant I have worked with . . . and those yet to come.

With deepest gratitude,
Stacy Keach

INDEX

INDEX OF PRODUCTIONS

ABOUT THE AUTHOR

Stacy Keach began his professional career with the New York Shakespeare Festival in 1964, doubling as Marcellus and the Player King in a production of *Hamlet* directed by Joseph Papp. He rose to prominence in 1967 in the off-Broadway political satire, *MacBird!*, for which he received the first of his three Obie awards. He has also won a Drama Desk Award, and in Washington, DC, he has earned three Helen Hayes Awards for Leading Actor. He played the title roles in *Henry V*, *Hamlet*, *Coriolanus*, *Richard III*, *Macbeth*, and most recently *King Lear* in Robert Falls's modern adaptation in Chicago and Washington, DC. Mr. Keach's stage portrayals of Peer Gynt, Falstaff, Cyrano de Bergerac, and Hamlet caused the *New York Times* to dub him "the finest American classical actor since John Barrymore." Keach has played to grand success in contemporary roles, from Arthur Kopit's *Indians* to Jon Robin Baitz's *Other Desert Cities*.

Perhaps best known around the world for his portrayal of hard-boiled detective Mike Hammer, Stacy Keach is also well known among younger generations for his portrayal of the irascible, hilarious dad, Ken Titus, in the Fox sitcom *Titus*; as the warden, Henry Pope, in the hit series *Prison Break*; and as the narrator of *Nova* and *American Greed*. Additionally, Stacy Keach won the 2011 Audie Award for Best Original Work for the Mike Hammer radio novel, *The Little Death*, where he reprises his role as Mike Hammer and also composed the musical score. He is an accomplished pianist and musical composer.

In 2013 he appeared in the film *Nebraska*, directed by Academy Award winner Alexander Payne, and voiced Skipper in the Disney animated feature, *Planes*. He has a cameo appearance in *Sin City 2: A Dame to Kill For*, directed by Frank Miller and Robert Rodriguez, which is scheduled to be released in 2014.

Mr. Keach attended the University of California at Berkeley and the Yale Drama School; he was a Fulbright scholar to the London Academy of Music and Dramatic Art. In 2012 he became the first Heritage Professor by George Mason University, teaching acting via online platforms.

For the past thirty years he has been honorary chairman of the Cleft Palate Foundation.

Mr. Keach has been married to his beautiful wife, Malgosia, for twenty-seven years, and they have two wonderful children, son Shannon, aged twenty-five and getting a master's degree in public relations at NYU, and daughter Karolina, aged twenty-three, currently studying at the Pepperdine University. Visit him at gostacykeach.com.